MYTH, MONSTER, MURDERER

Jack the Ripper: the victims, the crimes, the story.

JACKIE ANDERSON
CIARA WILD

The Book Guild Ltd

First published in Great Britain in 2022 by
The Book Guild Ltd
Unit E2, Airfield Business Park
Harrison Road
Market Harborough
Leicestershire, LE16 7UL
Freephone: 0800 999 2982
www.bookguild.co.uk
Email: info@bookguild.co.uk
Twitter: @bookguild

Copyright © 2022 Jackie Anderson and Ciara Wild
The rights of Jackie Anderson and Ciara Wild to be identified as the authors of this
work have been asserted by them in accordance with the
Copyright, Design and Patents Act 1988.

All rights reserved. No part of this publication may be
reproduced, transmitted, or stored in a retrieval system, in any form or by any means,
without permission in writing from the publisher, nor be otherwise circulated in
any form of binding or cover other than that in which it is published and without
a similar condition being imposed on the subsequent purchaser.

Typeset in 11pt Minion Pro
Printed and bound in the UK by TJ Books LTD, Padstow, Cornwall

ISBN 978 1913913 793

British Library Cataloguing in Publication Data.
A catalogue record for this book is available from the British Library.

CONTENTS

Authors' Note		vii
1	Catch Me When You Can	1
2	Monsters and Men: Jack the Ripper, An Urban Legend	7
3	The Media and the Monster	22
4	Beyond the Grave: Jack the Ripper's Victims	37
5	The Desperation of the Poor Amid the Wealth of Empire	61
6	Who Kills Whores? Victorian Attitudes to Prostitution	83
7	Violence Against Women, Then and Now	108
8	Women and Crime: Then and Now	123
9	Women's Mental Health and Treatment	139
10	A Comparison of Killers	158
11	Jack the Ripper: Suspects and Theories	178
Afterword		192
Bibliography		195

AUTHORS' NOTE

This book has been written by the authors over the last five years using publicly available information and contains references throughout. The thoughts, views and opinions of the authors contained in this book are our own and are not associated with any employer or organisation.

Wherever possible in this book, we have avoided sensationalising these crimes and crimes against vulnerable people. Instead, we have tried to understand why these crimes happened using social and psychological theory. We have aimed at all times to discuss the victims with the respect that they deserved and that had often been denied them but for some notable exceptions, both in life and since.

1

CATCH ME WHEN YOU CAN

'We, the women of East London, feel horror at the dreadful sins that have been lately committed in our midst and grief because of the shame that has fallen on our neighbourhood.'

From letter to the Queen by the women of East London,
published in the *Pall Mall Gazette* on 25th October 1888.

October 1888 was a remarkably cold, dark, dreary month. Despite the cold, despite Catherine Eddowes' destitution, her hand-to-mouth existence and her estrangement from her family, her murder at the hands of London's most notorious murderer added to the shock and sense of terror among those who lived in the East End with her. Catherine's sister, Eliza, distraught at Catherine's terrible death, made sure that her sister did not suffer the final ignominy of being thrown into a pauper's grave. Catherine's coffin was carried in a glass carriage, drawn by plumed horses, and followed by a second, mourner's carriage. Hundreds of the residents of East London lined the streets on the chilly afternoon of 8th October to pay their last respects to a woman many would have known personally, and others would have recognised from within their tight-knit community. Hundreds more crowded into the City of London cemetery along with many members of the Eddowes family to say their final farewell. The funeral directors and coffin bearers worked sombrely, moving quickly to keep the cold at bay and to put to rest the mutilated body of Catherine Eddowes, one of numerous women who had met their gruesome end on the blade of Jack the Ripper's knife.

Jack the Ripper. The very words to this day still conjure up images of dark corners in Victorian London's slum-ridden streets, of death, blood, gore, violence and terror. Days earlier, when still alive and walking those dank, crime-smeared streets, Catherine Eddowes would have felt that fear. She would have known the dangers that she faced, a woman alone, perhaps drunk to the point of being almost incapacitated, in the dark, perhaps looking for a trick or two so she could pay her room for the night. If she could not raise those few shillings, she would have no option but to find a dark, poorly frequented corner in which to huddle and take a few hours' sleep. She was no stranger to violence, nor was she a stranger to many forms of abuse. She would have been thinking that perhaps she would be lucky, perhaps she would not fall prey to the killer she knew stalked the alleyways of Whitechapel, who had already killed and mutilated. She would have sensed the panic in the local community; the streets and alleys, pubs and courtyards would have been buzzing with horrified accounts of violence, with the anger of those local people who felt that the police were not protecting their women, with muttered accusations at this suspect or that, this racial group or the other. But what was to happen to her that night, the night of 30th September 1888, was, in fact, the unthinkable. Jack the Ripper struck again, and Catherine Eddowes was consigned to the annals of notoriety because of her terrible death, carved open and butchered by one of the world's most notorious killers. Jack the Ripper, known by no other name, because his identity has never been uncovered beyond all doubt.

It was on a similarly bleak autumn day that Ciara Wild and I walked across the Wanstead Flats in the direction of the City of London Cemetery. The bite of the wind, unfitting somehow for the metropolitan sprawl that is London, was sharper than either of us had anticipated and we huddled into the collars of our coats. 'It was an exceptionally cold October in 1888, when Eddowes was buried', I remarked, having had a general interest in the Ripper and his victims for years. Ciara had already found herself drawn towards the mystery, partly from books I had strewn about our family home, and partly curious about the area of East London where she had lived and studied for a number of years. That was some five years ago. We talked of what we knew about the Ripper mystery as we walked. 'Eddowes is buried over there somewhere.' Ciara nodded towards the gloomy stone walls of the

City of London Cemetery, now streaked with the dirt of the London drizzle that seemed to slice through us in the wind. 'She had her left kidney removed.' He didn't just kill her: he hacked into her, he owned her, he overpowered her, strangled her, extinguished her breath. But that was not enough. He had to possess her so thoroughly that he ripped into her insides. It was violent in the extreme. It had to be driven by hatred or insanity or both. We speculated long after our walk and over a warming tea in a cake shop on the Leytonstone High Road. That is where our book was born.

The Jack the Ripper story is perennially absorbing, appealing in its gruesome fascination to millions of people around the world. If considered a theme on its own, the story has fed into fiction in the form of books, dramas and films and has been the subject of thousands of investigative books, articles and documentaries. There are hundreds, if not thousands, of websites with opinions, commentaries and some facts; there are conventions, lectures and a whole tourist industry in East London that specialises in tours, walks, ghost hunting... the story expands with every passing generation.

But this story of the Jack the Ripper murders is far more complex than a linear tale of an unknown, murderous monster who revelled in hacking down unfortunate women in the streets of Whitechapel, a monster who was never caught and just suddenly stopped the murderous spree; there is no clear beginning, middle or end to the Jack the Ripper story. There are victims, and there are characters, there are settings and locations, but otherwise, what we know about the murderer (or murderers, if you believe there were more than one) is limited.

We are as fascinated with the story of Jack the Ripper as anyone else, and after numerous years of research and the writing of this book, we continue to find elements of the story that merit even further exploration. The story has carved itself a place in the cultural identity of London – the London Dungeon tour, for example, has a section devoted to the Jack the Ripper story, much as it has to the Fire of London as well as to another perennially popular piece of fiction, the Demon Barber of Fleet Street. This latter is a well-known piece of fiction, but the Jack the Ripper story that is continually perpetrated by writers of factual treatises as well as of works of fiction does have some basis in fact, in events that did happen, that are relatively well-documented by contemporary sources and that can be researched. There are also clear parallels in the story to current times and it is that link to a contemporary reality that we found a particularly irresistible draw.

Stories inhabit our world in a way that is so pervasive that we are not aware that our narratives of our lives are expressed as stories. A story is a telling of a sequence of events, either true or fictitious, although at times those boundaries are not entirely clear, or can become blurred over time. The Jack the Ripper story, at its most basic level, is a recounting of the events that took place in Whitechapel, London, in 1888. These events were recorded in police reports, press reports and inquest reports. There are clear facts and there are versions of events that differ from witness to witness – such is the nature of crime that unless there is a full and truthful confession, specific events are sometimes open to interpretation.

Through stories, we explore meaning in our lives. The meaning of each story can be found in analysing its part in the greater whole. For example, the story of the Battle of Hastings can be better understood when examined in its broader context as part of the whole conquest of England by the Normans; it was far more complex and we learn far more about the time, the people and the repercussions when we look at the Battle of Hastings as something more than the story of a single battle where King Harold II was killed, and Duke William of Normandy becomes King. To uncover meaning in a story, we need to look at the links with all the other things associated with the story: the people, the places, the time. Of particular importance is the role of culture and society in deriving meaning from a story – as individuals we interpret stories from the basis of a shared understanding of our particular society. Groups, cultures, communities and societies gather and preserve collections of narratives in their myths, legends, folklore and histories – their own stories. These are used to develop a sense of narrative meaning which can be applied by communities to help make sense of their cultural origins and social rules. Over a period of time, meanings can become blurred, obscured by the retelling and by the countless interpretations that are added to it: stories are organic, they change minutely with each telling, and as the stories are passed from one generation to the next, they eventually evolve into myths, fairy tales, and enter the lexicon of the narrative of a social group. Thus, the Jack the Ripper story can also be viewed as the start of what is evolving into an urban myth, if indeed, it is not already so. The Jack the Ripper story seems to have become more fable than reality, yet the story is indeed rooted in reality, and it is through the bare facts of the story that we can examine the notorious, dark world that the so-called Ripper inhabited, get to know the characters involved as best we can and draw some clear ideas as to what the story tells us.

This book explores the role of women in the narrative as victims, not just the murder victims but the victims of social attitudes and of the way that society was organised and functioned. Whoever was responsible for committing the series of horrific crimes that became known as the Whitechapel murders was likely to have been as much a product of time and place as to have psychological and behavioural characteristics that would have predisposed him to murder and mutilation. In this book, we have explored the place and the social context in which the murderer may have lived or at the very least frequented and visited so regularly that he was intimately familiar with its labyrinth of criss-cross streets and alleys. Since the victims were all female, it is essential to also explore Victorian attitudes towards women, notably women who were in some way outside the constraints of a rigidly patriarchal society; in other words, women whose lives led them away from what was commonly accepted as the correct role for women in society, and this included divorced and women separated from their husbands, unmarried mothers as well as criminals, prostitutes and women who suffered from mental illness.

Their deaths were being exploited right from the moment their bodies were discovered – by the media and by other parties – and this exploitation has been going on ever since. The story is also pruriently voyeuristic as well as exploitative: the victims are dead and powerless; their stories are told not by those closest to them but by those who have been able to grasp those stories and use it for their own ends. Noticeably, and in keeping with Victorian attitudes towards women and in particular towards women that were prostitutes or were labelled as prostitutes – as we discovered, the term was used to label any woman who somehow ended up living outside the narrow constraints of the role of women as approved by society at large, and not specifically towards sex workers – the public telling of the story was male-centred, which is possibly why the victims were depersonalised at an early stage, and these days are merely part of the landscape of the Ripper's activities, providing the blood and the body parts rather than any form of humanity.

We know a great deal about how the women died, and the mutilations of their bodies after death, but we know comparatively little about how they lived, who they were as people. We wanted to explore the ways in which women lived at the time. We can't help but wonder if what these women experienced at the time continues to be reflected in the experiences of women in the twenty-first century. Through this book, we are looking at what the Jack the Ripper story tells us about society at the time, what life was like for those women and the lingering attitudes that are still recognisable today, where sex workers, single mothers, women who opt to have abortions, wives and mothers who also try to sustain careers, are still the scapegoats of society's ills. And when women challenge established morality, they are demonised further, especially in the media, much as they were in Victorian times.

Through this book, we explore how urban myths and legends arise and develop and ask the question as to whether the Ripper story is one of these legends, providing a way for communities to reflect upon and learn from the past. We look at the power of story to illuminate facts and illustrate in emotive and personal terms the darker and more easily hidden reaches of a particular period in history, or particular events. From this story, we see Jack the Ripper emerge as the epitome of a society where the worst that could possibly happen to a woman, happened to these victims. Thereafter, these women, who had lost their lives and the reality of their true identities, were then held by a prurient and manipulative media as examples of what *not* to be like as a woman.

This book is a testament to those women. It joins those other voices that aim to remind the world that these women represented the universal victimhood of the women of their time. It endeavours to elevate their lives and their deaths to a place beyond the murk of lurid tabloid stories and sordid tourist attractions. These were women who lived and loved, who laughed and cried, who knew pleasure and much pain, more pain than they deserved. They were victims of much more than the knife of the world's most notorious murderer; they were victims of a male-dominated society that would use them for pleasure and punish them for the same, victims of the poverty and the exploitative system they lived in, victims of the scandalous prejudices of a deeply religious and judgemental people. Victims of more than a psychopath stalking the streets of East London.

2

MONSTERS AND MEN: JACK THE RIPPER, AN URBAN LEGEND

'Sometimes human places, create inhuman monsters.'

Steven King, *The Shining*

"Life is so much more interesting with monsters in it," Mikel J. Koven, a folklorist, senior lecturer and course leader at the University of Worcester, has commented. The world's fascination with Jack the Ripper, the murderer, victims, locations, suspects and even with the researchers themselves, shows no sign of abating.

The story of Jack the Ripper has been told and retold year after year since the term was first coined (the origin of which is not known). It is probably better to restate that sentence: the story of Jack the Ripper has been told and retold year after year since the term was first made public. This is a more accurate representation of how Jack the Ripper, the legend, came to grow into the familiar story. The character of "Jack the Ripper" has been the subject of hundreds of books, websites, blogs, magazine and newspaper articles, as well as numerous films and plays, and this number increases every year. While much of this body of research and exposition aims at discovering or explaining the identity of the killer, the "Jack" that inspires terror, revulsion and curiosity in equal measure, this work focuses on what we do know about the story; we have decided to use the story to lead us to an understanding of the people and places of the time when the story began, and to a greater understanding of the human condition; a condition that appears to need archetypal monsters as much as humans need to be delivered from them.

The concept of archetypes as discussed in Carl Jung's psychological theories is based on the construct of human societies having a collective consciousness, rooted in the thought that over time humans have created a collective psychology containing the universal experience of what it is to be human. Within this collective consciousness resides what Jung calls "archetypes" which are universal, archaic patterns inherited from our most ancient of ancestors. Every human being has the capacity of each archetype but only those that are played out in each person's behaviour and interactions with the outside world are observable.

Jung identifies three types of archetypes: events, figures and motifs. Archetypal events are universal moments that we can all experience or relate to, such as birth and death. These in themselves are powerful motivators of action, with death representing dark and violent motivations. Literature, and more recently the wider media, is replete with representations of archetypal figures, such as the hero, the mother, the clown and so on. Stories can create caricatures of each of the archetypal figures and one that persists in most stories, especially in counterpoint to the hero of each story, is that of the villain. The need in human society to find balance, creates a psychological need to counteract each archetype with its polar opposite. Motifs in stories are themes or ideas that permeate human experience, such as creation stories and quest adventures, and to populate these, we use events on which to base them and create figures to act them out. The villain, therefore, is supremely important to humanity in order to allow us to understand and rationalise events that occur in our experiences, as individuals, but more importantly, the shared experiences of society or a social group.

The villains that have roots in this deep collective consciousness are those that are most readily related to by social groups. Villains, such as Jack the Ripper, and before him the London Monster, Spring-heeled Jack and Sweeney Todd, embody the archetypal villain, by conforming to the collective consciousness universal pattern of a typical villain existing in darkness and preying on the weak and vulnerable. This not only piques our curiosity at a deeper psychological level, but somehow connects us to the roots of the story in a sub-conscious way. Society seeks out the archetypal figures that are potentially connected to an archetypal event such as a death, and a violent death, in our social consciousness, relies on a villain in order to be explained. Villains, as well as heroes, underpin our society and allow society to articulate its collective thinking and experience of the event, and it is through the constant telling and retelling of the stories in attempts to explain and understand it, that urban legends eventually evolve. We could therefore consider, that as the Jack the Ripper story lacks a hero (or an anti-hero that has never been identified), in our collective social consciousness the story remains unfinished and therefore continues to hold us in its sway. The search for the true identity of the killer could fulfil this as the person who manages to achieve inviolable proof of identity would be the hero in the narrative and the story would come to its final conclusion. However, despite researchers' best efforts, this has eluded them and so the story continues, and we collectively continue without closure.

While archetype theory is just one of many that could explain how Jack the Ripper as the leading character of a mystery story has entered the social consciousness, it certainly helps us to understand how the unidentified murderer whom we call "Jack the Ripper" has entered our social consciousness and has gathered increasing infamy as a villain. It may also be that this way of viewing Jack the Ripper lends him a ubiquity which easily allows the translation of the legend internationally, with murders in the USA, for example, being attributed to Jack the Ripper's having moved across the Atlantic.

While viewing Jack the Ripper as an archetype is a useful way for then examining society's response to the murders, we also need to consider how and to what extent Jack the Ripper can be considered a stereotype, or, indeed, how stereotypes have entered the Jack the Ripper legend and influenced the original investigations and responses, and responses ever since. A stereotype is a thought that is widely accepted and taken up by society about specific types of individuals which are intended to represent the entire group of those individuals and attempt to explain their behaviours and attributes. Stereotypes may or may not reflect reality with any degree of accuracy. They are often considered dangerous with negative effects, related to prejudice and discrimination: racial or gender stereotypes, for example, are thought to be at the root of discriminatory thinking and actions against certain groups. However, human society uses stereotypes as a way to categorise, simplify, systemise and explain information, using stereotypes as shortcuts in order to explain their social context. The Jack the Ripper stories are full of stereotypes fallen women, alcoholics, Jews, the Irish, the poor, women beaters, gangs, doctors, midwives, foreigners, and the story is told frantically, bordering on panic, whilst society races to explain the events, and why they may have happened.

This is closely linked to the search for scapegoats. A scapegoat is an individual or group, or entity of some sort (demon or animal, for example) that is blamed for the wrongdoings, mistakes or faults of others. Scapegoating means that uncomfortable feelings such as guilt, anger, envy and so on, can be displaced onto others, these others often being a more vulnerable person or group. It was an instinctive reaction for the people of Whitechapel to seek a scapegoat for the murders and they sought small groups – foreigners, Jews, mad doctors – with the negative feelings of horror, shame, collective guilt, outrage and fear building up and fuelled by speculation, including speculation in the press, until the archetypal villain is created, emerging finally as Jack the Ripper, the urban legend.

Urban legends are an important part of popular culture. They provide a simple way of sharing and then embellishing and passing down a story through communities and through generations, and they are a way of explaining our fears and analysing the state of our society. Urban legends are distinct from myths in that a legend is usually based on a kernel of truth, whereas myths are fabrications, stories manufactured in order to explain how the world works and tend to involve resolutions that can only take place through magic or some supernatural intervention.

While there are numerous definitions of what makes up an urban legend, and explanations on how they are initiated and developed, there seems to be a general view that they are not usually entirely fictional, that they are based at least in a small part on an element of fact. As a story, the Jack the Ripper tale is typical of the way urban legends grow. The story is based on true events, the murders are documented and there is even photographic evidence of their veracity. The facts of the event were readily sensationalised and spread rapidly, embellished almost as soon as they were revealed. With embellishment comes distortion, which creates versions of events that could be deemed to be fiction, and as time distances us from the original events, unravelling the facts from the fiction becomes increasingly difficult.

However, stories and what is implied within them help us grasp an insight into the lives of a particular section of society in a specific time and place. Yet, unlike some of the great stories that we know and retell today, such as the tale of star-crossed lovers (*Romeo and Juliet*) or a regret-haunted hero (*Hamlet*), urban legends are not authored by individuals. They begin with a real, or sometimes imagined, event that was compelling and found to be worth repeating time and time again. Many are passed on by word of mouth from one generation to the next, and these days, via social media. Slender Man is a modern example where a meme of a fictional character, generated online, has developed into an internet based urban legend. Stories of him have been told across internet platforms using photoshopped images and have spread through a variety of narratives and media including literature and computer games. However, his legend as a supernatural being, typically involved in stalking, abducting and traumatising others, not only compels people's curiosity but in one instance it led to two teenage girls attempting to take another person's life as they were indoctrinated by the power of this legend.

Each time the story of an urban legend is retold it is changed very slightly, and we tend to remember and repeat the features of the story that are most striking and therefore most memorable. Urban legends put into words feelings that in essence are innate human fears. The stories that form the basis of urban legends tend to be exaggerated in places and minimised in others, glorified or vilified, ennobled and idealised or used as an example of how not to behave. As storytellers, we also have a tendency to avoid parts of the story that do not support our theories or our purposes in telling the story, and we simplify – a natural editing process. We also have a multitude of individual ways of organising and recollecting our thoughts, so that over decades, and over a myriad of media, for a multitude of reasons, stories are altered, with only very specific information remaining from the original story. The Jack the Ripper stories are often reduced to featuring dark, dismal, dangerous London, the dead of night and dead prostitutes, "fallen" women hunted down by a marauding monster. These are the features that ring the tills of the tourism industry in London and of book publishers across the world.

The Jack the Ripper story lends itself to easily developing into an urban legend. After all, it is a story where we do possess the basic facts through the extensive reporting of the media at the time, the police, inquest and coroners' reports and statements from witnesses. However, it is because the mystery remains unsolved, precisely because there is so much availability of records of facts mixed with records of conjectures and theories, both of the time and over the past 120 years, that discovering the truth is becoming ever more elusive. There are, however, some basic facts of the case that do not change and cannot change: there were a series of murdered women, tragic women who had a number of traits in common besides the fact that they were female; the murders all took place in a very small geographical area; the location for the crimes was in one of the most impoverished districts of one of the richest cities in the world; at the time, the prevailing social attitudes were skewed against the victims – violence towards women was known to be common, women had few rights, and social or medical care for women who were sex workers, mentally ill or were substance abusers was very poor or non-existent. These facts are unchangeable.

The development of the Jack the Ripper legend centres on whom the murderer might have been and why the murders took place at all. In these aspects, 'Ripperologists' have shown assiduous researching skills and have combined their findings with conjecture; some wildly imaginative while others have been intelligent, reasonable arguments. The very anonymity of Jack the Ripper lends strength to the enthusiasm with which so many people choose to carry out investigations, their own detective work on what has been a cold case for over a century. In turn, this has led to layer upon layer of conjecture to be laid upon the bare facts of the case – lists of likely suspects can be drawn up, many books have been published supporting one or other favoured theory, including conspiracy theories which implicate the freemasons and even the Royal Family as well as surgeons, sailors and persons from all classes, professions, locations and even various nationalities.

There are also a number of salient themes in the story or stories that abound on Jack the Ripper which lend themselves to fuelling the spreading of distortions that quickly became the stuff of legend rather than facts. For example, the fact that the victims were all or had been at some point or other in their lives, prostitutes, street walkers at that, desperate for money even simply to pay for a night's lodging in their lodging houses, that they all lived and worked in the same area and all were involved in alcohol abuse meant that we can very easily imagine and spread word of the images of Jack the Ripper as a sadistic, woman-hating monster stalking the streets at night in a state of bloodlust looking for the opportunity to kill and mutilate. The events take place in a backdrop of destitution, dirt and appalling living conditions, in the context of a violent existence where early and avoidable deaths happened every day, and in a place like a rabbit warren, full of alleys and yards, getaway routes and hidden places. Above this there is an overarching context of the politics of the day, where Whitechapel was a place crammed full of refugees from Eastern Europe, Polish and Russian Jews many of them, seeking safety from the vicious pogroms that drove them from their homes, and mixing with Irish immigrants, themselves fleeing poverty and destitution in their native land.

All stories, true or fictitious, have a setting, a context within which the events, or the plot, is played out. That, of course, is the simplistic view. In reality, the events of any narrative are unavoidably influenced by the context in which they are set. Would there have been so much crime and prostitution in the East End of late Victorian London if there had been less poverty, decent housing and reasonably paid, secure jobs? If the state had taken a role in ensuring housing was decent, hygienic and affordable, would it have been less easy for the Ripper to pick off women in dark corners? It is no coincidence that crime statistics show a reduction in theft and violent crime in more affluent areas. Poverty, lack of employment, lack of opportunities, poor education leading to low aspirations are all linked, and all of these act to foster crime and networks of criminal gangs. As Gray (2013) puts it when discussing this in the context of Victorian London, 'The Whitechapel murders represent an extraordinary crime of any period of history, but contemporaries believed that the area in which they occurred was a breeding ground for criminality of the basest sort.' Towards the end of the nineteenth century, social observers had begun to view criminal behaviour as a collective activity from a distinct group of people in society rather than just stemming from the personal failings of the individual. This group could be thought of as a class of its own, a subclass, or criminal class, existing in the shadows beneath the ordinary, decent working classes. This led to the beginnings of criminology as a science, with Henry Mayhew publishing his study of *The Criminal Prisons of London* (1862) and *London, Labour and the London Poor*, and in 1861–65, the Rev W.D. Morrison writing, "There is a population of habitual criminals which forms a class in itself." (Morrison, 1891, in Barrett and Christopher, 1999.)

This research added to the more elaborate anecdotes of criminals and criminal activities in the slums and helped to fuel the Victorian view that the slums were a breeding ground for crime. The Whitechapel murders added to those fears, propelling public concern to a state bordering on national hysteria. This was enhanced even further by works by the likes of Maudsley in England and Lombroso in Europe, who developed ideas on the link between mental illness and crime and speculated on a possible link between physiognomy and crime. Inevitably, this would have added another dimension to the speculation on what the Ripper might have looked like, leading to variations in the narrative through "imaginative" witness accounts that described possible suspects as "dressed as a gentleman" or "dark and swarthy like a Jew". Here, we have the beginnings of the stereotypical Ripper character – the top-hatted, dark, Victorian gentleman, or heavily coated Victorian doctor with his Gladstone bag full of sharpened knives that form the familiar figures of Ripper film and fiction.

Urban legends, with their strong appeal and their foundation on reality, can provide useful messages or morals. These legends are a useful indicator of what is happening in society, especially where information on the deeper echelons of that society is particularly inaccessible, such as the territories of certain gangs in inner-city estates. While we may have a good deal of material on what the middle and upper classes thought and wrote about London and in particular the poor of East London, we do not have a full insight into what those poor living in those squalid conditions in Whitechapel truly experienced. We can only conjecture based on the little evidence we have left, and on the basis of their fears and their reactions to situations such as the Jack the Ripper murders.

A particularly strong feature of urban legends is that of lack of information that surrounds the possible kernel of truth. 'The lack of verification in no way diminishes the appeal that urban legends have for us,' writes Jan Harold Brunvand in *The Vanishing Hitchhiker: American Urban Legends and Their Meanings* (1981). 'We enjoy them merely as stories and tend to at least half-believe them as possibly accurate reports.' Brunvand goes on to explain that the definition of an urban legend is a strong basic story appeal, a foundation in actual belief, and a meaningful message or moral. An information vacuum is usually filled in by society with rumour and speculation, fuelling fears. The response of society to this is to seek explanatory solutions through the extension of those legends. This is where fact becomes mixed with fiction and reality is obscured. This is the birthplace of conspiracy theories, with which the Jack the Ripper story is littered.

This open-endedness of the story, the lack of satisfactory resolution, is the hook that attracts its fictionalisation. As Clive Bloom explains in his 2007 essay "The Ripper Writing: the cream of a writer's dream" (Warwick and Willis, 2013), Ripper literature is not confined to the work of investigators, journalists and amateur sleuths. It extends beyond this genre and into fiction and film, an early work of fiction being *The Curse upon Mitre Square* by J.F. Brewster, published in 1889. Bloom draws an interesting parallel between the way the character of the Ripper has been drawn and speculated upon through both investigation and fictionalisation, as has Hitler, the twentieth-century "bogey man", citing the two sets of diaries, Hitler's Diaries and the so-called Ripper diaries, both of which have been proven to be fakes, as an attempt to identify and authenticate figures whose actions are both specific and documented, and at the same time legendary.

What does distinguish the Jack the Ripper story from other urban legends is that it is a relatively new construct. Victorian London was already home to a number of urban legends and figures of fear and terror. It would have been all too easy for society at the time to attribute the murders to legends such as Spring-heeled Jack, who allegedly sprang out from behind walls and bushes with devilish cunning and strength to attack his victims, although never with the ferocity and the gruesome results of the Jack the Ripper murders. Spring-heeled Jack is visualised in a similar way: dressed as a gentleman with a hat and long black cloak, and notorious for jumping out and "roughing up" women walking the streets at night. Sightings of this fiend took place in the 1830s and 1840s and, like Jack the Ripper, the perpetrator was never brought to justice. Sightings were not confined to London, and Spring-heeled Jack appeared all over Britain and in Europe, another monster with which to frighten children and, more importantly, a legend used to deter women from wandering about on their own in the late hours. Spring-heeled Jack was a villain, perhaps an archetype that represented society's fears of crime and the underworld, and, behind this, fears of the darkness of night and all the unknowns that reside in that netherworld we cannot see.

Gray (2013) uses the examples of this and two other significant urban legends, the London Monster and Sweeney Todd, to argue that Jack the Ripper is becoming an urban legend (if indeed the story isn't already so): 'The abundance of possible suspects, the destruction or renaming of the streets in which his victims died, and the purported "loss of evidence" from police files, the Ripper letters, a number of film and television series, and above all the mythmaking by both contemporaries and more recent contributors, has muddied the waters to the extent that the truth is now almost completely obscured.' Gray also warns readers, and we would reinforce the warning, that 'the mythologising of the past is a continuum within history writing and that we should be aware of it'.

An interesting side effect, as it were, of urban legends is how society can make use of them in order to exert some form of desired social control. In 1789, as Gray recounts, London was alive with rumours about "an unpleasant man" who followed women in the street, used foul, suggestive and abusive language, and stabbed them in the thigh before walking away. During the years that followed, the attacks became more frequent and increasingly outrageous, including being stabbed in the nose by a long pin concealed in a nosegay that women were invited to smell. The man was publicly called "The Monster", and wanted posters began to appear as Monster-mania gripped the city; the press was full of stories, conjectures and cartoons. Exacerbated by fears of the events in France in the post-Revolution era which horrified English society and which the media used to terrify the people into not rebelling against the English order and avoid a cross-channel imitation of the Revolution, the stories of the London Monster were used by many men to control the activities of women, insisting they only go out when accompanied by men. This reinforced, says Gray (2013), "paternalistic relationships in a period when enlightenment ideas were promoting democracy, freedom and liberation". Gray also, validly in this writer's view, refers to Bondeson, noting: 'The Monster phenomenon identified sexual liberty with bloody violence: his sexual deviancy could be linked to political anarchy.' Jack the Ripper was an ideal vehicle, one hundred years later, for society to use to represent a threat to society and in particular, to control the activities of sexually active women.

Another related urban legend is that of Sweeney Todd, the demon barber of Fleet Street. Despite the films and books, there is very little of the original tale of Sweeney Todd except stories of a barber who murdered a number of his customers. The legend works by exposing a number of fears: the voluntary exposure by victims of the throat and the vulnerability experienced that is instinctive in all mammals, and specifically, of the gentleman laying back and surrendering to the mercy of a servant, which played on class fears. This vulnerability parallels the vulnerability experienced by the prostitutes who would willingly agree to be taken into dark corners by men, one of whom could have been the Ripper. None of the villains of the urban legends described above have ever been identified and, despite enduring over a century of investigation by thousands of enthusiasts and academics, not to mention police officers and other professional investigators, our Jack continues to elude being pinned down to a specific identity.

The term "Jack the Ripper" was released by the press of the time, reporting on a letter that had been received by the police which was purportedly signed by the killer who named himself "Jack the Ripper". The letter has long since vanished and was one of numerous letters received by the police, apparently from the killer, many of which were considered to be hoaxes. It is not known whether the killer really did write the letter or call himself "Jack the Ripper". It is not a real name but a fiction, a nickname, with Jack being a name frequently given to simply anyone who was a man whose name was not known, and, indeed, even if their name were known, many men were called "Jack", for example, the habit of calling any sailor "Jack Tar", and there were "Jack the Lad", "Jack-O-Lantern", "Jack the Giant-Killer" among many others. If it was the murderer who coined the phrase, he certainly created a flurry of media attention that ensured that his real persona was never discovered. If it was a hoax, then the name "Jack the Ripper" and everything that has ensued since the story began is very much a story, a legend. Steven Knight refers to the term "Jack the Ripper" as a "misnomer", a term that conjures up images of a lone, monstrous, murderous stalker, for years throwing everyone off his scent or of those, who might have been the true killer – or killers – and Knight believes that there were three: two killers and one accomplice. Yet while that legend continues to excite attention, it is all too easy to set aside the real stories of late nineteenth-century Victorian Whitechapel and the many women that were its victims, not least the five who were thought to be killed by the one Ripper.

In considering the Jack the Ripper story as an urban legend, albeit one which is still evolving over time, we can set aside the need to search for a perpetrator. Suffice it to understand and accept that there was a killer, or possibly more, who didn't just kill the victim, but proceeded to mutilate the victims in a way which made sense to link at least five of these to the one perpetrator. That Jack the Ripper was not the only murderer stalking the streets of east London in the late 1880s is well known, and while the features of the murders and the psychological profile of the killer is a fascinating and useful investigation in itself, the story speaks volumes about the society that created the monster and the circumstances in which it was able to find and devour its victims.

When investigating the Jack the Ripper story, we find that what we are dealing with is an urban legend that, while rooted in reality, is replete with conjectures, fictitious constructs, assumptions and suppositions, all of which developed for a number of reasons, but essentially through the auspices of the media industry. It is worth noting that it is in the perpetuation of the mystery that the Whitechapel murders are at their most compelling. The discovery of the truth would bring the legend back down to earth, where the murders would be regarded as a sadistic and bloody episode in the East End of London, rather than as the mystery which fascinates millions, and the commercial money-spinner that it is today. However, the story serves as a useful tool with which to examine the Whitechapel and lives of East Enders of the time. We may never know definitively who committed those murders, but the story does aid a better understanding of the context in which those murders took place, and the social circumstances that allowed those murders to happen. It is through exploring this, that we can seek parallels and similarities in our own current circumstances and maybe even learn to prevent similar atrocities.

The Jack the Ripper narrative sits in the midst of this complex situation and plays to the fears that people experience daily: fears about the threat posed by different ethnic groups, fear of hunger, fear of violence, fear of destitution, poverty, ill health, among others. The different groups living in the East End of London in the late Victorian times felt and understood those fears, albeit from a range of perspectives. This makes the Jack the Ripper narrative a particularly useful tool for deflecting attention away from the shortcomings of the state which did not provide a reasonable environment for its own people to live and thrive.

It might be considered useful to the establishment to use the terror that this monster had conveniently unleashed to turn the focus and anger of the masses of the working class and discontented underclasses towards immigrants and away from the state itself. This is not dissimilar to the use of the media, and in particular social media, by twenty-first-century ruling elites, and can be observed in the way that attention from the effects of post-2008 financial crisis austerity policies in Europe was deflected towards pointing the blame for increasing hardship at immigrants, policies that have led to wider divisions in European societies and may well have led, at least indirectly, towards the United Kingdom's decision to exit the European Union. The UK's prolonged austerity measures, based in some degree on the Thatcherite call to "return to Victorian values", has resulted in greater poverty, low pay, job insecurity and an increase in gang violence, sex working and people trafficking. The UK may not quite be at the point of re-opening the workhouses, but housing conditions have greatly deteriorated, and homelessness has sharply increased. Access to welfare has also dramatically decreased. If living conditions and attitudes are enormously different, there seems to be a worrying rapprochement of the threads of the backdrop of the Jack the Ripper context, and of the current times.

The narrative of Jack the Ripper and the urban legend that grew around it also played a perfect hand to the patriarchy; the media sensationalising of the murders succeeded in terrifying the women of the East End – and of other cities as the story spread across the world. Women were frightened into staying indoors, to not stray out of the home without being escorted by a man. Women were thus electing to restrict their freedom of movement, to be dependent rather than reach out for their independence. The late Victorian period saw a steady strengthening of the cries of feminists to gain greater freedoms including political franchise, and the Jack the Ripper narrative served to curb support for female independence. Urban legends reflect the prevalent attitudes of society towards, and its assumptions related to gender. Heroes are always good, kind and strong, and usually male, whereas female characters in leading roles are usually delicate, submissive and willing to be rescued. They also tend to be pure and wholesome – especially important to an urban legend originating in Victorian times, given the Victorian preconception that a woman was to be pure and if not so in some way, must therefore be sinful and immoral, a "contagion". In the Jack the Ripper urban legend, we have women as victims, and the villain as a cruel, but ultimately powerful, male. The victims were murdered because they were walking the streets alone, away from honourable male protection, easily dubbed "prostitutes". The story points towards the inevitability of calamity from a monstrous villain that befalls women who emulate the victims of the Ripper story.

The fictionalisation of the Ripper legend has provided society with a means to explore the themes that the legend encompasses. Mental illness, for example, the insanity that is supposed to be at the heart of the Ripper's motivation and how this can be reconciled with the precise, logical and, to all consideration, perfectly sane way that the killer is able to evade capture, cover his tracks, find victims and clinically murder and mutilate them: "mentally defective and metaphysically gifted" (Bloom, 2007, in Warwick and Willis, 2013). The nature of evil is another such theme, of sin in the way that the violence is perpetrated and the sinners it is perpetrated towards; theological issues and the question of how society can balance the fact that the murderer is "disposing" of sinners in a way akin to society hanging other "sinners". The question, then, needs to be posed: is the Jack the Ripper story, having gone far beyond the question as to the murderer's identity, a means of "holding up a mirror to society", a way of entering the psychological space of that society, a complex, contradictory, often dark space which continues to exist in one form or another in the present time? 'The Ripper's script,' says Bloom, "has violence, eroticism, sentimentality and the supernatural: a text to live out the sensationalism of the modern." (Bloom, 2007, in Warwick and Willis, 2013.)

The mythologising of Jack the Ripper began with the first reports of the earliest of the murders, even before opinion had been settled on which victims formed the "canonical five". Gray (2013) opines: 'From the moment he started killing poor women, "Jack" became a cultural construction used to serve a multitude of diverse causes. He was a purifying angel, an enlightened reformer and a harbinger of revolution.' And the mythologising has continued ever since, creating possibly the most familiar urban legend of modern times.

REFERENCES

Barrett, A. and Harrison, C., *Crime and Punishment in England: A Sourcebook*, Routledge, London.

Bloom, C. (2007), "The Ripper Writing: the cream of a writer's dream", in Warwick, A. and Willis, M. (2013), *Jack the Ripper: Media, Culture, History*, Manchester University Press, Manchester.

Bondeson, J. (2000), *The London Monster: A Sanguinary Tale*, Philadelphia: University of Pennsylvania Press, in Gray, D.D. (2013), *London's Shadows: The Dark Side of the Victorian City*, Bloomsbury Academic, London.

Brunvand, J.H. (1981), *The Vanishing Hitchhiker: American Urban Legends and Their Meanings*, W.W. Norton & Company, New York.

Cherry, K. (2019), "The 4 Major Jungian Archetypes", 17th July 2019, retrieved from https://www.verywellmind.com/what-are-jungs-4-major-archetypes-2795439

De Vos, G. (2012), *What Happens Next? Contemporary Urban Legends and Popular Culture*, ABC-CLIO, Alberta.

Gray, D.D. (2013), *London's Shadows: The Dark Side of the Victorian City*, Bloomsbury Academic, London.

Mayhew, H. (1862), *The Criminal Prisons of London and scenes of prison life. With numerous illustrations from photographs*, London, British Library General Reference Collection 6057.i.7.

Mayhew, H. (1865), *London labour and the London poor: the condition and earnings of those that will work, cannot work, and will not work (Vol. 1–4)*, retrieved from https://www.gutenberg.org/ebooks/author/48614

Psychologist World, "Carl Jung: Archetypes and Analytical Psychology", retrieved from https://www.psychologistworld.com/cognitive/carl-jung-analytical-psychology

Robson, D. (2015), "What Makes an Urban Legend", retrieved from https://www.bbc.com/future/article/20150126-how-to-create-an-urban-legend

Sherman, E. (2016), "The Forgotten Lives Of Jack The Ripper's Victims", updated 11th September 2019, retrieved from https://allthatsinteresting.com/jack-the-rippers-victims

The Guardian (2017), "Slender Man case: girl who attacked classmate gets 25-year hospital sentence", updated 1st February 2018, retrieved from

https://www.theguardian.com/us-news/2017/dec/21/slender-man-case-anissa-weier-sentenced

Walkowitz, J. R. (1982), "Jack the Ripper and the Myth of Male Violence", *Feminist Studies*, 8, 3, 542–574, retrieved from https://www.jstor.org/stable/3177712?read-now=1&refreqid=excelsior%3Afa26ae946c3bc27ae516454dea68f9fb&seq=1

Wikipedia, "Urban Legend", edited 5th March 2020, retrieved from https://en.wikipedia.org/wiki/Urban_legend

3

THE MEDIA AND THE MONSTER

'The media's the most powerful entity on earth. They have the power to make the innocent guilty and to make the guilty innocent, and that's power. Because they control the minds of the masses.'

Malcolm X

The role of the media in speculation and conjecture and in the propagation of urban legends is undeniable and we need only refer to the uses of media by governments in the early twentieth century to see how social control was exerted in, for example, Nazi Germany and Fascist Italy. The popular press not only disseminates information, but information can be distorted and shaped to influence groups of people according to the ends that those in the media wish, or misinformation can be used to exert control over the mass of the population. Indeed, this book is being written under the clouds of "fake news" that is rife in social media – the modern-day version of the tabloids, perhaps – and already general elections are under scrutiny for the signs of influence by groups wishing to use the media to influence voting, undermining the heart of democracy. As Anthony Smith argues, journalism "became the art of structuring reality, rather than recording it" (Gray, 2013).

It was during the late Victorian period that revolutionary changes took place in the way the media operated and the role that it played in society, changes that led to the development of the type of investigative journalism that we recognise today. New technologies resulted in better quality and faster printing at lower costs, and, combined with growing literacy among the general population and a greater level of affluence overall which allowed more people to read the news, this led to a wider circulation of news stories, and therefore a greater opportunity to influence public thinking as well as to inform the public. Added to this was the intense competition that existed for newspaper sales and for advertising revenue. In London, this competition was at its highest, and there was a deep thirst for information, as well as for finding styles and stories that kept readers buying their favourite newspaper. The story of the Whitechapel murders was heaven-sent sustenance to the news hungry editors, who eagerly turned to "Jack the Ripper" as the perfect stereotype of a villain. By the late 1880s, the popular press had grown and was at the stage where it was filling its Sunday papers with gossip and sensational stories, and by October 1888, stories of the Whitechapel murders filled inch after inch of newspaper columns, not just across the country but across the world. Jack the Ripper sold newspapers, and newspapers sold the Jack the Ripper story to the masses.

The impact of the newspaper reports was further enhanced by the use of sensationalism. This was, as Gray put it (Gray, 2013), a way of writing that exaggerated the story in order to create a "startling impression". Sensationalism was being used in all forms of popular culture, from music hall theatre to literature, with sensation novels enormously popular, such as those written by George W.M. Reynolds and the classic *The Strange Case of Dr Jekyll and Mr Hyde* by Robert Louis Stevenson. Music hall songs and melodrama also aimed to appeal to a wide audience using sensationalism, much as do modern soap operas. Interestingly, Gray points to the stereotypes that are portrayed by these, where good triumphs over evil, the hero "gets the girl" and the girl is almost always a frail and vulnerable victim that needs to be saved. Gray also notes that Victorians appeared to like their villains as somewhat inhuman, or monstrous and limited in their humanity, or, as Gray puts it, "as unlike them as possible. This helps to explain why the Ripper is perceived to be an 'alien', whether foreign or from outside 'society' is perhaps irrelevant" (Gray, 2013).

The sensationalism used by the press to make their voices heard above the general clamour itself drew criticism from writers who believed that the stories were to blame for the corruption of the population and heralded its descent to greater evil and debauchery; the expression of the fear, perhaps, that the evil perpetrated by the "alien monster" that was the Ripper could signify some sort of contagion. On 20th October 1888, *The Lancet* published its attack on Fleet Street, accusing newspapers of exploiting the vice and the violence evident in the East End and suggesting that the "prurient and demoralising amplification of its sickening details" (Warwick and Willis, 2013) could corrupt readers and influence those of less sound mind. With this assertion, the way that the story had been taken from the reporting of facts and conjectures as to perpetrator can be seen to have been heightened to the realms of itself aggravating violence, and potentially being the cause of copycat crimes – the Ripper has now been elevated to the pedestal of a monster with unstoppable evil influence.

Besides colourful news stories with instant shock appeal, the Whitechapel murders also gave the Victorian press an immediate means of campaigning. There was a campaigning fervour in Victorian Britain among philanthropists and their supporters who wanted to draw attention to the plight of the deprivation endured by residents of those East End districts, and also from those moralists who wanted to "convert" prostitutes and alcoholics and turn them away from their depravity. This was excellent fuel for marketing newspapers where the editorials fanned those campaigning flames. Furthermore, because the Ripper had managed to elude the police despite their best efforts, the media was able to use the unsolved murder as a means to criticise the police, the commissioner of the Metropolitan Police and members of the government. The media was thus able to take on different types of effective campaigning, drawing on this unknown villain and his heinous actions for suitable ammunition because it inflamed public opinion, drew readers and sold newspapers. The media was able to sow what Stanley Cohen, an eminent sociologist and criminologist, referred to as "moral panic" in the streets of London.

Gray sheds some light on what might constitute a moral panic and the role of the press in developing this phenomenon. Drawing on Stanley Cohen's theories, Gray explains that moral panics begin readily with press reports on a sensational event or, more often than not, a series of events that catch their attention – or is usefully brought to their attention – and the press then exaggerates these. The exaggerations whip the public into a state of fear and frenzy, and then panic ensues, with actions being taken by frightened individuals that arguably would not have occurred should the original facts not have been exaggerated in the first place. These are then focused on by the relevant authorities as public opinion begins to swell and take voice.

The responses are not always adequate, nor are they always made to directly address the purported cause of the moral panic, but in order to address other motives.

Gray uses the matter of the London Garrotters to illustrate his point. He explains how in 1862, the press reported an unacceptable increase in attacks on London residents of the type that we would now refer to as muggings, claiming that the attacker or attackers took hold of their victims by the throat using rope or cloth or their arms. None of these reports were based on crime numbers, and the response from the Metropolitan Police was heavy-handed, only too eager to use this public outcry to arrest many of those on whom they had their eye: petty criminals, "ticket-of-leave" men (former prison inmates on parole), anyone, in fact, who appeared to belong in the so-called criminal class that some Victorians believed existed. The criminal class included anyone who did not share the tough Victorian work ethic and thus it seems as if the Metropolitan Police was pursuing its own agenda under the guise of responding to the outcry whipped up by press reports, which had effectively stirred up "moral panic".

There is a next stage to a "moral panic", according to Gray, and that is that the justice system proceeds to respond with tougher measures including harsher punishments in the hope that public fears will be quelled, and the panic will subside. After the garrotting panic of 1862, for example, the Security Against Violence and the Penal Servitude Acts of 1863 and 1864 respectively increased the severity of punishments meted out by the courts and harsher conditions in prisons across the country were permitted by the Prison Act of 1865. In terms of facts, the incidents of garrotting that were brought to court peaked in November and December of 1863 – by the time the legislation was enacted, the need for it had faded. The moral panic of 1862 was over. But the conditions in prisons and the harshness of the justice system remained. This moral panic enabled the authorities to impose legislation that they may have already wanted or intended to impose but needed first to create the context necessary for its widespread acceptance.

Gray looks at the elements that Cohen suggests constituting a moral panic and considers whether Jack the Ripper fits the category of being the folk villain that moral panics all seem to feature – Cohen applied his theory to the garrotting incidents in the 1860s in London and also to the Mods and Rockers fights in the 1960s among others (Cohen, 1972, in Gray, 2013). Gray concludes that there was certainly panic on the streets of Whitechapel and the wider area and that the murders received attention in the high echelons of power and indeed, through the auspices of the media, across the country, Europe and into the USA. For example, *Lloyd's Weekly Newspaper* of 9th September 1888 stated in page 7: 'There is no wonder that the whole neighbourhood is intensely excited, and that something very like a panic has seized the women of the district who are compelled to be abroad at night or in the early hours of the morning.'

The previous day, *The Star* had carried these headlines and opening paragraphs:

HORROR UPON HORROR.
WHITECHAPEL IS PANIC-STRICKEN AT ANOTHER FIENDISH CRIME.
A FOURTH VICTIM OF THE MANIAC.

A Woman is Found Murdered Under Circumstances Exceeding in Brutality the Three Other Whitechapel Crimes.

London lies to-day under the spell of a great terror. A nameless reprobate – half beast, half man – is at large, who is daily gratifying his murderous instincts on the most miserable and defenceless classes of the community. There can be no shadow of a doubt now that our original theory was correct, and that the Whitechapel murderer, who has now four, if not five, victims to his knife, is one man, and that man a murderous maniac. There is another Williams in our midst. Hideous malice, deadly cunning, insatiable thirst for blood – all these are the marks of the mad homicide. The ghoul-like creature who stalks through the streets of London, stalking down his victim like a Pawnee Indian, is simply drunk with blood, and he will have more. The question is, what are the people of London to do? Whitechapel is garrisoned with police and stocked with plain-clothes men. Nothing comes of it. The police have not even a clue. They are in despair at their utter failure to get so much as a scent of the criminal.

The Star, 8th September 1888

The papers and the community identified possible suspect types such as the mad doctor, the evil English gentleman, outsiders and foreigners, the mentally ill, and so on, and vigilante groups cropped up that took to hunting down potential suspects that they felt fitted these types, thereby identifying their own folk villains. With writing as dramatic as that of *The Star* as per the above example, press coverage heightened the community's sense of living under threat and this in turn resulted in an intense public interest, scrutiny of police activity and involvement in the investigation of the crimes. As Walkowitz puts it:

Media coverage transformed the unsolved murders of five poor women into a national scandal; and it incited a wide range of social actors to immerse themselves in the details of the cases, compelled by sexual titillation but also by the desire to extract meaning out of apparent disorder.

Walkowitz 1992

Gray, however, does argue that the facts of the murders were already well-documented officially and needed little exaggeration by the press – they were horrific murders – and feels it is unlikely the press was manipulated by authorities specifically to create a moral panic for its own particular ends. Perhaps quite the contrary – in the social tinderbox situation that Whitechapel was in, it may well have been in the authorities' interests to diffuse the panic and communal anxiety expressed in the media. The media could not but report the story and, in fulfilment of their need to sell ever more newspapers, they investigated, conjectured and used as much of the story and the sundry associated sub-stories for their own commercial ends.

One of the orchestrators of the moral panic of the 1880s – and not just those elicited by coverage of the Jack the Ripper story – was W.T. Stead of the *Pall Mall Gazette*. Widely considered to be one of the most important figures in the development of the investigative journalism that we are familiar with today, Stead's newspaper, under his guidance, provided a platform for exposing the social conditions and poverty experienced in the East End of London in the late Victorian period and for facilitating public social criticism of these conditions. It was Stead's relentless exposure of the situation that helped to fuel the growing public outcry over slum housing, poverty, crime and prostitution, in particular sex trafficking and the prostitution of minors. He published excerpts of *The Bitter Cry of Outcast London* (Mearns, 1883) and through his opening up of his newspaper columns to comments from socialist protesters and strike supporters he pushed outwards the boundaries of what could and should be brought to the public sphere.

Much of Stead's attention, joined as it was by others in the publishing sphere, was focused on the East End, which in the 1880s contrasted with increased starkness with the prosperity of the West End. The East End stood, and was vociferously portrayed, as a symbol of social unrest, of urban degradation, of a city in crisis, abandoned by the mechanisms of supervision by the gentry and middle classes, a breeding ground for immorality, deprivation and criminality. The East End was depicted almost as a separate city within a city, abandoned to its slow degeneration, a place of social disintegration, violence, wretchedness and moral degradation. Within the East End, Whitechapel itself, with its rookeries and slums, its violent crime and dirt, its gin houses and alcoholic prostitutes, represented the very essence of London poverty. With his 1885 publication of *The Maiden Tribute of Modern Babylon*, Stead shook the country. *The Maiden Tribute* was a scandalous account of child prostitution in London and exposed to the middle classes a depraved world of child abduction, sale to brothels and a rotten world where upper-class paedophiles engaged their perversions with mere children. Whether this literary and news media outpouring was of benefit to the people of the East End in the long run may well have been the case and there are academic arguments on the greater or lesser extent of this. The public outcry that followed the publication of *The Maiden Tribute* was tantamount to mass hysteria and obliged the government to publish the Criminal Amendment Bill, which raised the age of consent from thirteen to sixteen. The issue here is that the media played a vital role in contextualising the Whitechapel murders and in creating the indelible imprint on social consciousness that Jack the Ripper has become.

The highlighting of social conditions in London's East End may also have been a secondary motive on the part of some editors to highlight the plight of the poor of the East End and the moral crisis that society was experiencing, using the story to prick the consciences of those with the power to make a difference to living conditions in the East End. Ultimately, unlike Cohen's model, the Jack the Ripper episode did not result in any changes in the criminal justice system or in social legislation, save the fact that the Chief Commissioner of the Metropolitan Police resigned.

As a point of interest, Commissioner Warren resigned on the day before Mary Kelly's murder, at the end of a period when there were no new murders from the Ripper for the newspapers to report. From 1st October to 9th November 1888, when Mary Kelly's body was discovered, the Ripper seemed to have gone to ground, but the newspapers were not prepared to let the matter lie when sales were at stake. Instead, this period saw a time of reflection, if the media noise can be termed as "reflective". With no grisly murder details to fill the front pages and draw crowds of buyers, reporters and their editors instead sought to find angles, points of entry to the Ripper story that could keep the issue alive in the minds of the readers: the story, to use a modern analogy, was kept trending. Warren's resignation came at the height of newspaper criticisms of the police and their lack of success in catching the killer, although the angles of the stories included attacks on Warren and the way he policed the city, with a timely reminders of his sometimes brutal style, such as the piece in the *Daily Chronicle* of 8th October on the police repression of Bloody Sunday in 1887, and of his incompetence, such as the *East London Advertiser*'s editorial of 13th October 1888 which was headed: "Our Defective Detective System" (https://www.casebook.org/press_reports/).

For those five weeks, the media was rampant with criticisms and commentary on the police in an attempt to keep the "monster" as much in the public eye as possible. While it is easy to take a cynical stance and claim that it was all done for the sales figures, and certainly this was likely to be the main motivator, the media was also affirming its role in public service, not just in terms of providing information, but also in terms of providing a platform for public debate. Newspapers received a plethora of letters from the readership taking one side or another and expressing individual views, voicing, albeit in a limited way, the views of the general public. Some of these letters and opinions were published and added fuel to the public debate on the competence or otherwise of the police, although publication would have been carried out through the filter of the editor and the particular line that he wished his publication to take and the campaigning stance, if there was one, of his newspaper. Thus, there was an outcry on the "present reign of plunder and anarchy" on Gray's Inn Road in the front-page leader of the *Gazette* of 10th October 1888, which was headed: "Law and Order in London" (Warwick and Willis, 2013). Alongside criticisms, there were also calls for improvements to police resources, with the *Gazette*, for example, also claiming that the police were undermanned, overworked, demoralised and poorly led (Warwick and Willis, 2013). The parallels with modern media analysis and discussion in the wake of the continuing rise in knife crimes in London and other parts of the UK, or, indeed, after the terrorist attacks in Manchester and London in 2017, are striking.

Criticism of the police ran alongside a campaigning tone taken by some of the press which used the opportunity as a platform to campaign on the evils of poverty and slum living in the East End, with the more elitist media such as the medical journals running articles alongside the left-wing press. The *British Medical Journal*, for example, praised the Rev Samuel Barnett's campaign against the evils of poverty which he believed might "coalesce into a criminal class" (Warwick and Willis, 2013), stating that the "true causes" of the murders were being ignored, and that these "lay in the rookeries where there was a vast population… packed into dark places, festering in ignorance, in dirt, in moral degradation, accustomed to violence and crime, born and bred within a touch of habitual immorality and coarse obscenity". While attempts had been made to clear slums, the East End lay untouched and apparently abandoned, neglected by the authorities who had not even managed to light them at night and whose police could not successfully protect the women who lived there.

Also, during this lull in the Ripper's murderous activities, the newspapers gave way to the temptation of psychoanalysis and theorising on the state of mind and the motives of the killer. Overall opinion widely expressed, both in print and in conversations in the street, in pubs, across dinner tables and wherever people gathered, was that the killer was a homicidal maniac devoured by his own bloodlust, marauding the streets of Whitechapel hunting for prey. A psychiatrist of the time, Forbes Winslow, developed theories on criminal insanity that were widely cited in the press which gave him an arguably unfounded legitimacy and status of leading expert on the theme. It was Winslow who propagated the view that the Ripper was a "gentlemanly lunatic" who might recently have been released from an asylum. The debate was powered through exchanges in the letter's pages of the newspapers by more medical men who could not help but air their views. Though there was no overall consensus on quite the psychopathology from which the killer might be suffering, there was a general understanding that he was sufficiently cunning to lure his victims without much of a struggle into dark corners, kill them without attracting any attention and make a clean getaway, unidentified, with no pursuers.

The media debate moved on to the issue of sexual motivation after the double event, although these discussions were often reserved to the more audacious evening papers – the killer was disturbed before fully achieving satisfaction with one victim and went on to kill another within the same "expedition" in order to attain whatever gruesome fulfilment he required. In his essay "The Pursuit of Angles" (Curtis, 2001, in Warwick and Willis, 2013), Curtis refers to an article featured in the *Evening Post* of 15th October 1988 titled "A Medical Man" which discussed the kind of men who disembowelled women for "voluptuous" reasons, and which alluded to Krafft-Ebing's *Psychopathia Sexualis* which dealt with sexual and criminal abnormality. Other so-called experts of the time asserted that the killer's motivations arose from a rage derived from venereal disease – the idea of a mad syphilitic doctor arose from this, a killer bent on killing prostitutes to avenge his own infection. Meanwhile, a third contemporary hypothesis was that of the killer suffering from some form of epilepsy. Again, allusions to Krafft-Ebing and also Cesare Lombroso in the press, discussed the belief that in the course of an epileptic seizure, some men were overwhelmed by sexual desire and killed in a state of sexual frenzy.

It was during the lull in the killings during October of 1888 that the media were served with a perfect opportunity to revitalise flagging interest in the Ripper murders in the form of the portion of human kidney – the "ginny kidney", so-called because it was declared on investigation by Dr Thomas Openshaw, pathological curator of the London Hospital Museum, to be a portion of a kidney belonging to an alcoholic woman in her mid-forties who would have died at around the same time as Eddowes. The kidney had been sent to George Lusk, the founder of the Whitechapel Vigilance Committee, with a note purportedly from the killer who suggested that he had eaten portions of the bodies that had been taken from the corpses of Eddowes and Chapman, and who taunted Lusk, writing: "Catch me when you can…" and inscribing "From Hell" at the top of the letter. It was the perfect story from which to create sensational headlines and sell increasing numbers of newspapers.

Even this sensational story faded from the front pages along with the story of the murders as October entered its last week, with the theme being touched on in the form of reports on the petition to Queen Victoria by Henrietta Barnett, who had gathered the signatures of over four thousand concerned women. The letter accompanying the petition was printed in several newspapers, and "conveyed the revulsion felt by respectable women over 'the dreadful sins' recently committed as well as their sorrow and shame over the new notoriety attached to Whitechapel" (Warwick and Willis, 2013). The newspapers also printed the rather bland reply from the Home Secretary who said that the police commissioners were considering ways to 'mitigate the evils' but did not say how.

An analysis of the different stories related by the print media and how information was presented to the public, including the use of sensationalism in order to draw attention and gain sales, serves to illustrate how much of our current understanding and, in fact, knowledge – if that word can be used, albeit with caution, in this context – of Jack the Ripper can be directly traced back to the press reports and their versions of what was public thinking at the time. It serves to contextualise some of the many theories that have been pursued by researchers and enthusiasts over the course of the past century or so and can help us to understand why some of the strands of investigation were taken up: public debate threw up a number of "victim types" from a state of conjecture fuelled by a media seeking the greatest level of sensationalism as a platform from which to sell the maximum numbers of their particular newspapers. Darren Oldridge's assertion in his opening line of his essay "Casting the Spell of Terror: The Press and the Early Whitechapel Murders" (Warrick and Willis, 2013), "The Whitechapel murders of 1888 were, above all, a media event", can readily be understood.

Oldridge's essay explores the narrative created by the press that linked the crimes in the social psyche. Oldridge refers to the memoirs of Sir Melville MacNaghten, one of the senior police officers investigating the crimes, who opined that the press interest greatly exaggerated the facts and was unhelpful and misleading, encouraging panic in the city. He alludes to the press ascribing murders to Jack the Ripper that could not in reality be linked given the factual evidence. Oldridge refers to the existence of a publicly expressed "rumour" that there was a lone killer at large in the area responsible for a number of deaths, a story that was being spread in the press before the Chapman murder had been linked to Nichols' murder. By the time of Chapman's murder, some media reports already believed she was the fourth victim and this "allowed the *Star* to proclaim that 'London lies today under the spell of a great terror', as a 'nameless reprobate' – half man, half beast – is… daily gratifying his murderous instincts". Oldridge proceeds to discuss the view that the sensational coverage of subsequent events were rooted in these early reports of a killer, for which there was no concrete evidence, and which reinforced the early development of the story of Jack the Ripper as its own urban legend.

Oldridge also explored the main strands of the narrative based on which angle was taken by the various writers and editors, identifying these as, firstly, the focus on the terrible physical and social conditions in which the murders took place, and the accompanying public outrage and the resultant connection of the murders by ascribing them to the same killer, which also included the possibility that the killings had been carried out by gangs; and secondly, the assumption that there was a lone killer, a frenzied maniac hunting down women for prey, an especially popular theory that sold many newspapers. The strands were themselves linked: a depraved enclave of society would, in the public mind, inevitably sink into the unspeakable horrors of savagery, for example. There was a further link in that the victims were all destitute women at the very least occasionally working as street prostitutes simply in order to survive, and with alcohol abuse issues, making them one of the most vulnerable groups in society, but one which was the least likely to attract public sympathy. In Oldridge's view, it was this early coverage and the creation of narrative strands through which the story could be explored, and its various levels peeled back and exposed, that contributed to such a great extent to the development of the sensation that immortalised "Jack the Ripper". 'By crafting the story of the Whitechapel murderer from the deaths of Emma Smith, Martha Tabram and Polly Nichols,' writes Oldridge, 'the press launched the "Ripper industry" on an enthralled public.' He goes on to add that "since nothing connected these women except the overwhelming tragedy of their lives, the earliest stage of this industry illustrates the fundamental role of mythmaking in the process. It is hardly surprising, then, that myths about the Ripper have flourished and multiplied ever since".

Besides successfully communicating the complex backdrop against which the murders were acted out, media reports were also revelatory of the significant divisions in social class and social attitudes, in particular, as Judith Walkowitz so clearly highlights in *City of Dreadful Delight* (1992) and her essay in Warwick and Willis (2013) "Narratives of Sexual Danger", the media stories and public commentary also "exposed deep-seated sexual antagonism, most frequently expressed by men towards women" (Warwick and Willis, 2013). Simply by heightening fear and panic among the population of London, indeed throughout the country and in other cities of the world, the media elicited a response among the community that served to reinforce the image of woman as victim, woman as fully vulnerable unless "in her place" by the hearth or under the protection of a man. Where women were reported to be afraid to walk out alone, the social constraints on the free movement of women were strengthened, further restricting women and repressing their attempts to seek employment, independence and empowerment. This victim mentality is self-perpetuating and traps women into a cycle of weakness and fear which causes disempowerment.

One striking feature of the media reporting and the Jack the Ripper narrative is that more recent murders, such as the Yorkshire Ripper murders of 1975, are not as contextually different as might be expected, although responses by contemporary feminists to situations such as the Yorkshire Ripper murders and, more recently, the Harvey Weinstein sex scandal are different, more politically focused and played out against a backdrop of greater gender equality. However, in terms of social context, poverty and poor housing is still rife in pockets of inner cities throughout the country and notably in East London, and conditions worsening dramatically as we enter the third decade of the twenty-first century. Sex workers continue to be among the most vulnerable people in our society and people trafficking notably for sex and among this the trafficking of very young children, continues to plague society. As Walkowitz explains in her book published in 1992, the iconography of the Ripper narrative continues to be exploited and employs the imagery that provides a reference point for a society that still references male violence against women to the Ripper murders. The disempowering effect of media exploitation of horrific deaths continues to be felt today.

> *The Whitechapel murders have continued to provide a common vocabulary of male violence against women, a vocabulary now more than one hundred years old. Its persistence owes much to the mass media's exploitation of Ripper iconography. Depictions of female mutilation in mainstream cinema, celebration of the Ripper as a "hero" of crime intensify fears of male violence and convince women they are helpless victims.*
>
> Walkowitz, 1992

What does stand out in stark relief from this welter of sensation, story-making and newspaper-selling, is how quickly the focus on the tragedy that was each of those deaths fades into the background. Victorian attitudes to prostitution, despite the best efforts of journalists and social reformers such as W.T. Stead, were such that the victim was of little consequence compared to the prurient nature of fascination with the physical injuries. The media's reporting of the crimes moved from horror at the facts of the murder to the degraded nature of their lives, at which point, the victims begin to fade into the background of the narrative – they are steadily depersonified so that their life experiences outside and beyond the East End – their lives before misfortune had broken them – become inconsequential to the Ripper narrative. The media were concerned far more with the landscape of immorality in which the murders took place than with the fact that women, regardless of whether or not they had to sell sex in order to survive, had died in such awful circumstances. There was a media obsession with the location of the crimes, and this obsession opened the doors to the debate on reform and the causes behind intemperance and prostitution, linking closely to the Victorian conflation of the "broken woman" with the "fallen woman" – the former is a victim of unfortunate circumstances, the latter has chosen a life of immorality, but for Victorians, when it came to women, the two terms were easily merged to mean the same thing.

The victims were mourned by a few of their friends, families and acquaintances, persons whose consequence in society was minimal because they were part of an underclass that Victorian society preferred not to think about too deeply. Instead, the media flurry of speculation has left modern readers the legacy of a monstrous construct, a legendary villain whose identity will never be ascertained but whose presence continues to haunt newspaper columns, books, online articles, blogs, film and television. This is the legacy left by the media for the victims – their deaths are reworked day after day in tourist "attractions" and "Jack the Ripper", tours and replayed for the unrelentingly prurient public. The media successfully turned the Whitechapel murders into a tool for controlling the behaviour of women, not just in the 1888 aftermath of the killings but into the present.

REFERENCES

"Attacking the Devil", W.T. Stead Resource Site: https://www.attackingthedevil.co.uk/pmg/tribute/

Cohen, S. (1972), *Folk Devils and Moral Panics. The Creation of Mods and Rockers*, MacGibbon, London, in Gray, D.D., (2013), *London's Shadows: The Dark Side of the Victorian City*, Bloomsbury Academic, London.

Curtis, L.P. (2001), "The Pursuit of Angles", taken from *Jack the Ripper and the London Press*, Yale University Press, in Warwick, A. and Willis, M. (2013), *Jack the Ripper: Media, Culture, History*, Manchester University Press, Manchester.

Gray, D.D. (2013), *London's Shadows: The Dark Side of the Victorian City*, Bloomsbury Academic, London.

Gregg, J.J. (2013), "Murder, Media and Mythology: The Impact the Media's Reporting of the Whitechapel Murders had on National Identity, Social Reform and the Myth of Jack the Ripper", University of Warwick, Undergraduate Research Paper, retrieved from https://warwick.ac.uk/fac/cross_fac/iatl/reinvention/archive/bcur2013specialissue/jones#notes

Lloyds Weekly Newspaper (1888) retrieved from https://www.casebook.org/press_reports/lloyds_weekly_news/18880909.html

Mearns, A. and Preston, W.C. (1883), *The Bitter Cry of Outcast London: An Inquiry into the Condition of the Abject Poor*, James Clarke & Co, London, retrieved from http://www.gutenberg.org/ebooks/55316

Ryder, S.P., Anderson, R., Chisholm, A. and Scott, C., "Casebook: Jack the Ripper", copyright Stephen P. Ryder and Johnno, 1996–2021, Thomas Schachner, retrieved from https://www.casebook.org/press_reports/

The Star (1888), retrieved from https://www.casebook.org/press_reports/star/s880908.html

Warwick, A., and Willis, M. (2013), *Jack the Ripper: Media, Culture, History*, Manchester University Press, Manchester.

Walkowitz, J.R. (1992), *City of Dreadful Delight: Narratives of Sexual Danger*, University of Chicago Press, Chicago.

Wescott, T. (2014), *The Bank Holiday Murders: The True Story of the First Whitechapel Murders*, Crime Confidential Press

4

BEYOND THE GRAVE: JACK THE RIPPER'S VICTIMS

*'Crime and bad lives are the measure of a State's failure,
all crime in the end is the crime of the community.'*

H.G. Wells

Jack the Ripper's murder victims were all women. More specifically, they were women who bordered on complete destitution, and from time to time had resorted to selling sex on the streets of the East End of London or exchanging sex for some sort of security or place of safety. It is probable that they had been prostituting themselves just before they were killed, and their bodies mutilated. Prostitution was as prevalent in cities across the globe during the supposedly prudish days of the Victorian era as it is in our current, so-called permissive times. We have discussed the nature of the Victorian's attitude towards prostitution in Chapter 6 and through our research we uncovered a society with conflicted views on sex, prostitution and morality. The victims were also exclusively drawn from the ranks of the working class – or the underclass, those who could not find work that paid sufficient wages for basic survival. This was typical of Victorian prostitution; while clients came from all the classes and backgrounds, the women and girls serving them were largely those who could not otherwise afford to fend for themselves, and many of these had no real choice but to sell sex in exchange for food and shelter. Gray (2013) refers to Bracebridge Hemyng's study of the London poor. Hemyng divided prostitutes into three classes, although he also qualifies Hemyng's division by suggesting the lines probably often blurred:

> *those women who are kept by men of independent means; secondly, those women who live in apartments, and maintain themselves by the produce of their vagrant armours; and thirdly, those who dwell in brothels.*
>
> Hemyng 1861

Prostitution was seen largely as a threat towards the moral health of the nation by the Victorians. Sex workers were classed as somehow less than human because they were women that had cast aside their roles of wives and mothers, roles that would preserve their purity and reserve this only for the husband, the man that legally, and morally, possessed them. For the more liberally minded middle- and upper-class Victorians – those who had some degree of understanding of the devastation that could be caused by poverty and destitution in a society that did not provide any form of state support to the poor – prostitutes were "fallen women", "unfortunate", worthy of some pity. Many more, however, regarded prostitution as a form of disease, a corruption of body and soul, and prostitutes were anathema to the workings of a civilised and Christian society. Yet men did not shy from using the services of these sex workers and society tended to believe that men required the services of prostitutes to relieve their powerful "manly" urges. The victims of Jack the Ripper's murder spree were part of the ugly, seething Victorian underbelly, used and abused by the wealthier classes, and either ignored or despised and, at best, pitied at a distance. Whether they were regular sex workers or whether they had to supplement their meagre incomes with sex working, they were judged and categorised by the police, the media, the middle- and upper-class commentators of the time, by generation after generation of those fascinated with the events and possibly by the Ripper himself.

Given the sheer numbers of prostitutes working in the East End at the time of the murders, it stands to reason that the death of a prostitute would not attract the kind of media attention that these murders received. Victorian Whitechapel was seething with criminal gangs that ran "stables" of street prostitutes, protection rackets, smuggling and thieving. The gangs were often responsible for violent crimes, assaults, and murders. Prostitutes working on the streets at night were vulnerable and open to assaults, as much from their own pimps and traffickers and whichever gang controlled the streets and alehouses where they worked as they might have been from rival gangs or even random strangers. Besides being some of the poorest and most abused members of society, street prostitutes were also the most likely victims of all sorts of crimes including assault, robbery and murder, something that is as true today as it was during the Victorian period.

That Jack the Ripper's victims were prostitutes is usually the first thing we learn about them. There is something distastefully prurient about the focus on this fact, as if we have not yet, one hundred and fifty years later, managed to disengage the moral judgements on sex working from the unequivocal fact that the victims were all women. They were, each and every one of them, daughters, wives, sisters, neighbours, friends, and some were also mothers. Why else, is the silent question that screams at us from across a century and a half of investigation and analysis, would any other woman be wondering out in the small hours of the night in the dark and dismal labyrinth of grubby alleys that was Victorian Whitechapel? The sense of victim-blaming still pervades how we look at these women and is an undercurrent in much of the Ripper literature still being produced. It has influenced the equally prurient, almost voyeuristic tourist attractions that have arisen from society's continued fascination with the Jack the Ripper story – from guided Ripper Walks to an exhibition at the London Dungeon tourist attraction, to the opening of a Ripper museum in 2015 in Aldgate. We wanted to take a different look at the women who became Jack the Ripper's victims, and this chapter focuses on their humanity.

That the victims were living in poverty, in the squalid lodging houses of Whitechapel and had been involved in prostitution, and probably touting for trade when they made their fatal encounter with the murderer, has not, until more recently and only by a very few writers and academics. been under dispute. There remains to this day, however, heated debate on which of the murders that took place between the spring and early winter of 1888 could realistically be ascribed to the one murderer that we term "Jack the Ripper". The police list the names of nine dead women: Emma Smith, Martha Tabram, Mary Ann Nichols, Annie Chapman, Elizabeth Stride, Catherine Eddowes, Mary Jane Kelly, Alice McKenzie and Frances Coles. However, there is a general acceptance that only five of those – largely because the nature and extent of their injuries fit the accepted mould of "ripper" mutilations – have been attributed to "Jack the Ripper" and are known as the "canonical five": Nichols, Chapman, Stride, Eddowes and Kelly. However, we have taken the view that regardless of whether these nine women were murdered by the same perpetrator, they are nonetheless also victims of a murderous city and of dangerous circumstances, victims of time, of place and of their own misfortune.

Emma Smith's murder received little publicity. It even went unreported by the doctor in whose care she died of her horrible injuries for a number of hours after her death. In fact, the police did not hear of the crime until 6th April despite the attack being on 4th April, which is when the coroner's office reported that an inquest was to be held on 7th, leaving precious little time for the police to obtain detailed reports from their constables on duty on the night of the attack. It is notable that neither the police had made any record of observing Emma Smith on the streets and bleeding from her attack, nor had any report to the police been made either by other residents of the lodging house, nor by the hospital, despite the sheer brutality of the assault that she endured.

Emma was a forty-five-year-old mother of two and on occasions was a sex worker. She was attacked in Osborn Street just off the Whitechapel Road on the bank holiday of 2nd April 1888, by a group of three men who had made off with all her money. Her attackers had left her with horrific injuries but still living, and despite these she had managed to stumble in agonising pain back to her lodging house at around 5am. She went to her friend, Mrs Mary Russell, whom she had known for two years. With the pain and bleeding between her legs not abating, Smith was escorted to hospital by Mary Russell and a second friend, Annie Lee, showing them where she had been attacked, although she was unable (or unwilling) to describe her attackers. She was admitted to the care of the house surgeon, Mr George Haslip, who gave evidence at the inquest, which was presided over by Mr Wynne Baxter, the Coroner for East Middlesex.

Smith had received cuts and abrasions about the head during the attack and one ear had been almost torn off. She was reportedly knocked unconscious and lay for a while on the ground before making her way back to her lodging house. The cause of her death was due to the rupture of the peritoneum caused by a blunt instrument having been thrust forcefully into her vagina. She died of peritonitis caused by the rupture on the morning of April 4th. The jury at the inquest returned the verdict of "wilful murder against some person or persons unknown".

On the surface, Emma Smith's murder does not immediately relate to the later Ripper murders, and it is easy to see why she has been dismissed as a Ripper victim by investigators over the years. She was not ripped or even stabbed by a knife and death was caused by a blunt instrument. However, the attack was ferocious: Wescott refers to a report in the *Lloyd's Weekly News* of 8th April: 'Dr. [Haslip] described the internal injuries which had been caused and which must have been inflicted by a blunt instrument. It had even penetrated the peritoneum, producing peritonitis, which was undoubtedly the cause of death, in his opinion… He made a post-mortem examination and described the organs as generally normal. He had no doubt that death was caused by the injuries to the perineum, the abdomen, and the peritoneum. Great force must have been used. The injuries had set up peritonitis, which had resulted in death on the following day after admission.' (Wescott, 2014.) It is not known whether there were any cuts on her body other than the fact that her ear had been almost torn from her head. Whether Smith had been attacked by the Ripper in the early stages of his development into a serial killer still refining his methods and selecting his preferred tools is open to speculation. But it is evident that brutality and death was being meted out to destitute women in East London in a way which still haunts its streets.

Nor was violence that night confined to prostitutes. Dr Haslip had also been tending Malvina Haynes, a woman who had been savagely beaten on the same bank holiday night as Smith, incurring severe injuries about the head. She had been standing near the Leman Street railway when she was attacked, and she was later discovered unconscious by a constable. Like Smith, Haynes was taken to the London Hospital and placed in the care of Dr George Haslip a few hours before Smith arrived. However, in Haynes' case, the hospital immediately contacted the police. Malvina Haynes was a married woman whose husband was a painter. The couple lived at 29 Newnham Street, Great Alie Street in Whitechapel and had been out with friends that day seeing the sights of their city. Having returned home earlier in the evening, Mrs Haynes popped out, whereupon she was viciously attacked. The police found her, took her to hospital and the hospital quickly reported on her injuries. This text-book example of cooperation between the hospital and the police immediately failed Emma Smith, and the failure was especially severe because Smith died of her injuries, yet while she was alive and conscious, the police were not given the opportunity to obtain evidence which might have led to the apprehension of her attacker, who became her murderer. Whoever he might have been, he was, through negligence – intentional, possibly, because there might have been a fear that this attack was carried out at the behest of a local gang – of Dr Haslip, free to attack again. The suspicion that this was because of the different moral status of each woman, one a wife, one a prostitute, cannot be avoided.

Part of Emma Smith's personal tragedy is that there is so little known about her other than that she might have died at the hands of the Ripper, and there is even doubt about that. She had friends who shared her lodging house at 18 George Street where she lived for the last eighteen months of her life. She was thought to be a widow, although this was often a claim made by women who had separated from their husbands, and many of those had been abandoned by their families because of their alcoholism or infidelity or had fallen into alcoholism as result of being separated from their husband and the support of their families; the issues were often combined. However, Smith did claim openly that she had left her husband some ten years prior to his death so it is plausible that she was telling the truth. What is more certain, is that for some reason, or a number of reasons, she had left her previous life and fallen into a hand-to-mouth existence, impoverished in the East End of London, relying on prostitution to stay alive. That she suffered from alcohol abuse is corroborated by Russell's evidence at the inquest, describing Smith as a "'mad woman' when drunk who earned her living as a prostitute and would often return home with bruises and black eyes" (Wescott, 2014).

Testimony at the inquest was also provided by one of Smith's friends, another prostitute, Margaret Hames. Hames told the inquest that she and Smith had decided to spend their bank holiday at Limehouse which was some two miles away from their home. Prostitutes would have been perfectly well aware that Limehouse was closer to the docks and on a bank holiday evening would have been teeming with eager, recently paid sailors ready to buy sex. At midnight, Hames was walking home alone and was punched in the face by two youths. Hurrying back along Burdett Road, Hames claims she saw Smith on the corner of Farrance Street talking to a man dressed in black and wearing a white scarf, although she simply walked on and did not stop to talk to her. Hames also referred to having had to spend twenty days in the Whitechapel infirmary the previous December after having been attacked on the street and being left with injuries to the chest and face.

We are not going to speculate on the rights and wrongs of why Mrs Malvina Haynes was treated differently to Emma Smith, nor on whom the attacker might have been, or whether this attack was by the Ripper himself or otherwise. Rather, we consider this an issue of the prejudice that was demonstrated by both the medical profession and the police in their responses to the plight of the two women. The expectation of prejudice was clearly high in Emma Smith's mind when she hesitated in presenting herself to the hospital. She might have feared running into her attacker again or being caught in gang rivalries and considered as a liability for having approached the doctors who were bound to report the incident to the police. Mrs Haynes – a more "respectable" woman and less likely to be involved in this underworld – had less hesitation in seeking medical help. Furthermore, when she did so, this was quickly forthcoming, as was the police investigation into the attack. Attitudes clearly influenced the degree, extent and speed of response shown by the authorities.

While the nature and extent of Emma Smith's injuries meant that she was not included in the "canonical" five, she was the victim of a ferocious and eventually fatal attack. Her murder was never solved, and it was certainly the case that once other murders had been committed, the police referred back to her case and for a while linked her to the series. Wescott (2014) points to the fact that Inspector Reid believed that Smith's murderer was the Ripper, and while this remains in the realm of conjecture, the view of someone as deeply involved with the Ripper cases as Reid was, cannot be loosely dismissed.

Martha Tabram, also an impoverished woman likely to have been relying on occasional prostitution to supplement her meagre an only occasional income as a street hawker with a history of alcohol abuse and also attacked on a bank holiday, died in the early hours of 7th August 1888. If the murderer was the same attacker who killed Emma Smith, it seems as if he had refined his methods, improved on his choices of weapon and killing so that his mutilation of the body could receive a greater degree of focus and therefore allow him a greater degree of satisfaction. But this is mere speculation, and it is believed by many that Tabram's murderer was probably not the same attacker as had left Smith for dead and not the Ripper.

On the night of 6th April 1888, Tabram had been out drinking with her friend, Mary Ann Connelly, also known as Pearly Poll. They were with two soldiers at The Angel and Crown, a pub close to George Yard Buildings. The four paired off and at around a quarter to midnight, the two pairs, each woman with their own client, wandered off, Tabram into George Yard, an alley that connected Whitechapel High Street to Wentworth Street. Her body was found by a resident of George Yard Buildings, Mr Albert Crow, who was returning home from work as a cab driver at 3.30am and found the body lying on the landing above the first flight of stairs. At first, he thought she was a vagrant in a drunken sleep, so he walked on to his room. It was not until 5.00 that a dock labourer on his way to work, John Reeves, realised she was dead. Reeves called the police, and the doctor was sent for. Tabram was found to have died some three hours earlier. She had been stabbed thirty-nine times in the body and neck, including in her lower abdomen and genitals. She was found lying on her back, her clothing in disarray, the bosom of the dress torn away, raised to her middle and exposing her lower half, indicating a sexual position and recent intimacy, although Dr Killeen, who had examined the body at the scene and went on to carry out the post-mortem, could not find any evidence of intercourse. He did find that she was well nourished, with fat around the heart, and the brain, kidneys, stomach and liver were healthy. Besides the stab wounds which the doctor believed might have been carried out with at least a knife and a dagger, he mentions a "deal of blood between the legs". There is no more detail than this, but then, with the cause of death being attributed to loss of blood, and Victorian courts preferring not to discuss the intimacy of injuries to female sexual organs if it was not strictly necessary, these details have been withheld.

Martha Tabram was born Martha White on 10th May 1849 in London. She was the youngest of five children whose family was eventually abandoned by their father, a warehouseman called Charles White. In 1869, on Christmas Day, Martha married Henry Tabram, but six years later they were to separate because of Martha's heavy drinking. For some time after their separation, Henry Tabram paid her a weekly maintenance but reduced this when he discovered she had been prostituting herself. In 1879, Henry Tabram discovered that Martha had taken up living with Henry Turner and he stopped the allowance altogether. Turner, who lived with Tabram for some nine years, also found her heavy drinking to be a problem. The couple separated three weeks prior to her death, although he saw her three days before she died and lent her some money to buy "stock" for her to sell. There is little to distinguish the course of Tabram's life from those of the other victims: misfortune, drink, poverty, dysfunctional relationships, destitution, violence, death.

It was only after the murder of Mary Ann Nichols (also known as Polly) on 31st August that the police began to suspect that something extraordinary was taking place and linked the previous murders, although, as we know, these were subsequently dismissed as not being linked. It was then that the media, and with it the public imagination, caught light. The stories and speculation became a conflagration that continues to burn today.

The forty-two-year-old Polly Nichols was found murdered in a narrow, cobbled street – Buck's Row – at 3.45am on Friday 31st August 1888. The witness who found her, Constable John Neil, had been going about his patrol along Buck's Row towards Brady Street when he came across her lying on her back with her eyes wide open and blood around a wound in the throat. He noted that she was still warm to the touch and thought that she might just about have still been alive when he came across her but died as he was seeking help. Shortly after Constable Neil found the body, Dr Henry Llewellyn arrived, and finding that she was dead, he ordered the body to be removed to the mortuary, where he then lifted her clothing and discovered the extensive mutilations of the abdomen. His report to the inquest claimed that in his opinion, she could not have been dead much more than a half hour. It is possible that the murderer was still nearby when she was found, perhaps still in the process of making good his escape, although a local person or a person with thorough local knowledge of the labyrinth of passages and alleys in the Whitechapel of the time could easily have traversed quite a dizzying distance in a short space of time.

The inquest into Nichols' murder was presided over by Mr Wynne Baxter, the Coroner for South East Middlesex. Nichols' body was identified by her father, Edward Walker of 15 Maidwell Street, Albany Road in Camberwell. He had not seen her for three years but identified her by a mark on her forehead which she had as a child, and by one or two missing teeth that she had had taken out. Nichols had been married for twenty-two years to William Nichols, a printer's machinist, from whom she had been estranged for some eight years. The couple had five children, their relationship apparently turbulent, with references made to William Nichols having had an affair and eventually separating from Mary because of her drunken habits and accusing her, rightly or wrongly, of prostitution. William Nichols was supposed to pay her an allowance despite their estrangement, which he apparently did until 1882 but stopped when he heard that she was working as a prostitute, the law not obliging him to do so if she was earning money through illicit means. For a while, Mary lived with her father, but left after a quarrel and eventually moved in with a blacksmith in Walworth. She moved in and out of workhouses, her problem of substance abuse never overcome probably because of her circumstances. Early in 1888 she finally found a position as a domestic servant in Wandsworth, but by then she was an alcoholic, and her employer would not stand for it. She left, allegedly stealing some money from her employer, and eventually found her way back to the lodging houses of Whitechapel. Nichols' story is not untypical of those of thousands of women trapped in poverty and substance abuse, then and now.

Like the other of the Ripper's victims, Polly Nichols had spent time in and out of lodging houses, living on the margins of society. She had been staying at lodgings with an Emily Holland for some six weeks, although she had not been there for the ten days or so prior to her murder. Mrs Holland was possibly the last person to see her alive, at around 2.30am on the Saturday morning, and she observed that Nichols appeared very much the worse for drink, trying to make her way eastwards through Whitechapel. Just one and a quarter hours later and only three-quarters of a mile away, she was brutally murdered.

With the murder of Annie Chapman being investigated at the time Polly Nichols' murder came before an inquest, it is at this point that the coroner and the police linked several murders. According to reporting from Marriott (2007) in his book *Jack the Ripper: The Twenty-First Century Investigation*, the coroner, Mr Wynne Baxter, said:

> *We cannot altogether leave unnoticed the fact that the death that you have been investigating is one of four presenting many points of similarity, all of which have occurred within the space of about five months, and all within a very short distance of the place where we are sitting. All four victims were women of middle age, all were married, and had lived apart from their husbands in consequence of intemperate habits, and were at the time of their death leading an irregular life, and eking out a miserable and precarious existence in common lodging-houses. In each case there were abdominal as well as other injuries. In each case the injuries were inflicted after midnight, and in places of public resort, where it would appear impossible but that almost immediate detection should follow the crime, and in each case the inhuman and dastardly criminals are at large in society.*
>
> *Marriott 2007*

In his summing-up at the inquest of Nichols' murder, Baxter, again as reported in Marriott (2007), goes on to draw a greater similarity between the murders of Chapman and Nichols:

The similarity of the injuries in the two cases is considerable. There are bruises about the face in both cases; the head is nearly severed from the body in both cases; there are other dreadful injuries in both cases; and those injuries, again, have in each case been performed with anatomical knowledge. Dr Llewellyn seems to incline to the opinion that the abdominal injuries were first, and caused instantaneous death; but if so, it seems difficult to understand the object of such desperate injuries to the throat, or how it comes about that there was so little bleeding from the several arteries, that the clothing on the upper surface was not stained, and, indeed, very much less bleeding from the abdomen than from the neck. Surely it may well be that, as in the case of Chapman, the dreadful wounds to the throat were inflicted first and the others afterwards. This is a matter of some importance when we come to consider what possible motive there can be for all this ferocity. Robbery is out of the question and there is nothing to suggest jealousy; there could not have been any quarrel, or it would have been heard. I suggest to you that these two women may have been murdered by the same man with the same object, and that in the case of Nichols the wretch was disturbed before he had accomplished his object, and having failed in the open street he tries again, within a week of his failure, in a more secluded place…

Marriott 2007

Although there have been strong criticisms of Baxter in the Ripper literature, partly based on the idea that as a senior freemason Baxter would go on to protect the identity of the Ripper, another freemason, through misleading juries and the public and general obfuscation of facts (see Robinson, 2015), this summing-up does summarise quite neatly that there was a series of similar ferocious attacks on a certain group of women in the streets of East London and that the likelihood was that these were being perpetrated by one person. From our own analysis, we suggest that the murderer was most likely to have been a man, named by the popular media of the time as Jack the Ripper. Baxter's summing-up also points to the similarity of the victims as "unfortunate" women, if not entirely of the crime itself. This would lead us to suggest that the motives for the crimes were similar and probably linked to violent sexual deviancies. And this leads us to the idea that the motive and the type of victim points to the one killer for all these women, or, just as possible, two or three killers who shared a similar ideology and possibly psychological profile.

Mary Nichols was buried on 6th September 1888 at the City of London Cemetery. Her grave is now marked by a plaque and is situated on the edge of the current Memorial Garden.

Like Mary Ann Nichols, Annie Chapman was found dead in the early hours of the morning with her throat so deeply cut that her head was almost completely cut off her body. Her body was found in the backyard at 29 Hanbury Street on 8th September 1888. Chapman was last seen alive at around 5.30am talking to a man near to where her body was found. She had been disembowelled, and at the time of the post-mortem, her uterus was found to have been cut out and was missing. Her intestines had been removed from her abdomen and placed over her right shoulder, with other parts of her digestive system placed over the left. The significance of this ritualistic style of killing and disembowelment, the careful setting-up of the corpse and its organs, has also been the subject of much speculation and has fuelled much of the literature relating to the masonic nature of the killings, which in turn has pointed to the identifying of various suspects who also were freemasons, with particular emphasis given to the report by Dr Phillips, who examined the body at the scene and also carried out the post-mortem examination, saying:

> *Obviously, the work was one of an expert – of one, at least, who had such knowledge of anatomical or pathological examinations as to be enabled to secure the pelvic organs with one sweep of the knife, which must therefore have at least 5 or 6 inches in length, probably more.*
>
> Marriott, 2007

Also known to have worked as a prostitute, the forty-eight-year-old Annie Chapman died, like Polly Nichols, in the month of her birthday. For over four years she had lived in and out of various lodging houses in Spitalfields and Whitechapel, and spent her time around Brick Lane, Flower and Dean Street and Dorset Street. Since many of her fellow victims were of similar age and lived so locally to each other, it is highly likely they know each other, possibly even well enough to have been friends.

Annie Chapman was a mother and a widow, although she had been separated from her husband for many years as he could no longer live with her because of her dependency on alcohol, something that may have developed or become worse after the death of one of her two children. Although unable to live with her, her husband continued to support her, sending her a regular income until his death some eighteen months prior to her murder. When examined in post-mortem, Chapman was found to be carrying the bruises of earlier violence, was sick and had two teeth missing, her clothing simple, old and dirty. Chapman's life, even before her dreadful end, was already marked with tragedy.

For the four months before she died, Chapman lived at 35 Dorset Street, William Crossingham's house, before which she lived at a large lodging house operated by John McCarthy at 30 Dorset Street. It was here that she made friends with Amelia Farmer, whose husband was a former dock foreman. Chapman had lived there with John Sievey, an iron sieve maker, sharing the bed next to the Farmers'. Chapman was a heavy drinker, according to Amelia Farmer, and used prostitution as a way to earn enough money and add to her meagre income from knitting and selling items. However, she was not always penniless and was known to like to rent double beds in the lodging houses she stayed at, and not always in order to accommodate one of her regular clients.

At the post-mortem, it was discovered that Annie had lung and brain disease, which would have killed her fairly quickly had she not died under the Ripper's knife. Her life on the streets of East London was harsh. Annie Chapman walked to Stratford on most days to sell whatever items she could gather. She did not do so on the day before she died, because she claimed to be feeling unwell. It could be she was unwell as the symptoms of her illness made themselves felt. Or this could have been because she had been assaulted by an Eliza Cooper, another resident of the locality and one who had given evidence along with Pearly Poll and Elizabeth Allen regarding the Nichols murder. Chapman and Cooper had confronted each other on previous occasions, once at the kitchen of their lodging house and once in the Britannia Pub. The fight in the kitchen took place on 4th September and it was based on a disagreement over a bar of soap that Cooper lent to Chapman so that a Ted Stanley, one of Chapman's regular clients, could wash himself in the lodging house's outside lavatory. The bar of soap was never returned to Cooper and the women fought when Cooper asked for it back. The altercation at the pub involved Cooper – according to Chapman – kicking Chapman in the chest, the resulting bruise being witnessed by Amelia Farmer. Again, the animosity between the two women had arisen over another of their joint clients – Harry the Hawker – and some money.

As will be noted from our discussion on women and domestic violence during Victorian times in Chapter 7, violence against women by the men in their lives, and between two women, was not unknown. In fact, it was almost an established and expected fact. However, the degree of violence against a woman could be deemed by family, friends and neighbours as entirely unacceptable. While violence against prostitutes was commonplace and might not have raised an eyebrow, people, including the inhabitants of the slums of East London, found the Ripper murders horrific. At thirty-nine years of age, Cooper led a similar life to Chapman and to other of the Ripper's victims: poverty-stricken, relying on prostitution to survive, and with dubious acquaintances and clients, with violence often a feature of their lives. It would also be worth noting that the Britannia Pub was a favourite location for the women of Dorset Street to gather; Annie Chapman drank there, and so did Mary Kelly, and if they did, it is highly likely that Cooper, Pearly Poll and Polly Nichols did too.

Annie Chapman was buried at the Manor Park Cemetery, Forest Gate, on 14th September 1888, early in the morning and in secret, with only her close relatives and the police knowing about the arrangements. Her grave no longer exists but the place where it was is now marked with a plaque.

In his book, Wescott (2014) has highlighted some information on the company kept by some of Jack the Ripper's victims. Cooper and Pearly Poll were linked to several of the victims. Both were known criminals, and both were known to have provided false information about the murders, casting suspicion on people subsequently dismissed as suspects. While deeper investigation into the possible identity of the Ripper is beyond the scope of this book, we should note here, that the fact that these women, who were well known by the victims, provided misleading information to the investigating authorities points to them also knowing, or at least suspecting, the true identity of the Ripper and making moves to protect him (or them). This could be for numerous reasons, including fear that they might be next on his list and not least linking the Ripper to a local gang – although writers such as Bruce Robinson link the Ripper, with not insubstantial arguments, to one of the biggest secret gangs in the country, the freemasons. At the very least, it shows that Jack the Ripper was probably well-known in the locality, either as a local man, or as a client who used the prostitutes' services regularly and knew the area very well.

Elizabeth Stride was also a prostitute and also around forty-five years of age and was the first of two victims killed on the same night of 30th

September 1888, something that became known as the "Double Event" after it was described in this way in a letter received by the police on 1st October 1888 signed by "Saucy Jack". Stride's body was found by a salesman returning home with his pony and cart at about 1.00am in Dutfield's Yard. The pony shied at entering the yard, and, sensing something was wrong, the salesman himself entered the yard which was so dark he could barely see. He probed about with his whip and eventually found the body of a woman lying on the ground, at first believing her to be drunk and asleep. He went into the local working men's club, whose rear entrance opened into the yard to ask for help rousing her, but when he returned with two men, they found she was dead, with her throat cut, a packet of cachous pills still in her hand, her body still warm. Since then, it has been generally believed that the salesman was heard approaching and the killer was frightened off, his grizzly ritual of mutilating the corpse disturbed. He might even still have been in the yard while the salesman probed about because the pony continued to display signs of nervousness. Somehow, and probably when the salesman went to seek help, the killer escaped.

Stride was known to have stayed at 32 Flower and Dean Street, a notorious lodging house in a notorious street, and one which links some of the victims and some of the people who knew them: Eddowes and her partner John Kelly lived at 55 Flower and Dean Street, for example. Stride was born Elizabeth Gustafsdotter, the daughter of a Swedish farmer, Gustaf Ericsson and Beata Carlsdotter, in Gothenburg, Sweden. She was nicknamed "Long Liz", perhaps because she was very tall, perhaps because of her married surname. Unlike some of the other Ripper victims, she did not become a prostitute after a failed relationship and a subsequent fall into prostitution. By the time she was twenty-two years old, the Gothenburg police already had her recorded as a prostitute and she had been treated for a sexually transmitted disease. She was also known to have given birth to a stillborn girl in April 1865 in Gothenburg.

She then moved to London, possibly entering domestic service, and in 1869 she married John Thomas Stride, who was thirteen years older than her, a ship's carpenter from Sheerness. They lived in Poplar for a while and ran a coffee room, although this, and possibly their relationship, was not successful as she entered the Poplar Workhouse in March 1877. By 1881 it appears that she and her husband were separated, and John Stride died of tuberculosis in 1884. There are no records of there being any children of the marriage.

After separating from her husband in the early 1880s Stride took up with a Michael Kidney and lived with him from time to time. She resided, like the other Ripper victims, in and out of lodging houses, earning odd bits of money with activities such as sewing and cleaning as and when she could, and supplementing this with proceeds from her prostitution. Like the others, she was known to have behaved in a drunk and disorderly fashion from time to time, having made some appearances at the Thames Magistrates' Court, and she did once lodge a complaint of assault against Michael Kidney but never pursued this, which was not unusual in relationships at the time.

Elizabeth Stride lived a harsh life and died a violent death. She was buried on 6th October 1888 at the East London Cemetery at the expense of the parish in a very sparse service.

At 1.45am on that same night of 30th September, the body of Catherine Eddowes, sometimes also known as Kate, was found in a dark corner of Mitre Square. Although bordering Whitechapel, Mitre Square fell under the control of the City of London police. It is also only some ten to fifteen minutes' walk away from Berner Street, where Elizabeth Stride had been murdered a short while earlier; Eddowes' body was found some forty-five minutes after Stride's. Her throat had been cut so deeply that her head, like that of Polly Nichols, had been almost severed from her body. Her torso was slit open from breastbone to stomach and her intestines had been cut out and placed over her right shoulder with a portion of intestine placed between the body and the left arm – a meticulous arrangement of innards that has led to much comparison to ritual and the speculation that the Ripper might have been a freemason. The post-mortem would show that her kidney and her uterus had been removed. Her face had also been severely mutilated.

Catherine Eddowes was forty-six years old, born in Wolverhampton and also thought to be a prostitute. Her father was a tinplate worker and her family moved to London when she was about a year old. She then moved back to Wolverhampton and worked as a tinplate stamper but when she lost this job, she moved back to London with former soldier Thomas Conway and had two daughters and two sons with him. Here, she took to drinking and also to prostitution to supplement her meagre income as a hawker. Her relationship with Conway fell apart and he moved away, taking their sons with him. Friends described her as around five feet tall, with fair brown hair and hazel eyes, very intelligent with a fierce temper when roused, and also "a very jolly woman, always singing" (Marriott, 2007).

Eddowes had last been seen alive at 1.35am with a man, as reported by three witnesses, Joseph Lawende, Harry Harris and Joseph Hyam Levy. She was identified by her sister, Eliza Gold of 6 Thrawl Street, Spitalfields, who was widowed. She reported that Catherine had been living with a man called John Kelly at a lodging house known as Cooney's in 55 Flower and Dean Street, although she was not married to him. John Kelly claimed to have last seen Eddowes on the afternoon of the Saturday in Houndsditch, saying that she was heading for Bermondsey to get some money from her daughter, Annie, promising she would return by four o'clock, except she never made it back. When she did not return, he set out to find out what might have happened and discovered she had been arrested in Bishopsgate Street worse the wear for drink and heard that she would be released on the Sunday, once she had sobered up. He claimed that she did not often drink and as far as he knew she did not prostitute herself. Kelly and Eddowes were described by the deputy of the lodging house, Frederick Wilkinson, as not violent and not prone to drinking. He also told the inquest that Eddowes made a living hawking and also cleaning among the Jews in Whitechapel, nor did he know her to walk the streets at night.

It was at around 3.00 on the night of Eddowes' murder that Constable Alfred Long of the Metropolitan Police, who was on duty in Goulston Street, found an apron with some blood on it lying in the passage leading to the staircase of Nos 106 to 119. On the wall, he discovered writing in chalk: "The Juwes are not the men who will be blamed for nothing", although in his evidence at the inquest he stated that the writing said: "The Jews are the men that will not be blamed for nothing". DC Daniel Halse of the City of London Police also observed the writing on the wall in Goulston Street and noted it down. Instructions were given to have this photographed but the writing was cleaned off before it could be examined. This has given rise to the controversy of the statement and why this might have been erased on the orders of the Metropolitan Police in case the implication of the Jewish community in this murder might lead to riot or outbreak of violence, opening up the doors still further to conspiracy theories associating Sir Charles Warren, the Metropolitan Police Commissioner at the time.

Catherine Eddowes was buried on Monday 8th October 1888 in the City of London Cemetery, in an unmarked grave 49336, square 318, a public grave. The funeral was attended by John Kelly and Eliza, Eddowes' sister. Nowadays, square 318 has been converted into part of the Memorial Gardens for cremated remains. Eddowes now lies beside the Garden Way in front of Memorial Bed 1849, marked since 1996 with a plaque, a public recognition of another tragic life brutally ended.

Mary Jane Kelly, often considered the Ripper's last victim as she is the fifth of the "canonical five", was a bit of a departure from the "usual" type of victim. Although known to be a prostitute, she was young, only twenty-five years old. Only Frances Cole, a woman murdered in 1891 and linked by some to the Ripper murders, was younger. She was also the most savagely mutilated. Murdered in her own private room, the Ripper appeared to have had the time to set about the most gruesome of mutilations.

Mary Kelly's background is a little more mysterious than those of the other victims. She was known by various names, including Mary Jane Kelly, Mary Jeannette Kelly and Dark Mary. Her early life is obscure, and it is likely that Mary Kelly embellished some of the facts or told different people different things about herself. Most recently prior to her murder she had been living with a Joseph Barnett, a fish porter who had lived with Mary Kelly for just over a year and a half, the last eight months of that period at 13 Miller's Court, at the back of 26 Dorset Street, until 30th October. At the time of the murder, he had been living with his sister at Gray's Inn Road and just prior to that, at Bishopsgate. At the inquest, he claimed he had left her only because she had introduced a woman of bad character to the room at Miller's Court and he objected to it.

Kelly was, like the others, poor, always struggling for money and had a habit of drinking, and she was known to be a prostitute. She had told Barnett that she had been born in Limerick, Ireland, but that her family moved to Wales when she was young and that her father worked in an iron works there. There are contradictory stories about her, some saying that she was highly educated, while Barnett himself claimed she was illiterate and often asked him to read from the newspapers to her. In around 1879, Kelly claimed she married a collier called Davies who was killed a few years later in a mine explosion. She stayed in Cardiff for some months after that and then moved on to London. It was around this time that she began a life of prostitution, because she had nothing else to keep her alive. For a while she worked in a brothel in the West End and was invited by a client to travel to France with him. It appears that she spent a few weeks in France but did not like it and returned to England, this time to the East End of London. It is plausible that Kelly, in around 1884 still a very young woman, had been the victim of trafficking and returned to a life of hiding from the traffickers in the slums of the East End. That she continued prostitution and took to drink is the most plausible part of her life story, other than the fact that she liked to sing, was quarrelsome when drunk and was considered to be very physically attractive.

Like the other murder victims, Kelly would have been only too aware of the dangers that lurked in the streets of Whitechapel that autumn and of the horrific ways other prostitutes – women she would probably have known – had been killed.

Kelly was killed on the night of 8th November 1888 at 13 Miller's Court off Dorset Street. The post-mortem found no sign of a struggle – her outer clothes were found neatly folded on a chair and what was left of her was lying on the bed in a light undergarment – yet she was dismembered, disembowelled and her face disfigured in an orgy of blood.

Mary Jane Kelly was buried on 19th November 1888 at the Roman Catholic Cemetery at Leytonstone. If there were any mourners at the funeral is not known. What is known is that the Telegraph reported that there were no family members at the funeral (*The Daily Telegraph*, 20th November 1888, page 3).

There then seemed to come a lull in the murders. Not a lull in the press, however; this continued in its speculation and no doubt, the communities in the East End were not ready to easily forget the atrocities, especially in light of the police not having caught the murderer.

Then on 17th July 1889, Alice McKenzie died in Castle Alley. She was found dead at 12.50am with wounds to the left side of her neck and mutilations to her abdomen. Although the injuries were largely superficial, there were similarities in method and in possible weapons used to the Ripper murders. Dr Phillips and Dr Bond, who both examined the body, disagreed as to whether the murder could be attributed to the Ripper, with Dr Bond believing that the murder of Alice McKenzie showed evidence of similar design in the cut of the throat and mutilation of the abdomen to be able to consider this the hand of the Ripper. Besides Dr Phillips, Robert Anderson, the Assistant Commissioner of the Metropolitan Police, also disagreed with him. The controversy still runs to this day.

Alice McKenzie was about forty-five years old and thought to be a prostitute. The body was identified by John McCormack, with whom she lived for about six years. He recognised her by the scars on her forehead, the clothes and boots she was wearing, and by her thumb, which had been crushed by machinery, causing her to lose half the nail. McCormack stated at the inquest that she had told him she came from Peterborough and that she worked very hard as a washerwoman and charwoman to the Jews. During the afternoon of the day she was murdered, he gave her a shilling and eight pence with which to pay the rent and to enjoy as she pleased. He then alluded to the fact that she had not been at work during the previous day, although she had told him that she had, and that they had a few words which upset her. Little more is known about Alice McKenzie. Generally considered not a victim of the Ripper, she has disappeared into the dark underbelly of Whitechapel crime history with barely a trace.

Some eight months after the murder of Alice McKenzie came the death of twenty-three-year-old Frances Coles, a prostitute younger even than Mary Kelly. She died in the early hours of 13th February 1891 under a railway bridge in Royal Mint Street. She had her throat deeply cut just minutes before being found at 2.15am by a policeman who heard footsteps walking away but who stayed with Frances because he thought she might still be alive. She had last been seen just half an hour earlier by a fellow prostitute Ellen Gallagher in Commercial Street. Ellen had just passed a man in a cheese cutter hat that she knew as a violent man. She warned Coles but Coles proceeded to solicit the man and headed with him towards the Minories, never to be seen alive again.

Again, there are doubts that Coles was a Ripper victim. The knife used to cut her throat was blunt, unlike those in previous Ripper murders, nor was there evidence of mutilation of the abdomen. Had the Ripper left London for a while? Did he just stop killing and was this the work of someone else? Copycat murders are not unknown. It is highly unlikely that a serial killer, whatever the motive or preferred method, simply stops killing. Usually, the crimes cease when the killer is caught, or dies, or leaves the area, although murders can be found elsewhere including in other countries. Ripper investigators have looked into crimes as far afield as New York and Germany in their search for the identity of the murderer.

Meanwhile, in London, women, notably prostitutes, continued to be victims of violence, assault and murder. On 20th December 1888, prostitute Rose Mylett, who was also known as Lizzie David, was found strangled in Clarke's Yard off Poplar High Street. She was twenty-nine years old and had lodged at 18 George Street. While the doctors who examined her body thought she had been murdered, Robert Anderson believed that she had accidentally hanged herself on the collar of her dress when drunk. Dr Bond examined the body on the request of Anderson and agreed. Commissioner Monroe, who by then had replaced Warren, felt that in the absence of signs of struggle, the victim had committed suicide or had died by accident. Interestingly, the jury, despite being advised by the coroner, Wynne Baxter, that there was no evidence to show the death was the result of violence, the jury returned a verdict of wilful murder. Although the case was added to the Whitechapel case file, that is where it was left, and no murderer was ever found. This and a multiplicity of police inadequacies that are not within the scope of this book, inspired Bruce Robinson to write his detailed theory that the Ripper was none other than prominent freemason Michael Maybrick. The theory is exquisitely researched by Robinson and although we are not in this book contesting or supporting any theory on the most likely suspect, we do acknowledge the possibility of Robinson's assertion that, 'The Ripper hadn't stopped killing at all. What had stopped was the police associating him with his crimes.' (Robinson, 2015.)

There were other murders, where again links were made with the Ripper and then dismissed by the police along with many Ripper investigators, although we believe that they are relevant to this book because the corpses of these victims are part of the story of the women of London of the period.

On 10th September 1889 at 5.15am a woman's torso was found under a railway arch in Pinchin Street in Whitechapel. Despite a search of the area no other body parts were found and the victim was never identified. There was disagreement as to the cause of death, with the police through Commissioner Monroe and Chief Inspector Swanson believing that there had not been a cutting of the throat as there was blood still in the torso, and pathologist believing that the general lack of blood in the vessels and tissues indicating that the victim bled to death. There was speculation in the newspapers that the body was that of Lydia Hart, who had disappeared at that time, until she was found in hospital, while another theory was that the body was that of a missing girl called Emily Baker, although that, too, was refuted as the torso belonged to a taller, older woman, perhaps someone around thirty to forty years of age.

Instead of linking the Pinchin Street torso to the Ripper murders, and not without some degree of logic, the police suggested a link to the Thames Torso murders of Rainham and Chelsea and to the Whitehall Mystery. There could also be links to the Battersea Mystery of 1873 and 1874, when two women were found dismembered, and the Tottenham Court Road Mystery of 1884. These demonstrate different modus operandi to the canonical Ripper murders and could have been perpetrated by someone else. It is not unknown for serial killers to change their modus operandi, although this is not so likely. Nevertheless, the vulnerability of street prostitutes, and the lack of police detection of the murderer, is breath-taking – unless it is taken into account that the predominant attitude of Victorian males towards prostitutes was that they were sinful, dirty, less than human and therefore not worthy of the attention and time that solving a case would require. We should, however, add a caveat in fairness to the efforts of the investigators of the time. It is all too easy for modern recounting and investigation of the Whitechapel murders and the Ripper story to criticise the police methods of the time; however, this was a relatively young force concerned more on keeping public order and incarcerating known criminals than in detecting and solving crime. Forensic science, criminology and investigative methodology were in their very early stages of development, and this included systems such as recording observations, questioning of suspects, recording and keeping items of evidence, and so on. The police and detective services were still in infancy and still learning, not least through the many, and often justified, criticisms of incompetence in the press of the time.

The "Ripper Murders" were not the only ones that were perpetrated around 1888/89 in the East of London. This was a harsh place to live, where those whose living was to be found on its pavement, narrow alleys and dark yards were at risk from violence and all sorts of degradations. They are, however, especially brutal murders with a sexual element that probably has been one of the main contributory factors of the enduring fascination with the unidentified killer, a fascination which writers like Walkowitz allude to as a form of prurient voyeurism that was perpetuated by the press and served as a form of social control over women. The murders came about because of the state of mind of a particular individual who exerted power, including sexual power, over a particular type of victim. However, as we will explore in further chapters, that perpetrator's actions were further facilitated by the place, the social context, the pervading attitudes of Victorian London. These worked together to create victims from those who were already victims, tragic women who led devastated lives, whose personal identity was limited by history to be the "unfortunates" of East London: prostitutes, alcoholics and murder victims. History has somehow set aside that they were daughters, sisters, wives, friends, women who struggled to survive day in day out, women whose mental and physical health wavered under the onslaught of poverty, poor housing, gang life on the streets of Whitechapel, trafficking and more. Women whose tragic stories echoed those of so many others, the Ripper victims, canonical or otherwise, are remembered, sadly, for their gruesome, horrific deaths, and the way in which society focused on avoidance by women themselves through not wandering about the city unaccompanied rather than through efficiency of investigation or through eliminating the root causes of poverty and slum living.

Poverty and slum living may have lessened during the course of the twentieth century but is increasing in the twenty-first after nearly a decade of strict austerity measures which have targeted austerity on the poor who are growing in numbers, including in pockets of East London. Poverty gives ample fodder for the growth of gang culture, and trafficking, both of which are linked. Young women with backgrounds of abuse are still falling into prostitution and into the hands of trafficking gangs. Women are still having to sell sex in exchange for accommodation; a recent scandal that is growing is the open call from landlords willing to reduce rental costs in return for sexual favours from their tenants. In London, where rents are notoriously high, this is especially prevalent. A similar situation is seen among students, where young women are selling sex in order to be able to fund their education as fees and living costs increase and student finance does not keep pace. Women are finding it impossible on zero-hour contracts or low wages to keep their families and resort to food banks, charity hand-outs and selling sex. Not only has society not caught Jack the Ripper, but his shade begins to loom large again as the conditions which facilitated the crimes and gave the murderer the perfect context in which to act out his depraved fantasies once again are appearing to haunt the streets of London. If the memory of these women serves to ensure that those conditions are reversed, perhaps their lives and their deaths will not have been in vain.

REFERENCES:

Gray, D.D. (2013), *London's Shadows: The Dark Side of the Victorian City*, Bloomsbury Academic, London.

Marriott, T. (2007), *Jack the Ripper: The Twenty-First Century Investigation*, John Blake.

Robinson, B. (2015), *They All Love Jack: Busting the Ripper*, Fourth Estate, London.

The Daily Telegraph, 20th November 1888, page 3, retrieved from https://www.casebook.org/press_reports/daily_telegraph/dt881120.html on 3rd June 2020 and https://www.britishnewspaperarchive.co.uk/ on 3rd June 2020.

Wescott, T. (2014), *The Bank Holiday Murders: The True Story of the First Whitechapel Murders*, Crime Confidential Press.

5

THE DESPERATION OF THE POOR AMID THE WEALTH OF EMPIRE

Amidst such poverty and squalor it is inevitable that one should be constantly confronted with scenes of heart-breaking misery – misery so pitiful that men whose daily duty it has been for years to go in and out amongst these outcasts, and to be intimately acquainted with their sufferings, and who might, therefore, be supposed to regard with comparatively little feeling that which would overwhelm an unaccustomed spectator, sometimes come away from their visits so oppressed in spirit and absorbed in painful thought, that they know not whither they are going.

Andrew Mearns, from *The Bitter Cry of Outcast London*, 1883

This was the London of Jack the Ripper and his victims. This outcast London with its "poverty and squalor" and "scenes of heart-breaking misery" was the place from which the women that became the Ripper's victims could not even dream to escape, the London to which they were born or were drawn to at some point in their lives and in which they barely survived from day to day. Whoever Jack the Ripper was, he was familiar with this outcast London, with the underbelly of the capital of the Empire. Whether he lived among the whores and the destitute of Whitechapel or whether he was a frequent visitor and able to come and go as he pleased, it was this London that he encountered and that drew him. And it drew from him the most horrific acts of carnage that have lived long past his own death. These were the conditions in which his victims lived and died.

With his famous 1883 report exposing the housing conditions in south London, the Rev Andrew Mearns struck a chord in the hearts and minds of many a Victorian. Sub-titled "An Inquiry into the Condition of the Abject Poor", the pamphlet received extraordinary attention. It was a penny pamphlet of some twenty pages which began with descriptions of housing conditions of some of the poorest communities in the country and ended with a call for social reform. While the Rev Mearns did not skimp on the sensationalism of his text, drafted for the specific purpose of eliciting sufficient emotional response to create a movement for the social reform that he believed was necessary in order to save the poor from the degradation of the immorality to which they inevitably sunk as a result of their conditions, the pamphlet was also powerfully promoted by W.G. Stead, the editor of the *Pall Mall Gazette*, publishing a reader entitled "Is it not Time?" The response from the public filled pages of the printed press for weeks to come and generated a detailed public commentary that culminated in the 1884 Royal Commission on the Housing of the Working Classes and the Housing Act that emerged from this. Its impact was immediate and, for its time, revolutionary. And yet, for all the furore, for all the questioning and debating and legislating, in 1888, while Jack the Ripper sharpened his knives, destitute women wandered the dark alleys of Whitechapel and other slum districts of the capital, the heart of the richest Empire the world had known, avoiding the desperation of homelessness and the degradation of the workhouse. The longer-term effects of the social reform demanded by Mearns, Booth, Hill and others eventually led to greatly improved life opportunities for the working classes. But in 1888, it was all too little too late for most of the victims of poverty.

In 1888, London was a city of contrasts. Capital city of the greatest empire the world had ever known, its West End glittered with opulence and the wealth extracted from that empire. London was also a city in whose dark corners and shadows, notoriously in its East End, there lurked all manner of despair, degradation and crime. Queen Victoria, now elderly, sat on the throne in all her splendour and Robert Cecil, second Marquis of Salisbury, sat in the Houses of Parliament at the head of the Conservative government of 1886 to 1892. London was at the height of its fame and powers as a trading city. It was the hub and focus of Great Britain and the leader of the world in transport. Everything from across the Empire could be brought to London and everything from Great Britain could be transported to anywhere else on the globe from London. In 1888, London's underground railway was already a quarter of a century old, while the Paris metro was still in development and New York's subway was not to start operating until 1904. The wealthy of London had access to anywhere in the world that they wanted to travel, and, with enough money, could buy almost anything they desired from almost anywhere in the world. And, much as it is today, London was alive with art and entertainment, with theatres, music halls, clubs, bars, opera performances, circuses, magic shows and spectacles that catered for all tastes and for all budgets.

If the West End glowed like fairy lights on a Christmas tree with its splendour and ostentatious luxury, the East End stood in stark, coal-stained, dirt-splattered contrast, overshadowed by the depth and desperation of its poverty, and with the crime and degradation that went along with it. By the mid-1880s journalists, social commentators, philanthropists, prominent Christian clergymen and leaders of charitable organisations had already visited, explored and investigated the East End and posited numerous theories as to the causes of the inequalities that resulted in such deep poverty. More often, they also debated the potential long-term effects on the moral welfare of the nation of increasing poverty and, by and large, the resultant social discontent was left unchecked and untreated.

Prominent social researcher and social reformer Charles Booth was one of those eminent figures highlighting the extent of the poverty in East London. In 1886, he carried out a major survey of London life and work which added to the information and campaigns that led to eventual reform. Booth's "Life and Labour of the People in London" is considered one of the founding texts of British sociology. His innovative contribution to the study of societies included the mapping of poverty to demonstrate the spatial components of poverty. This added environmental context to the empirical study of the issue of poverty.

Much of the outrage that was publicly expressed in the wake of these investigations and reports were motivated by more than just altruistic concern at the plight of the poor and the crushing effect of destitution. A particularly important concern was the fear that the moral degradation that accompanies poverty and the crime associated with the poorer districts would spread, like an infectious disease, to the wealthier and more respectable classes. The causes of poverty were of a more muted concern and never publicly attributed to the rampant capitalism of the age, nor the untrammelled exploitation of the working classes by those middle classes and wealthy philanthropic businessmen among whose ranks those same social investigators could be counted. The Victorian establishment's obsessive fear – not without some realistic cause – of revolution was one of the motivators of reform but this same fear would also reduce the apportionment of blame on the functioning of the exploitative class and economic systems that ensured its exorbitant wealth and luxurious comforts.

That the dire housing conditions in which the poor of London lived contributed to their degradation was not lost on the establishment. A combination of high rents for reasonable housing, low wages and unstable employment made it difficult for many in the working classes to live anywhere other than in very poor, overcrowded and unsanitary housing, prey to precariously built properties and ruthless landlords, alongside the threats to public health from highly infectious diseases. While in the twenty-first century the current situation for the working poor and unemployed in London and other areas of the UK may not be quite as extreme, the essential ingredients for a similar situation continue to exist, and have risen to the fore in recent years: high rents, low wages, zero-hour contracts and the gig economy with its unstable employment, ruthless landlords with greater powers of eviction and a dilution of tenant rights, and cash-strapped local authorities that do not have the resources to tackle landlords that do not keep their properties fit for human habitation.

In the Victorian period, the writings of social reformers such as Octavia Hill opened a window onto families living a dozen to a room, just a few feet above the fetid waste of human sewage spilling into the property's basement; into lodging houses where beds were rented for the night and bedding only infrequently laundered; privies shared between so many people that it was often easier for inhabitants of these slum buildings to relieve themselves in one of the many dark corners of the yards and alleys of the slums. Octavia Hill eventually found that in order to help the poor, she had to become a landlord herself, leading her to pioneer social housing and housing management.

However sensationalistic writing such as those of Hill, Booth and Mearns might have seemed – and there was use of scandalous words such as "incest" in Mearns' seminal text, which caused uproar among the middle classes horrified that this immorality was occurring because of the squalor and the overcrowding of poor people's housing conditions – these influential social reformers were not imparting new information. The East End was already notorious for its poverty, decadence and crime. There had been an ongoing public discussion for decades on the living conditions and the moral welfare of the working classes. Nor was the interest of the media kindled only by sensational events. By the time of the Ripper murders, the public, government ministers, parliamentarians and peers were aware of the poor quality, unsanitary and overcrowded lodgings in which many of London's residents were condemned to reside, as well as the exploitative practices of landlords. There had already been previous attempts at reform, with legislation such as the Torrens Bill of 1868, but these had been often so watered down by the time they had been filtered through parliamentary readings and amendments – unsurprising, of course, given the numbers of land-owning landlords among the members of parliament and peers deciding on the exact detail of the legislation – that many of the measures were either weak, or unenforceable, or back-tracked. Specifically, in the case of the Torrens Act, the legislation created an excuse for the wholesale clearance of areas of slum housing with no recourse to the rehousing of sitting tenants. These slum clearances came in cycles, the displaced poor suffering even greater deprivation than they had and with no recourse but the streets, the workhouse, or lodging in increasingly overcrowded and filthy conditions. The driving ethos of the authorities was to clear the iniquitous den of crime and moral depravity by demolishing decrepit homes and opening the areas up to the sanitary inspectors, police and reformers. But by not providing any viable alternatives, the poor simply congregated in other, similar properties where they might be able to afford minimal rent and that meant appalling living conditions.

If living conditions were appalling, these were mirrored by the working conditions of the working classes, or those of the lower classes fortunate enough to have a job. Despite the inordinate wealth that entered the country partly through foreign trade, but increasingly through the growth of financial services, in the 1880s Britain was still in the grip of a prolonged depression. While it is outside the scope of this book to look into what and why of this, the depressed economy had a great impact on the lives of the working classes and the poor in East London.

What was once called the Long Depression was triggered by a financial crisis in Europe and North America in 1873. The depression that followed saw a dramatic fall in manufacturing and in foreign trade as demand for goods across much of the "civilised" world decreased. This immediately meant unemployment in the streets of British cities, and in a time when there was no welfare to fall back on, people who were already poor, became destitute. Where there was employment, there was a downward pressure on wages as employers sought to hold on to their profit margins and secure investment from shareholders. Many jobs became less secure, with employers taking workers on in the morning for that day only – a Victorian equivalent to the current "zero-hour contract" which has contributed to the rise in the numbers of working poor in twenty-first-century Britain. The economic depression resulted in many bankruptcies, the halting of infrastructure projects as investors fell shy of committing funds and crippling unemployment. While the wealthy licked their wounds from losses of business, the working classes were subjected to crushing poverty.

The poverty of so many Londoners went hand in hand with the atrocious housing conditions and therefore attracted the attention of social investigators such as Charles Booth. Considered one of the founding texts of British sociology, his "Life and Labour of the People in London", published in 1889, applied numerous methods of study including quantitative methods and qualitative methods such ethnography. The study also included Booth's mapping of poverty, which looked at the spatial aspects of poverty, of interest in particular to those involved with the issue of public health. The thoroughness of the investigations was impressive and influential, and led to campaigns to introduce old-age pensions among other social reforms.

The poor in London made up about 8% of the population. This included the "working poor", people who worked long, hard hours but simply did not earn enough to make ends meet. The term "the working poor", which is coined regularly in modern UK to describe people who once again struggle with low wages, insecure employment and high rents and living costs, is apt for describing many of the working classes – simply having a job was no guarantee of being able to go beyond sheer subsistence. The 'very poor' were another 11% of the population. These included those who could not rely on regular work but turned up at the docks or at factories daily in the hope of obtaining piecework.

Life for the very poor was incredibly difficult and they frequently experienced the anxiety of not having any secure homes even among the slum dwellings of places like Whitechapel. Then there was a further stratum of humanity, the "underclass", those who were utterly wretched. These were the "down and outs" the "dossers" who did not even have enough to secure themselves a bed regularly at one of the lodging houses. These mainly homeless and destitute people made up some 2% of the population. When they could afford it, they would rent a bed at a lodging house, and when they did not have the coins necessary, they would need to sleep in the cold, filthy, crime-ridden streets. Or as was the option believed to be taken by Jack the Ripper's victims at least from time to time, they could sell themselves for sex and at least they could sleep in relative safety – provided they made it back to the lodging house alive.

The lodging houses (sometimes also known as "doss" houses) were the last resort for the poor before they permitted themselves to sink to the degradation of the streets, which for some was preferable to the degradation of the workhouses. These lodging houses were like those at Dorset Street or Flower and Dean Street and Thrawl Street where some of the Ripper's victims and their friends resided. The lodging houses were home to all those whose lives had been brought low through a series of circumstances sometimes beyond their control: widowhood, alcoholism, child abuse, lack of employment, sexual abuse, ill health, mental health following traumatic events such as the death of a child – any number of life events could have the effect of causing those just about managing to slump into near-destitution.

The American writer Jack London, disguised as a sailor, spent some time exploring conditions in the doss houses of the East End in 1902, ironically describing these as the "poor man's hostel". Earlier, in 1886, Howard Goldsmith had done similar, finding himself deeply disturbed by the cramped conditions, the poor food, the foul language, the filth, the drunkenness – the descent of the inhabitants into an "abyss" (London, 2007). Jack London went so far as to describe the smaller, privately run doss houses as "unmitigated horrors".

In late Victorian Britain, there was no social housing nor provision of homes for the poorest in society by the state; this did not happen until after the end of the First World War and then only in a limited way. Instead, the provision of the cheapest accommodation was left to market forces and inevitably this resulted in the cheapest accommodation being provided only by the worst of landlords. In a lodging house, a bed could be rented for as little as five pence per night. In really desperate situations, it might even be possible to share a bed and share the cost. Needless to say, given the rate of turnover in these places, hygiene was not necessarily prioritised, and sheets could see many a change of tenant before being laundered. Disease was rife. While some social reformers rightly saw the need to improve access to better quality accommodation and developed model dwellings and garden cities, it was only in the slums and in these doss houses that the poorest in society could resort to live if they were to avoid the workhouse or the open streets.

The term "dosser" was linked to the people who had to live in the doss or lodging houses and carries with its connotations of idleness, preferring squalor to an honest day's work. Certainly, this might have been true of some "dossers" and some others might have given this impression because they were suffering the debilitating effects of illness or alcoholism or other substance abuse. However, in a way similar to the current-day misconceptions of people who have to claim welfare benefits, this was not entirely the case. Goldsmid was able to describe the occupants of the Beehive lodging house in Brick Lane as coming from diverse backgrounds:

> *Many have seen better days; respectable artisans whom the waves of trade-depression have overtaken and submerged; clerks elbowed out of a berth by the competition of smart young Germans; small shopkeepers ruined by the poverty of the working-folk among whom their business lay; even professional men – land surveyors, solicitors, surgeons – are now and then to be found among the motley crowd in a "kip-house" kitchen.*
>
> Goldsmid in London, 2007, and Gray, 2013

The East End of London also suffered from the huge problem of intense overcrowding which exacerbated the difficulties caused by low wages, intermittent employment and the insanitary conditions of the doss houses and slum dwelling inhabited by the poor. Huge rent increases in the East End saw the overcrowding worsen considerably: if people could not afford their own homes, they had to crowd in with others. This concentrated the problems that already were rife in society, where honest, hardworking but poor people had no option but to share their living space with others with less than desirable lifestyles, and perhaps would fall into ways of living that they might not have under better conditions: petty crime or even serious crime, prostitution, gang life, drunkenness, disease.

To make matters worse, living in overcrowded and insanitary conditions would often lead to people spending as much time as they could out of their "homes". Many people would resort to spending as much time as they could, and unfortunately spend what little spare they had, in pubs and taverns. This led to an increase in the problems associated with alcoholism and heavy drinking, including brawls, fights and even worse cases of violence, as well as disease, ill health and the crime associated with the manipulation of people with substance dependency, including prostitutes. The East End, with its close proximity living, squalor and poverty, also intensified the tendency towards violence. That the most horrific series of murders that took place in England occurred one swiftly after the other in the East End could be seen as a culmination of factors – location (the dark alleys in between tenements), the poverty and the despair which drove women into the streets in the night willing to have sex with strangers in exchange for a few coins. The East End was a place where violence was commonplace if rarely this extreme, where every vice and depravity was available, almost, it seemed, on every corner.

Although the lodging houses offered some dire living conditions to those whose lives were already encumbered with all manner of misfortunes, they were nevertheless preferable to living in the harsh conditions of the open streets, or to submitting to the iron rule of the workhouses. If the Poor Law Union Workhouses had long had a dreadful reputation, by the 1880s they were completely unable to cope with the social problems resulting from intense industrialisation, migration – both internal migration from rural to urban areas and external migration from the Empire – and swift population growth. The fear of the workhouse for those whose lives teetered on the verge of destitution was intense. In general, workhouses were run to extremely strict rules where some of the clerks in charge could easily (and did) resort to cruelty. Here, the "inmates" were fed a poor diet of gruel, bread and cheese (not always in adequate quantities or even fresh) in return for working. In other words, the poor who succumbed to the workhouses surrendered their freedom in return for shelter, poor food and hard labour. Families entering the workhouses would be separated, they would be given workhouse clothes, they had to follow the workhouse rules and if they actually had the right to vote, they would surrender this along with any personal dignity that they might have had left. Not only would husbands and wives be kept apart in different sides of the workhouse, but children were taken away from them to be "educated", apprenticed or even given away in forced adoptions.

If the result of economic depression was an increase in unemployment and widespread abject poverty, it also had appalling effects to working conditions:

insecurity in the business environment simply would not serve to encourage employers to make improvements in wages or the conditions in which the workers carried out their tasks. To the contrary, economic difficulties tend to lead to an erosion of working conditions as the desperation of workers leads to acceptance of work at all costs. These costs are usually to the health of the workers. This exploitative situation was illustrated dramatically by Annie Besant on 23rd June 1888 – just as the Ripper was beginning to warm to his spree of bloodletting and carnage in the streets of Whitechapel.

Annie Besant was a campaigner for women's rights and welfare, and on 23rd June 1888 she published an article called "White Slavery in London" in her halfpenny newsletter, *The Link*. In the article, she draws attention to the terrible conditions of the women workers, the match girls, in the Bryant and May factory in the East End of London. The article revealed the poor wages and the appalling conditions suffered by the match girls. Not only were their wages so low they could barely subsist on them, but they could be fined and have their wages docked for the slightest infringements including arriving late or talking to other workers. Their working conditions were also incredibly dangerous. They worked with phosphorous, which gives off poisonous fumes which caused necrosis or what was known as "phossy jaw". This awful and often fatal condition started with pain and swelling of the jaw, gums and teeth, and eventually foul-smelling pus formed. The jawbone gradually rotted, and the girls' jaws would turn green, black and eventually, if the face could not be operated on to remove the affected area, the girl would die. The conditions the match girls worked in was likened to slavery. The Victorians were appalled. Slavery had been abolished in 1833 and that British girls suffered in a way slaves had once suffered shocked the respectable establishment.

In its initial response to the article, Bryant and May were furious and sacked the workers they believed had spoken to Annie Besant. Besant's response was to help the girls form a trade union, which immediately called a strike. The striking match girls received support from the press and from the general public, who donated funds to help them survive the strike. Despite Bryant and May's initial threats to replace all the striking workers, they eventually conceded and by August all the striking workers had been reinstated and a union formed, and the company had agreed to improving working conditions and increasing rates of pay.

The Match Girls' Strike was only one in many campaigns in the long struggle for workers to achieve improvements in pay and working conditions, but it does serve to illustrate the intense difficulties faced by the working classes, in London but also in other cities across the country. Even if able to secure employment, this might be uncertain due to the economic conditions, and likely to be very poorly paid. Women and girls were exploited not just for their work, but very possibly for sexual favours from factory over-seers and managers, much in the same way as young women in domestic service were often subject to sexual abuse from their employers or indeed had to supplement their income by working as a prostitute.

That many of these women turned to alcohol and other substances in order to numb the awfulness of their living conditions and the hopelessness of their fate is unsurprising. From here, it was only a small step towards addiction and prostitution: the former because of the nature of the alcohol or the laudanum when they could get it, and the latter because of a desperate need to supplement their income in order to avoid the workhouse, and, of course, to be able to buy more of the substance to which they were addicted. The women were trapped in a cycle of poverty, distress, anxiety and in, all probability, with symptoms of mental illnesses, in a society which appeared to care little and provided very little in the way of care, except by the community among whom they lived. Many of those having to use the lodging houses would struggle to find even the few pence per night for a bed. Nichols, Chapman and Eddowes were murdered when out in search of some money for a bed. Victims of alcoholism would have found it almost impossible to hold on to even the few coins they might earn in less dangerous work. Supplementing meagre wages or managing the outcomes of alcoholism was almost impossible without resorting to prostitution for women mainly, while men would resort to illicit "working" for the many gangs that preyed on the unfortunate as much as they preyed on those from whom it was worth to attempt to rob.

Squalid housing, low paid, insecure work in appalling conditions, disease, crime and the hopelessness experienced by many of the working classes and those even poorer combined with new ideologies that were permeating even the hordes of uneducated workers of the East End and created the sparks for civil unrest and burgeoning social discontent that led to demonstrations and riots in the late 1880s. Marxist and socialist ideologies were being brought to the heart of the Empire by travellers, by those returning from service in the military scattered across the world to find themselves struggling to resettle in their home country and abandoned by the establishment they had served, and by the waves of immigrants arriving in London, many refugees from despotic regimes and revolutionary turbulence across Europe. The seeping of these ideologies into British social consciousness coincided with a period of increasing levels of education among the working classes. Education was a means whereby the upper and middle classes sought to encourage greater Christian godliness and temperance among the poor. Charities and churches established schools of the children of the poor, taught them to read, to work, to live clean and moral lives, and they also taught them to think. Wider levels of literacy and education led to the rapid growth of the printed press, opening the workforce further to thinking, deliberation and to events both across the world and in their own cities. Penny pamphlets and leaflets were distributed by many organisations, including those with revolutionary ideologies. Workers were able to meet in the evenings in social and educational clubs to take classes and among entertainment such as music shows, could also debate economics, rights, industrialisations, capital and exploitation, which led to a greater awareness and acceptance of those Marxist ideologies that inflamed the continent and terrified the establishment. In Whitechapel alone there were some twenty or more clubs that encouraged education among the workers, such as the United Brothers Club in Commercial Street, Spitalfields Working Men's Club in Hanbury Street and Whittington Club in Leman Street.

The summer of 1887 was particularly hot and restless. Many of the lowest-paid workers in London chose to sleep in the open and save the cost of renting a bed or a slum room in a crumbling tenement building, and many came together in Trafalgar Square, which to a degree stood at the boundary between the poor East End and the opulently wealthy West End of London. The homeless gathered in growing numbers, starting around the base of Nelson's column and spreading outwards, using the fountains for a quick face and hand wash in the morning before setting off to find work again.

Trafalgar Square was also a place where numerous groups, many of them with political interests, often held public debates and demonstrations, such as the Fair Trade League and the Social Democratic Foundation. This latter was already causing alarm to the establishment because of their "espousal" of seemingly "dangerous" Marxist ideas. However, the situation was not a simple issue of leftist or right-wing ideologies clashing – there was no clear-cut dichotomy and groups of people could demonstrate for any reason that took their fancy at any particular time, altering their allegiances as they saw fit or to coincide with a particularly influential speech by a particular group.

Any or a combination of these groups could easily have motivated the mass of gathered individuals, and also the enormous numbers of disadvantaged and disaffected of East End poor:

> *East London's politics was a volatile mix of ideologies and pragmatic demands for change; its poorest classes could be exploited to swell the ranks of demonstrations for any number of causes.*
>
> Gray, 2013

However, it was situations such as the occupation of Trafalgar Square by the homeless that brought the impact of deprivation on society to such stark relief in the eyes of the rest of society. Londoners, and in particular those of the upper and middle classes, could see with their own eyes, how volatile society had become because of the intensely difficult living conditions of so many people. The mishandling by the police of the Trafalgar Square occupation and a number of demonstrations that resulted in rioting, also resulted in a scepticism among wider society that the establishment really could control the situation, fuelled by the increasing awareness of the plight of London's poor. As Gray puts it:

> *Beyond the concerns with the ability of the policing authorities to quell any attempts at socialist revolution and unruly demonstrations was a more deep-seated fear of social unrest caused by the deprivation experienced by thousands of Victoria's subjects. The occupation of Trafalgar Square and Saint James' Park was an ugly reminder of the plight of London's poorest.*
>
> Gray, 2013

That there then arose the most brutal and horrific of murders, where the injuries were considered too distressing to be publicised in any explicit detail or even described in relation to the mutilation of sex organs in the inquests, the fear, the panic and the clamour for action that arose from society at large can be better understood. It was inevitable then, that the establishment became deeply involved in the media storm that followed the Ripper murders. Not, in any likelihood, because of any great altruistic desire to protect the women who might be the likely victims – after all, these were mere prostitutes, in their eyes, and as such, a dirty reminder of the establishment's sins and moral weaknesses, prostitutes on whom the descent of the middle- and upper-class men who were their "tricks" into moral decline or even disease could be blamed. The main motivation of the establishment's desire to solve the crimes and calm down the horrified and angry East End was much more likely to be motivated by the fact that the Ripper murders and the police incapacity to apprehend the murderer and bring him to justice might incite another wave of social unrest. Demonstrations and riots in London were at the time only too familiar; the ranks of the rioters were swollen by the dispossessed poor and destitute who had nothing to lose among those working classes who were genuinely indignant at police failures and the failure of the capitalist economic system to work for them as well as for the lucky few and that was causing the poverty in the first place. The system, by its very nature, resulted in the majority of people having to settle for less in order for a very few to be able to have more. Social unrest was only a few steps away from inflaming into full-blown rioting in the wake of the Ripper murders.

Not only were social and political tensions running high during that summer of 1888, when the memory of the Trafalgar Square riots were still fresh, but the Ripper perpetrated his ghastly murders under the cloud of intense racial prejudice underpinned by the fears that so many immigrants had flocked to London and continued to arrive in the Empire's capital city. These fears were rooted in age-old, deeply ingrained prejudices against certain racial groups, in particular the Jews and the Irish, and fuelled by the nervousness felt by the establishment and very effectively communicated to the masses of working class and poor that these groups of immigrants were responsible for plotting dissent, revolution and causing unrest. The British ruling classes were already cautious to the point of alarm at the spread of Marxism and similar revolutionary ideologies spreading throughout Europe, and an influx of European immigration was potentially an opening for the contagion of socialist views to enter Britain and spread from London and other cities throughout the country. It was clear to the British ruling classes that the extreme deprivation of living conditions in the East End along with the many immigrants crammed into its slums and the ease of communication with the European mainland through London's docks provided a perfect environment for the fomentation of social unrest and the spread of dangerously revolutionary ideology.

Prejudice was, and arguably still is, deeply ingrained into Britain's social fabric. While vigilante groups were set up in Whitechapel to try to protect women and served as a physical expression of a complete lack of faith in the police force's capability to protect the community, and while social unrest simmered under a cracked and violent surface, the police managed to both antagonise community groups and then feebly to attempt protection – for example Warren's order to clean off the "writing on the wall" in Goulston Street on the night of the double event, the murders of Catherine Eddowes and Elizabeth Stride, apparently to avoid inciting public hatred against the Jewish community. On the night of the murder, at around 3.00am, Constable Long of the Metropolitan Police Force discovered a dirty and bloodstained piece of an apron in the stairwell of a tenement block, 108–109 Model Dwellings at Goulston Street. The cloth was later confirmed to be part of Eddowes' apron. On a wall above where the cloth was found, was seen the now-famous piece of graffiti: "The Juwes are the men who will not be blamed for nothing". Enormous controversy followed Warren's decision to have what could be prime evidence erased, although a copy was taken and reported to the inquest.

This sudden desire to protect the Jewish community came in the wake of some heavy-handed police interrogation of members of the Jewish community and the acceptance of witness statements claiming to have seen Mary Ann Nichols with someone looking like the archetypal Jewish man shortly before being found murdered, with intense suspicion having fallen on a local Jewish man, John Pizer (also known as Leather Apron) who was arrested but released when one of his alibis was corroborated. However, as the tension in East London appeared to be increasing by the day, this graffiti sentence, which seems to reflect the local London accent, could be deemed to be highly inflammatory and incite violence towards the Jewish community. If, taking into consideration the East London common use of the double negative, the Jews, by implication, were not blamed for nothing, they might get away with even this heinous murder. The writing might point the East London masses towards a possible perpetrator among the many Jews crowded into the East London slums.

London's Jews, many of whom were Polish or Russian, refugees from the pogroms of their homeland, were a particularly compact community living largely in East London; about 90% of London's 60–70,000 Jews lived in the East End, and Whitechapel alone had a population of around 30–40,000. They were a hardworking community, and, as Charles Booth noted, they made the most of the few opportunities that came their way:

> *They are set down on an already over-stocked and demoralized labour market. They are surrounded by the drunkenness, immorality and gambling of the East End streets... in the midst of the very refuse of our civilization, and yet... whether they become bootmakers, tailors, cabinetmakers, glaziers, or dealers, the Jewish inhabitants of the East End rise in the social scale.*
>
> Warwick and Willis, 2013

It has to be kept in context that the police and all other members of the ruling system, including politicians and the government, were also affected by deeply ingrained prejudices against numerous other racial groups as well as Jews. In addition to this, there were prejudices against the poor, the unemployed (commonly considered as idle), the homeless (thought of as layabouts) and prostitutes (probably at the very bottom of a heap of humanity that simply was considered not good enough to be part of the British establishment). In fact, the prejudices against prostitutes were especially harsh – they already suffered the prejudices against women of a rampant patriarchy. Prostitutes were tainted by the widely held belief that women were inferior to men and attitudes towards them were coloured by the guilt felt by men at using the services of a prostitute. These prejudices against prostitutes were further conflicted by social attitudes that claimed that extra-marital sexual activity was immoral but forgivable because it was a natural, male urge to require sex and satisfaction. The Jack the Ripper story fed into these prejudices. The murders played out in a most horrific way those conflicted male fantasies of all-consuming sexual power over a female figure worthy of extreme hatred because she embodied all the guilt and sin and prurient fascination aroused in the male.

Another racial group that attracted intense prejudice were the Irish. The Irish had long been migrating in and out of England but, while distinctive in many ways, the Irish were not necessarily quite as openly marked out by their appearance or mode of dress as other racial groups such as the Jews. The Irish were largely Roman Catholic, had different accents and traditions, and, because of centuries of discrimination and negative stereotyping, also tended to be among the poorest. They frequently found it much harder to find regular employment or holding on to work, a feature which was quickly used against them to reinforce the negative stereotype of being lazy, unreliable, intemperate and given to brawling. Because of this deep-seated prejudice, the Irish lived in some of the worst conditions among the London poor. Gray quotes one observer as describing the living conditions of the Irish in Whitechapel in 1872:

> *In the neighbourhood of Whitechapel or Bethnal Green is congregated the vast army of Irish toil or Irish misery whom the accursed Land system rooted out of their happy homesteads by the Barrow or the Blackwater, the Foyle or the Shannon, the Liffey or the Slaney – some of them struggling manfully and hopefully against the bitter decrees of destiny... that sink of moral pollution in which wallow the lowest dregs of English society.*
>
> Henrick, 1872

Although the Irish were the victims of negative stereotyping, it was very much the external immigrants – external to the British Isles – who were among the very poorest and those living in the worst conditions. In the late 1870s through to the latter end of the 1880s, the British economy was slowly recovering from a depression leading to a lack of employment, and where there was work, this was often piecework and insecure. The ranks of Irish immigrants in London swelled as they fled from continuing problems with potato harvests which was causing famine, along with the numbers of Jews who were at the same time escaping the vicious pogroms of Eastern Europe. The regular failures of the potato crops year after year were exacerbated by the inhumane protectionist policies of the English ruling classes who were the largest landowners in Ireland.

Many Irish immigrants were successful in finding work and restarting their lives, but the less successful gravitated to those places where with their meagre means they might be best able to survive, and in London, this meant the East End, where the docks would attract people seeking casual labour. Many of the Irish immigrants managed to find work in tailoring and shoemaking, trades that involved very long hours and very poor pay. Many young Irish women found work in domestic service, where the negative attitudes towards the Irish meant that they would be considered ill-mannered and not as capable as their English counterparts, and therefore they would tend to be appointed largely to the lower-paid jobs. Not only was domestic work low paid and precarious, but it was also a risk for young women and girls in terms of the predatory males either employed in higher positions in a household or being part of the household themselves. For many young Irish women, work as a domestic would end in coerced seduction and an unwanted pregnancy, loss of work and destitution with a choice of either the workhouse or prostitution. Mary Kelly was typical of so many young Irish girls in that she tried and failed time and again to obtain and keep a position in domestic service in a London household.

In terms of politics, the "Irish Question" was one that was to dog the British government for generations and persists today as evidenced by the Brexit crisis post EU Referendum of 2016, where agreement for withdrawal from the European Union hung on the question of what to do about the border between Northern Ireland and the Irish Republic. Violent unrest in Ireland during the 1870s was thought by British politicians to be caused by radical republicans stirring up unrest and riots. While the details of the political situation in Ireland and the acts that the British establishment considered to be Irish "terrorism" need not concern us here, it is important to note that this would have coloured the view that the authorities took towards any possibility of unrest in the overcrowded streets of East London where the numbers of slum dwellers were inflated by Irish immigrants, among whom there might have been any number of republican activists and terrorists.

It is telling of the negative stereotyping of the Irish in England as lazy, drunken, brawling, thieving, wife-beaters that the view that Jack the Ripper might himself have been Irish took hold for a while in the public's imagination when the press published one of the many notorious Ripper letters, this one dubbed "From Hell", reproduced below:

From Hell
 Mr Lusk,
 Sor
 I send you half the Kidne I took from one woman praserved it for you tother piece I fried and ate it was very nise. I may send you the bloody nife that took it out if you will only wate a whil longer
 signed
 catch me when you can Mishter Lusk

There's a touch of Irish dialect in the spelling of "Sor" and "mishter" and the name Lusk is of Irish origin. It is highly probable that the letter is a hoax and being used to divert attention from the real investigation, including police attention. Besides this and some investigations into possible suspects who were Irish, there is little to support the view that the Ripper was any more Irish than he might have been an Eastern European, a Jew, a doctor or a crazed midwife, or any other such suspect. However, Irish nationalism was considered a threat, and it behoved the authorities to take any suspicion seriously and to keep under consideration, the inflammatory nature of some, often wildly inaccurate reports in the press.

In fact, as far as immigrants were concerned, London was home to many other close-knit ethnic groups including Chinese, Indians and Africans, to add to the predominantly Irish and European Jewish mix. Immigrants from Europe posed a particular threat to Britain and its leadership was gravely concerned. Many revolutionary thinkers left their home countries to live somewhat more safely in Britain but did not let go of their politicising. Britain became home for political figures such as Karl Marx and Friedrich Engels. Among the immigrant communities of the East End there were to be found radicals, anarchists and socialists, many of whom were put under surveillance by the authorities. The Empire, it was felt, was under threat, and if European revolutionaries were a realistic threat, far greater was the threat of rising Irish nationalism.

Irish Nationalist activists, many of whom were Irish American, gravitated to major European cities, and to London in particular. In December 1884, James Gilbert Cunningham arrived in London from New York having smuggled 60lbs of American-made dynamite. Soon afterwards he was joined by an equally fervent Irish American nationalist, Henry Burton. Both men plotted an attack on a number of high-profile locations, including the Houses of Parliament. The first of the bombings took place on 2nd January 1885 on the underground railway from Aldgate to Hammersmith. While very few people were hurt and no-one seriously, the explosion served as a nasty reminder to the nation that the situation in Ireland was becoming increasingly febrile. At the same time, intelligence officers were finding that information was beginning to dry up with "Fenian" informers becoming increasingly scarce as anti-English sentiment grew. A series of terrorist bombings in London led to strong criticism of the police. Although the capture and conviction of Cunningham and Burton gave the police a brief reprieve, they were soon in hot water over their handling of the Trafalgar Square demonstrations.

Furthermore, there was trouble brewing in the internal politics in the Metropolitan Police as a result of a clash in views between the Commissioner,

Sir Charles Warren, who favoured the deployment of uniformed, disciplined troops over plain clothed men, and his Assistant Commissioner, CID James Monroe. This fracture at the top of the force led to inconsistencies in policing which resulted in a lack of thoroughness and coordination which then went on to plague the Ripper investigations. In August 1887, Monroe resigned as head of CID and was replaced by Sir Robert Anderson, who already had the experience of dealing with "Fenian" terrorists. However, Anderson was unwell and had to take time off to convalesce in Switzerland, which Gray points out was quickly picked up by the *Pall Mall Gazette*:

> *In his [Anderson's] absence the Criminal Investigation Department is delivered over to anarchy plus the incessant interference of Sir Charles Warren. Now Sir Charles Warren is a very able General and a very excellent man, but Sir Charles Warren presiding over the Criminal Investigation Department is like a hen attempting to suckle kittens. He does not know the A B C of the business.*
>
> Gray, 2013

Anderson was absent from the force from before the death of Mary Nichols and essentially, the CID was leaderless during the height of the murders.

The investigations into the Ripper murders took place against this backdrop of anti-Semitism, racism, xenophobia, degradation and depravity. When that backdrop is understood, there is little left in the way of surprise that the murders took place. And yet they horrified a society, rich and poor alike, that might have easily considered itself immune to this type of violence or tragedy. The horror was such that doors were opened to police for investigation, the people of the East End willingly cooperated and gave up what information and testimony they could, they clamoured for protection of their women, regardless of their moral status, and when they felt they were not receiving this, they created vigilante groups to try to find the killer and make their streets that bit safer. There was, despite the images that have come down to us over the decades, a strong sense of community, where people, especially those who shared such difficult living conditions in slum dwellings or who suffered borderline destitution through piecework that did not pay the rent let alone food, looked out for each other, helped each other when they could in whatever way they could. Not all slum dwellers were layabouts and idle alcoholics. Many would have been intellectual, educated, but had suffered some unexpected turn of life that resulted in their inability to find work or to find work that paid sufficient for them to improve their lot. It was this community, accustomed to violence and every difficulty life had to throw at them, that so abhorred the extreme violence to which the Ripper's victims were subjected.

This is the dark and difficult world that Jack the Ripper's victims inhabited. Jack the Ripper may well have been born of the difficult world that was the East End; however, we can have some confidence that the East End was the familiar haunt of the Ripper himself, whether he lived in it or was such a frequent visitor that he was intimately familiar with its streets and alleyways, the bars, pubs, nooks and crannies where could best work, undisturbed and make good his escape leaving only sufficient traces to keep the police on his trail so he could have the satisfaction of keeping one step ahead of them and keep the media's interest fully fuelled.

Prostitution was the inevitable outcome of poverty, mental illness and abuse. It was an attempt by women to survive in an extremely tough environment, where work opportunities were few and poorly paid and exacerbated by the fact that women had no real, tangible rights. Women were a vulnerable group, and prostitutes much more vulnerable in their own right. They lived and worked the streets in a place where there was poor lighting, ready to have sexual intercourse with anyone who would offer to pay them in a labyrinth of dark alleys and ready escape routes. It is inevitable that crimes were perpetrated in these places and against these women. That these crimes were so particularly horrific were, nevertheless, not caused by the place or the circumstances, but by the mental state of the murderer. That he was never caught, never identified and that a tourism industry thrives as a result of the murders, is a sad indictment of a society that continues to devalue the lives of the poorest and most vulnerable women in our cities.

REFERENCES

Goldsmid, H.J. (1886), *Dottings of a Dosser: Being the Revelations of the Inner Life of Low London Dossing Houses*, T. Fisher Unwin, London, in London, J. (2007), *People of the Abyss*, The Echo Library, Middlesex.

Gray, D.D. (2013), *London's Shadows: The Dark Side of the Victorian City*, Bloomsbury Academic, London.

Henrick, H. (1872), *A Survey of the Irish in England*, edited by Alan O'Day, The Hambledon Press, London.

London, J. (2007), *People of the Abyss*. The Echo Library. Middlesex.

Mearns, A. and Preston, W.C. (1883), *The Bitter Cry of Outcast London: An Inquiry into the Condition of the Abject Poor*, James Clarke & Co, London, retrieved from http://www.gutenberg.org/ebooks/55316

Walkowitz, J.R. (1992), *City of Dreadful Delight: Narratives of Sexual Danger*, University of Chicago Press, Chicago.

Warwick, A. and Willis, M. (2013), *Jack the Ripper: Media, Culture, History*, Manchester University Press, Manchester.

6

WHO KILLS WHORES?
VICTORIAN ATTITUDES TO PROSTITUTION

People imagine the brothel fills itself.

W.T. Stead, 1885

To the moralist prostitution does not consist so much in the fact that the woman sells her body, but rather that she sells it out of wedlock.

Emma Goldman, 1910

I am down on whores and I shan't quit ripping them till I do get buckled.

Jack the Ripper "Dear Boss" letter to *Central News Agency*, 27th September 1888

Prostitution was a major concern for the Victorians. It touched the lives of every class of society in some form or other and attitudes towards prostitution were mixed, despite the overall prevalence of the general disgust in which prostitutes were held in the public eye.

Victorian attitudes towards prostitution can be broadly divided into three main threads: condemnation, regulation and reformation. Condemnation was largely linked to the moral view of sexuality and sexual mores. Regulation was linked partly to the paternalistic approach of the Victorian ruling class towards the rest of society, meaning that it was deemed necessary to regulate their moral conduct. Condemnation was also linked to regulation in order to control the spread of contagious diseases; venereal disease was something that caused the Victorians a great deal of concern. Reformation was important to the Victorians because of their moral and moralistic evangelising role they believe they had a duty to carry out. Reformation of prostitutes formed part of the cry from the powerful chorus of social reformers who believed that prostitution could be reduced, possibly even eliminated, through social reforms which would see improvements in the lives of those impoverished women who felt driven to selling sex in order to earn enough to survive.

However, it tends to be the moralistic perspective that overshadows other Victorian discussions about prostitution, largely because the Victorians expressed such mixed feelings towards sex and sexual activity in general. The prostitute was considered the public symbol of female vice who stood in conflict to popular beliefs that the role of women was to be pure and virtuous. Prostitutes were considered to be amoral and sinful, the polar opposite of the "pure" and "good". Prostitutes stood in direct contrast to the Victorian ideal of the middle- and upper-class woman who represented the embodiment of a purity that was so complete they did not even know about sex.

However, the prostitute was able to permeate some of the boundaries between the classes. It did not matter to the male customers of sex workers what class they came from when they were in the throes of enjoying their services. For example, it was widely recorded that male upper- and middle-class men used prostitutes including those in East London as much as soldiers, sailors and men from other classes. It is important to note, therefore, that the possible perpetrator of the Jack the Ripper murders might have been anyone, from any class or background – a working-class person who lived in Whitechapel and enjoyed the services of the prostitutes that walked the streets there, or an upper-class "gent" who frequented the district in search of sexual gratification and who was familiar with the geography of Whitechapel's labyrinthine streets and the women that worked them.

It was thought that this "vice" was also common amongst people working in middle-class homes such as nannies and domestic servants, as well as shop girls and factory workers, most of whom needed to supplement their incomes in order to be able to get by. In his pamphlet of 1870, "Prostitution Considered in its Moral, Social, and Sanitary aspects", William Acton attempted to give some estimate of the number of prostitutes in London at the time. These estimates ranged from 6,371, as stated on the returns the constabulary force presented to parliament in 1839, to an estimation by the Bishop of Exeter "of prostitutes reaching as many as 80,000". Through a series of calculations, Acton proposed that there were many more: '219,000, or one in twelve, of the unmarried females in the country above the age of puberty have strayed from the path of virtue.' Whatever the official number, prostitution was widespread in Victorian England, particularly in London.

'Once a woman has descended from the pedestal of innocence, she is prepared to perpetuate every crime.' This quote by James Beard Talbot (1844) from his survey of prostitution in the UK concisely describes the prevalent view of women. They were perceived as bastions of purity while anything that detracted from that purity, or anyone that strayed from that pure state, must be evil beyond redemption. However, in contrast, and arguably the product of a male-dominated society, those men who were purchasing the services of a prostitute were not tarnished with accusations of impurity although they were not entirely immune from impunity. Walkowitz (1980) writes in her book that, in Victorian society, male sexual license among the upper class appears to be accepted but prostitution developed into a moral panic of sorts. The response from the ruling classes was to endeavour to control the moral behaviour of society, hence the legislation which followed in the 1860s and 1880s and discussed later in this chapter. This dichotomy of opinion over what is essentially the same act, we believe derives from the concept that females must be utterly pure in order to be socially acceptable. Purity of the female is more important than the buying and indulging in sexual pleasures by the more "naturally licentious" male and the undermining or destruction of that purity by the selling of sex constituted a serious sin or moral degradation.

This also appears to occur at a time when upper-class attitudes to the poor were particularly hostile and this led to intervention from the higher classes in order to control the behaviour and the lives of the "unrespectable poor". It is likely that this fear grew from a number of influencing factors, including a widespread fear of criminality and the Victorian criminal underclass. There would also have been an influence to enhance that fear from other social factors of the time such as increased migration from areas such as Ireland and Eastern Europe. This latter also added a fear of Judaism as discussed in Chapter 5 and the growth of civil unrest and workers' movements. The social "underclass" was seen as degraded and powerless yet potentially threatening and disloyal. In order to control the lower classes and protect upper-class social morals and the structures of privilege, social ideology, including those that pertained to sexuality, were embedded in laws, institutions and social policy.

Victorians were a combination of prudish and lascivious, the latter being hidden, tucked under the surface and only glanced at askance, or avoided wherever possible. Victorian prudishness avoided open discussion of matters of "poor taste" – for example, the inquests into the Jack the Ripper murders skirted around a direct discussion of the details of injuries to female genital organs for fear of causing offence during these public hearings. Victorians tended to look at moral reasoning as a factor that engendered or influenced crime, poverty and prostitution, rather than give full consideration to environmental, social or economic reasons.

Investigation and consideration of the moral aspects of society were led by a religious revival or temperance movement during the eighteenth century which brought clerics to the forefront of the prostitution debate, as prostitution is forbidden in the Christian Bible (Tait, 1840) and considered a "sin against God". Religious movements of the Victorian era included: Non-conformism, a mainly middle-class congregation opposed to drinking, gambling, prostitution, etc.; Evangelicalism, which waged a holy war against prostitution; and Puritanism, which influenced the Contagious Diseases Acts, further amendments to these acts and increased policing of prostitution in the early 1880s. Prostitution was a target for these upright moralists as prostitutes did not adhere to idealised gender roles; prostitutes were believed to subvert the ideal of womanhood and in this way, posed a threat to the social and moral order of the time. To add to their vitriol against prostitutes, it was also evident that prostitution flourished largely in urban areas, and, with venereal disease a constant scourge, especially among the armed forces, prostitutes were considered a source of disease. 'The prostitute's body became equated to a pollutant of the city which needed to be regulated or removed to preserve the health of the populace.' (Fisher, 1997.)

Prior to the 1880s, prostitution was largely tolerated by society. Having been "of service" since time immemorial, prostitutes were an accepted part of life, as was venereal disease, and there were even instances of men demonstrating violently against the conviction of prostitutes (Fisher, 1997). The debate on the "great social evil" (Fisher, 1997) demonstrates tolerance of prostitution without acceptance of it. In the 1880s, this tolerance changed to a complete repression of prostitution after the 1885 Criminal Justice Amendment Act.

However, even though prostitution was largely tolerated during much of the nineteenth century and prior to that, there was also concern as to the large number of prostitutes working in the major cities across Britain. For example, as well as brothels being tolerated, it was believed that many women from all classes in society used sex as a way to increase their income, although the common conception was that it was most rife in the servant classes. This would have been outrageous at the time as servant classes worked in the upper- and middle-class houses and were therefore bringing impurity into the homes of "pure" women and children. There were also deep concerns about child prostitution (Fisher, 1997), and the trafficking of British women to the continent to work as prostitutes in brothels there (this was known as white slavery). One exposé called *The Maiden Tribute*, carried out in 1885 by journalist William T. Stead, identified examples of children and women being taken to work as sex slaves. *The Maiden Tribute* caused a huge outcry amongst the populace of London (Stead, 1885).

W.T. Stead began by writing dramatic reports in journals and newspapers with a particular point of directing the reader towards feeling anger towards the upper classes and their abuses of the lower classes. To carry out the research that resulted in *The Maiden Tribute*, Stead took this one step closer to what we know as investigative journalism and dressed himself as a man of the upper classes to visit brothels and prostitutes on the streets. He went on to relate to readers a story of upper-class "monsters" which had an insatiable sexual need and took advantage of the poor working women. In his disguise, he entered into negotiations to see if he could buy a prostitute for himself with the aim of demonstrating to the reader, the horrors of white slavery. He recounts stories of a drunken mother and father selling their daughter to a brothel owner for a sovereign and the cruelty of the brothel. These articles had such a dramatic impact, that the government of the time had to debate the legislation on the age of consent. Stead himself also faced possible charges of entrapment.

What these dramatised articles did was play into society's attitudes towards prostitution and the class divide and fed into feminist and puritan arguments for the end of prostitution (Walkowitz, 1992). There is a sense, when reading about these fears and the beliefs that upper-class men were taking advantage of women from the lower classes, that Victorian society had some hedonistic attributes whereby if you could afford to pay for sex, you could help yourself to it regardless of any moral shortcomings. This sits in total contradiction to the more overt puritanical and religious social attitudes. What we are left with observing, is a conflicted society, where prevalent attitudes contrast with the realities of day-to-day life for many, and where change is muted by the inability to directly address matters which were considered to be of poor taste or unspeakable because of their link to impurity and immorality.

In this conflicted social context, the Contagious Diseases Act[1] (1864) was set to limit prostitution because of the fear of sexually transmitted infections affecting the army. The act resulted in a backlash from women's groups for a number of reasons, including believing that women were being exploited by the army in the selection of women free from disease to work as prostitutes, and in the overall ensuing repression of women by men for no pre-evidenced reasons. The act allowed the police to arrest women in their local area purely for being outdoors unaccompanied and to have them medically checked without evidence that they were prostitutes. This meant that non-prostitutes could be arrested and subjected to highly invasive physical checks without their consent and women with any vaginal disease could be locked away for up to three months without trial.

The Contagious Diseases Act generated intense opposition because it was seen as a double standard by non-regulationists. As a piece of legislation, it appeared to be content to accept male sexual access to a class of "fallen women" and penalised women for engaging in the same activity as the men. Men were also not subject to these enforced health checks, meaning that they could continue spreading sexually transmitted diseases, while their contracting any venereal disease would automatically be blamed on the prostitutes (Walkowitz, 1980). Prostitutes, not their male clients, were identified as the primary source of disease and pollution. Outrage amongst women's groups led to the establishment of the first-ever women's political movement, the Ladies National Association (Fisher, 1997).

Despite the Victorian era seeing some major advancements in medical science, such as Dr John Snow's discovery that cholera is waterborne rather than spread through "evil miasmas" in the air and Louis Pasteur's laying of the foundations of the germ theory of disease, the mortality rate through disease stayed relatively stable, and, to modern ways of thinking, unacceptably, high. As the nineteenth century progressed, there was an increasing understanding of – and therefore legislation on and regulation of – public health in order

---

[1] https://archive.org/stream/b22298423/b22298423_djvu.txt

to reduce the many epidemics that afflicted the highly populated urban areas. Along with advances in scientific knowledge and the development of improved procedures and technological equipment to both investigate and treat diseases, there came an advancement in the education and training of doctors, with the setting up of the British Medical Association 1856 and the General Medical Council in 1858, and also the establishment of nursing methods through the work of Florence Nightingale and her colleagues.

The mid to late Victorian period also saw the building of numerous hospitals and clinics, including Poor Law infirmaries, most of which were aimed at treating the poor sick since the wealthier patients tended to opt to be treated at home. However, healthcare, especially the services of well-trained doctors and the more effective medicines, was expensive and usually out of the reach of the working classes. Not only did the working classes live and work in poor, dangerous and unsanitary conditions, where their exposure to disease was heightened, and not only was their general health poor due to lack of appropriate nutrition and clean air, but the poor could rarely hope to access health care in any form other than through "quack" doctors, of which there were many, or through the services of the charitable infirmaries and new "free" hospitals. Since quality medicines were too expensive for most of the working classes, the newspapers were full of advertisements for all sorts of tinctures, lotions and potions, many of which could be downright dangerous, but which were more likely to be within the reach of the susceptible working-class sick.

With these limitations in place, it would have been extremely difficult for prostitutes to protect themselves from contagious venereal diseases, incidences of which saw a steady increase during the Victorian period, and which afflicted mainly the working classes and the armed forces. Acton (1870) states: 'Surgeons to the Royal Free… agree that the proportion of venereal diseases is very large, and that even the physicians see among their cases a large proportion of syphilitic complaints, affecting not only the external but the internal parts of the body.' Acton also makes an interesting allusion to the fact that in private practice, doctors were generally seeing far milder cases of venereal disease as the century drew on. We can generally attribute this to the fact that patients attended an increasing number of doctors more readily and treatments had improved. However, this was not necessarily the case for the poor who could not afford a private doctor and who would resort to the services of doctors in hospitals such as the Royal Free. Instead, there were many patients who had to resort to the ministrations of so-called "quacks", a fact which Acton rails against, adding his own subjective view of the activities that led to the disease:

> *I am often obliged to remind nervous patients who complain of tardy cures, that though they have to thank advancing science for such mild results as now form the penalty of their frailty, they must not expect a day when the complaint is to be divested of all pain or annoyance. Neither the disease nor our treatment are in general so much to be blamed for the worst phases which the former even now occasionally assumes, as the naturally bad constitution of the sufferer or the perverse industry he has applied to the debilitation of a sound one. He has oftentimes his own neglect to thank for doubled and trebled suffering – often his own folly in bringing to us only the reversion of a case complicated, and perhaps aggravated, by one or other of the villainous quacksalvers who are still permitted to flaunt their nostrums in the public face, to gull, to swindle, and to kill.*
>
> Acton, 1870

The issue of venereal disease is one that has been associated with Jack the Ripper since the start of the murders in 1888. Prostitutes were often blamed for the various infections, classed as the pollutants of the armed forces and of men (who, according to Victorian attitudes towards sexual desires, were merely relieving themselves of urges that might otherwise become harmful). The Contagious Diseases Act allowed society to control all women and, in particular, to treat with severity, those who were found to be infected with venereal disease (or a gyno-urinary condition that might be considered sexually transmitted, whether that woman was a prostitute or not). The sexual nature of the Ripper murders could not be avoided and in the Victorian mentality, while appalled at the mutilations of the victims, a link could readily be formed between the murderer, the prostitute and the social contaminants represented by the prostitute's body.

The macabre and sexual elements of the mutilations fascinated the Victorian readership of scandal-mongering press reports, although there was some restraint shown in reporting whereby some of the worst details of the mutilations were withheld from the public as these were considered in poor taste. It could also be argued that there was a general feeling among the ruling classes that publicising these details meant that the pure women of the middle and upper classes reading the reports might themselves be somehow "morally contaminated". The parts of the female genitalia, for example, were not mentioned; the word "vagina" was not used but instead references were made to "lower parts" of the body. In his mutilation of the female genitalia, Jack the Ripper became a symbol of deviant sexuality, destroying the prostitute, since the prostitute, in her spreading of disease and immorality, herself was responsible for destroying men. In the public imagination, Jack the Ripper became linked with vengeance against the prostitute and against the spread of venereal disease. 'I am down on whores,' says the author of whoever penned the letter purportedly from Jack the Ripper to the *Central News Agency* on 18th September 1888, 'and I shan't quit ripping them till I do get buckled.' There were also contemporary theories that the Ripper or perhaps a close family relative had been infected with venereal disease by a prostitute and that the killings were some form of revenge (Gilman in Warwick and Willis, 2007).

In 1885, the Criminal Justice Amendment Act[2] was passed. This made prostitution illegal. It was the culmination of years of campaigning from women's and puritan groups after the Contagious Diseases Act was repealed following pressure from women's rights activists. The 1885 act also saw the establishment of National Vigilance Associations (NVA), who closed down brothels and prevented women from sex working in particular areas. This bears an interesting impact on the social context of the Jack the Ripper murders. Where the NVAs obliged brothels to close, prostitutes were forced to seek their income through sex working directly on the streets, where they were exposed to much greater physical danger. The prostitutes were some of the poorest and most vulnerable women in society working in poor, working-class areas in particular, though not exclusively. By closing the brothels, they lost the relative safety and protection of working under shelter and in the company of many others. Lone street working is still one of the most dangerous forms of work known. On the streets, lone prostitutes, or even prostitutes walking in pairs, were vulnerable to being attacked, mugged, robbed, abused, raped and, as Jack the Ripper showed, murdered and mutilated. Police attitudes to prostitutes also became less tolerant and more brutal and this suggests that the NVAs, the Puritan campaigns and the new legislation, focused attitudes to prostitutes as "fallen women" and a blight on society and therefore society

---

2   https://www.bl.uk/collection-items/the-criminal-law-amendment-act-1885

no longer cared how prostitutes were treated or what happened to them. To an extent, prostitutes were dehumanised by the legislation combined with social attitudes; they were now the pollutants of the city.

There were a number of social factors which contributed to the emergence and maintenance of prostitution in the Victorian era. For example, at the time, middle-class men were not permitted to marry until they could financially support a family. As relationships were not permitted outside of matrimony, prostitution was considered a necessary evil to enable these men to fulfil their needs whilst working towards a more financially stable future. Similarly, men in the armed forces required permission from senior officers in order to marry, and this was rarely given as it was thought that having a wife and children would detract from a man's ability to fight well. Furthermore, most enlistment contracts lasted some twenty-five years and more men could not easily seek sexual fulfilment except through prostitutes, which is why prostitutes were frequently part of daily military life. It was through the Contagious Diseases Acts that much of the tolerance of prostitutes in locations close to military installations was reduced, as was the ongoing "casual" healthcare that was meted out by military doctors to prostitutes to try to limit the spread of venereal disease among the military.

The industrial revolution had led to a rapid rise in urbanisation and the migration of thousands of people towards towns and cities. The rise in the population of urban areas saw a corresponding rise in the numbers of prostitutes in these areas. As people flocked to the cities and the population grew, the supplies of adequate housing, means of employment and sources of food were strained. In order for many women to be able to afford food and lodgings for themselves, their children and even for their husbands, or to compensate for lack of male employment or the extremely low wages that were earned by many in the working classes, they had little choice but to supplement what meagre income they had by working as prostitutes in the city. There are examples of women coming from the countryside to seek their fortunes in the city and working as prostitutes, working women and married women supplementing their incomes by sex working. There are also examples of men from the middle and upper classes visiting prostitutes in the lower-class urban areas, creating a pseudo sex-market economy of supply and demand for prostitutes.

Theories of prostitution to date tend to explore the action in the context of society; for example, functionalist theories of prostitution, including in

Victorian times, believe there are two main reasons why a person would become a prostitute: sexual morality and social contribution. Their argument was that our sexual morality system condemns some sexual acts and sexual contact such as prostitution, homosexuality (in years past), oral and anal sex, but excuses the use of prostitutes to engage in these acts. This means that "meaningful", moral sexual acts are reserved to be conducted with a wife since, through wedlock, the wife remains pure and does not become a "fallen woman". This may motivate men who desire these acts to seek the services of a prostitute, who, in not being a wife or middle class, was already immoral and "fallen" so that the man in question need not carry any form of guilt in terms of being responsible in any way for her moral "fall". In doing this, the second reason for prostitution comes into effect: that men should be permitted an outlet for their sexuality in sexual acts of their choosing, and therefore prostitution has a valid role in society – the servicing of men so that they can continue to function in a healthy "masculine" way. If one extrapolates this theory outwards to other elements of Victorian society, it implies that crimes such as baby farming were simply parts of the functioning of society at the time and were therefore tacitly accepted as an unavoidable outcome, a necessary evil.

Feminist theories of prostitution argue against the functionalist theories, suggesting that functionalism accepts that men are permitted by society to exploit women for their own sexual needs and are protected by the patriarchal society. Feminism views prostitution as the ultimate embodiment of the oppression of female sexuality by the patriarchal society (Scoular, 2004) and is linked to a system of male power and privilege. In the Victorian era, feminists were criticised from both sides of the argument, with a suggestion that it was the feminist response of branding prostitution "evil" that helped to reinforce the patriarchal social structure of women's dependence on men. However feminist theory also demonstrated that prostitutes earned their own money and so did not confirm to this patriarchal structure. Feminist theory argues that, in fact, prostitution is an example of male exploitation and control of women including the control of women of all classes by dividing them into the sinful and the pure. There are, of course, differences in the theories depending on the type of prostitution, such as prostitution forced under duress, or prostitution by choice, both of which are beyond the scope of this book to discuss in detail.

Criminological theories posit an alternative to feminist and fundamentalist theories by suggesting that prostitution is the product of social strain and is viewed as a crime not because it violates the law, but because it outrages the public (Durkheim, 1997). If one takes the prevalent Victorian attitudes regarding the fact that a vital part of womanhood was purity and that prostitutes were "fallen" women having lost their morality and combines this with the estimated numbers of prostitutes in London being in the tens of thousands, it is not surprising that the fact that prostitution was so widespread sparked public outrage. General Strain Theory (Agnew, 2006) suggests that crime arises out of strains in one's life such as poverty, lack of opportunity, starvation, lack of housing, unemployment and even dissatisfaction and an inability to achieve one's goals. In both Victorian society and in society today, the strains placed on families and individuals can lead to people making a choice to commit a crime in order to survive or deal with intense stress, and for some people that stark choice meant entering into prostitution.

One such example was given by Henry Mayhew (1861, reprint 2005) in his exploration of the Victorian underworld in London. He reports speaking to a young woman and asking her to relate her story on how she ended up as a prostitute. She reported that she and her father had moved to London from Rochdale so that he could find work. He found work on the docks in East London, and they were living in the Spitalfields area (just north of Whitechapel). Some three weeks before her meeting with Mayhew, her father had an accident at work where a small keg of spirits slipped from a crane near to where he was standing. He broke his arm and injured his spine and was in the Royal London Hospital in Whitechapel. The girl was working as a hat binder but in the three weeks that had passed since her father's accident, she had been unable to find additional suitable employment to cover the loss of his income and help pay their daily and weekly living expenses and for his treatment. She says this about her decision to work as a prostitute:

> *I tried everywhere to get employment, and I couldn't. I ain't very good with my needle at fine needlework, and the slopsellers won't have me. I would have slaved for them though, I do assure you sir; bad as they do pay you, and hard as you must work for them to get enough to live upon, and poor living, God knows, at that. I feel very miserable for what I have done, but I was driven to it; indeed I was sir. I daren't tell father, for he'd curse me at first, though he might forgive me afterwards: for though he's poor, he's always been honest, and borne a good name; but*

now, I can't help crying a bit sir, I ain't thoroughly hardened yet, and yet it's a hard case as ever was. I do wish I was dead and there was an end of everything, I am so awfully sad and heartbroke. If it don't kill me, I'm sure I will get used to it in time. The low rate of wages I received has often put it into my head to go wrong; but I have always withstood the temptation, and nothing but so many misfortunes and trials coming together could ever have induced me to do it.

Mayhew, 1861

In this extract we see that the girl had been pushed to sex working due to poverty and dire circumstances. The extract explains some of her thought process and how she came to the decision, and it can be seen that economic and social strain has forced her hand. What we also see is that she takes no pleasure at this time, from this type of work and appears deeply ashamed.

A separate but related theory known as Labelling Theory (Becker, 1963) suggests that society's desire to control behaviour using a moral code results in the labelling of others as amoral with no possibility of redemption. The impact of this is that those given the label then fulfil this by identifying with the constructs of the label they have been given; it acts as a self-fulfilling prophecy. Labelling theory poses a different question which links back to the media, community groups, religion and wider social norms about the nature of women in society and the label of the prostitute as the "fallen woman". Would this have propagated continued prostitution as the women began to identify with the label? Would this have encouraged exploitation and even violence with the women being seen as having fallen from grace and therefore something lesser than society, a creature that society need not concern itself with, less, indeed, than human?

Proponents of functionalist theory (a theory also often attributed to Emile Durkheim but amalgamating other social theories of the time) would suggest that prostitutes are sexual deviants and devoid of morals and in doing so are perpetuating the label themselves and legitimising the belief from others that these women can be exploited or harmed without moral impunity. This links into the puritan views of prostitution as something that was influenced by the increasing industrialisation of society which led to changes in the role of women in society including their entering into new roles in the workforce.

The puritans, who believed man to be the epicentre of moral learning and the family's moral grounding, also believed that their purpose was to work to restore the patriarchy and the power of the man in the family. To them, prostitution was the antithesis of proper Victorian society. If women were living aside from the familial oversight of a patriarch, then they were exposed to becoming devoid of morals and exposing other precious, pure women to immoral influences.

Mayhew gives another example of a young woman who is in employment but also works as a sex worker. This young woman works in a printing office and states: 'I get enough money to live on comfortably; but then I am extravagant and spend a great deal of money eating and drinking, more than you would imagine.' This young woman explains that she is attached to a man and will be married one day but that he does not suspect that she is working as a prostitute and has been for the last three years. She justifies her actions in the following way:

> *I am nineteen now, and have carried on with my "typ" for nearly three years now. I sometimes go to the Haymarket, either early in the evening, or early in the morning, when I can get away from the printing; and sometimes I do a little in the daytime. This is not a frequent practice of mine; I only do it when I want a little money to pay for anything. I am out now with the avowed intention of picking up a man or making an appointment with someone for tomorrow or sometime during the week.*
>
> Mayhew, 1861

In this example, this young lady makes a rational choice and chooses what she considers to be an appropriate additional employment in order to earn more money to support her lifestyle. What isn't clear is how she came to the decision originally, but in the extract, she doesn't appear to see herself as "fallen" as the young lady in the earlier extract did, and she does hint at the reason that she continues to work as a prostitute is to be able to maintain a lifestyle that she enjoys. The puritan movement would consider this as immoral and that the power of the man in her life has been diminished by her immoral ways.

However, Social Exchange Theory (Thibaut and Kelley, 1959) implies that there is a two-sided, mutually contingent and rewarding process involving transactions or simply exchange. In the example above, it seems clear that there is a mutual exchange of goods and services whereas the first example suggests that an exchange is occurring but at the cost of the young lady's social and emotional self.

Landels (1858, in Ryan, 1939) argues that prostitution in Victorian Britain was perceived to be worse than any other crime and that women who fall from the ideal of purity cannot be redeemed and cannot regain their respectability. The literature demonstrates a language of hate that was employed at the time against prostitutes, but not against the men who used their services. Hateful language and labelling have been demonstrated to have effects on the general public and on the group or person being given the label. In employing this language of hate and labelling prostitutes as unredeemable and fallen women, society depicted them as less than human. In so doing, those parts of society using these labels and this language of hate, became participants in the violence that prostitutes have had to endure either from their customers or from vigilante groups.

This language of hate and of labelling women as prostitutes is further linked to Victorian ideas as to the role of women in society, which, as we have seen, was a highly constrained role of virtuous, meek woman submissive to a man whether married to that man and therefore placed on a pedestal as wife and mother, or under the care of a father-figure who would thus safeguard her continuing purity. Women who fell outside of this constrained definition of a valid role, whether through unavoidable circumstances or by choice, would readily be grouped together under the label of "prostitute", denoting a woman whose morality was open to question regardless of whether they actually exchanged sex for money in any way. If there were differences between women who chose to sell sex, those who sold sex in the relative safety of a brothel, those who sold sex occasionally to garner sufficient money to eat or pay a rent and those who chose to live independently of men, or left their husbands, or lived with a man outside of marriage, or chose any other alternative lifestyle to the rigid concept of what was normal and acceptable for women, were readily labelled as prostitutes. It is for this reason that Hallie Rubenhold (2019) calls into question whether the Ripper's victims could indeed be considered prostitutes in the full sense of the word that we understand today.

Rubenhold discusses the effects of divorce and separation from a husband on a Victorian woman. To be "cast aside", whatever the reason, and whether she felt obliged to leave the family home because of abuse or adultery, was to be placed in an extremely difficult position, which all too frequently led directly to destitution and the workhouse. Divorce in Victorian England was extremely difficult and costly, meaning that divorce was not usually available to the working classes, least of all to working-class women. Although there were some reforms in the later Victorian period, such as the Married Women's Property Act of 1870, which aimed to alleviate some of the financial distress caused even to wealthy women by divorce, the scales were very much weighted in favour of the husband. Leaving a husband and children, regardless of reason such as abuse or adultery, was a dangerous step for a woman, who immediately had to abandon any pretence to the label of "respectable". In the eyes of the moralistic and highly judgemental society that was Victorian England, any divorce arose as the result of the failure of the wife in her role, regardless of where the cause of the failure of a marriage actually lay. As Rubenhold describes it, to leave the family home rendered the woman "unfit, immoral, a specimen of broken womanhood".

Leaving a husband positioned a woman at the threshold of destitution. Her choice would be to enter the household of a close male relative and rely on him for her protection and to take charge, especially, of her moral welfare. The only mitigation to this potential destitution was that the law viewed the upkeep of a wife, even an estranged wife, to be the responsibility of the husband, largely in order to save the Poor Law the cost of her upkeep. Through the workhouse system, the Poor Law Guardians could enforce this, but it would mean that the estranged wife would have to surrender herself to the indignity of the workhouse system, much as Rubenhold shows that Mary Ann Nichols had done. Without a male protector, a woman had no choice but to enter the workhouse. In the Victorian world vision, a woman could not be both pure and independent of a man. Jack the Ripper's victims, although some were involved in relationships with men, were "independent" of men. They were widows or divorcees, or they did not have a male protector for a variety of reasons. Through circumstances usually outside their full control, the victims had made attempts to set up friendships, mutually convenient alliances and relationships with men, sometimes romantically, because both could benefit from pooling their meagre incomes. However, in the eyes of Victorian society, these women would have been thought of as prostitutes and the epithet has clung to them.

While Rubenhold claims that the Ripper's victims were not prostitutes – it is likely that at some point every one of those victims had to rely on some form of remunerated sexual activity in order to survive their straightened circumstances – it is equally likely that these women were as much victims of being labelled as such because of the way that their lives had pushed them outside the narrow constraints of female respectability, as they were victims of the socioeconomic conditions they were obliged to endure, and ultimately, victims of a murderer. It is highly likely that because of the nature of occasionally having to walk the streets to exchange quick sexual favours for the coins needed for a lodging house bed, that Jack the Ripper, whether he was specifically targeting each victim or was an opportunist stalking the street for that chance to kill, was readily able to take advantage of these women being out on the streets in the dead of night.

The language used to discuss and describe prostitutes generated a culture which excused violence or poor behaviour towards these women. In Hilary Kinnell's book (Kinnell, 2008), she describes a similar situation in an area of Birmingham where the use of language against prostitutes by police and the media led to public vigilantism and sometimes violence against prostitutes. These sex workers were already vulnerable, and the use of hateful language positioned them as less than human and as anti-society, immoral and a danger to children and families. Kinnell also argues that sex working is perceived to be a one of the most unacceptable crimes for women to commit and the language used in the past by the police and MPs created a culture which excuses violence towards sex workers to the point where it was acceptable to turn a blind eye to their victimisation. Regardless of the competing theories or with whom the blame lies, Victorian middle- and upper-class attitudes led to an increase in public condemnation of prostitution which led to an increase in police activity to "deal" with them. This is comparable to examples in modern Britain, where increases in public condemnation for prostitution has led to increased police activity in those areas including arrests, and in some cases has led to vigilantism (Kinnell, 2008).

The Ladies National Association (LNA), and the National Association (NA), the men's version of the LNA, worked with women's issues and defended prostitutes as victims of social injustice rather than as criminal miscreants. They believed that prostitution was not "pathological" but rather a rational choice given the limited options for living conditions and employment; prostitutes were a product of their circumstances. Prostitutes were often lower-class working women trying to earn extra money, not sexually deviant, pathological criminals, as feminist repealers would have had them. These groups of feminists were often frustrated by the fact that the women would not give up their sex work because they needed the money, which meant that they had made a rational choice to trade sex for money. The LNA and NA opposed police repression of solicitation on two grounds: it would constitute a dangerous extension of state power, and it was directed solely at women rather than also including males using prostitutes. Male and female feminists did however support certain legal measures that would restrict the trade in vice such as raising the age of consent and punishing seducers and those who would traffic and sell the women to buyers. LNA and NA members warned that the repression of brothels might render prostitutes homeless and further accentuate their status as social outcasts (Walkowitz, 1980).

Contrary to popular belief, the main customer for sex work in Victorian Britain, according to data (Walkowitz, 1980) were working-class men, members of the armed forces and transient male workers, and not the middle classes. This has an interesting impact on the Jack the Ripper murders as on the balance of probabilities, it would suggest that the culprit may have been a local working-class man. Prostitutes catered to the clientele close to where they lived (Walkowitz, 1980), according to data obtained from police returns of 1857 and 1869 (Tait, 1870). Music halls and pubs were the locations where prostitutes could meet their more respectable customers. They were often tolerated by their neighbours in working-class areas where they were able to live and work until pressure was placed on them by government legislation or police to leave the area. This would have had an impact on wages and work, particularly when prostitutes were no longer tolerated (Finnegan, 1979). The Poor Law Guardians who refused outdoor relief to widows and unmarried mothers, the merchants who grossly underpaid their needlewomen, and the shopkeepers who hired men instead of women, all helped to force women onto the streets and into prostitution.

Furthermore, the 1834 Poor Law Amendment Act compounded the suffering of single mothers. Under the Bastardy Clauses of this Act, evidence of paternity had to be material, which meant that more women were being left by sexual partners with no evidence to demonstrate paternity. This meant that the men were under no obligation to pay or to provide for their offspring and the women would have to have the child and raise it alone. If they were unable to support their illegitimate children, then the children might have had to enter a workhouse. What the act did was to try to make extra-marital sex and pregnancy unattractive to women. However, this begs the question of why there was no corresponding law or act to prevent or deter men from also having extra-marital sex. Perhaps this situation exemplifies the Victorian acceptance that men had sexual needs which were natural and acceptable, but that women's sexual needs were rooted in the evil of lust and that women should only be virtuous, pure and innocent.

These laws were particularly controversial and were diluted in 1839 and again in 1844 to allow women to again petition courts over paternity and gain much needed fairness and support from the magistrates. Although these changes would have helped, there was no effective reduction of the pressure placed on women who fell pregnant outside of marriage or even those who were married but could not afford to support a child. Being pushed into prostitution was a means of affording to support one's child but the pressure placed on women also led to more extreme actions by women desperate to deal with their situation through the use of baby farms and by infanticide, both of which are discussed in another chapter.

Despite the puritan movements criminalising prostitution, the Jack the Ripper murders caused utter outrage among the public, but instead of condemning the women victims and the ranks of prostitutes from which they came, there was a movement to protect local working women. Vigilante groups walked the streets of Whitechapel with the aim of catching the killer and protecting the women. They understood that these women were going to work despite the risks because they had to, because they were desperate. Whilst the literature suggests that the middle and upper classes were often content to leave the underclass poor to die out, there were others working hard to try to protect these women and children who were at risk.

This state of affairs continues to be mirrored today where sex workers are openly condemned by the public and ostracised from society, but no civilised society wishes the harm to come to them that murderers such as Jack the Ripper, Peter Sutcliffe (dubbed the Yorkshire Ripper) and others have brought against them, and outrage is expressed whenever this form of extreme violence occurs. In these instances, the public draws together to find ways to support the police and encourage these women to move off the streets and out of danger whilst intuitively understanding these women's need to continue working. However, what these murders reinforced in Victorian society was that it was not safe for women to be out alone, and constraints continued to be placed on women in the public sphere all in the name of protecting them. We know from the court statistics that in the 1880s (discussed in Chapter 7) it was still the case that men were more likely to be killed than women by a stranger in the street. However, it was women who were considered weak and defenceless, who were constrained and constricted in the name of their own safety. Whilst this may seem an appropriate and considered response, it fuelled the view of women as vulnerable and weak, and it gave society open permission to continue the monitoring and controlling of women in public.

Beyond this, prostitution continued to be condemned and made illegal with the onus and the blame being placed squarely on the prostitute rather than on the customer. It is only in recent years that prostitution and the act of selling sex has been deemed to be legal, while soliciting, the act of purchasing sex, has been made illegal, which demonstrates a shift in attitude that recognises the vulnerability of the women. This way of looking at sex working in modern times acknowledges the desperation, the lack of choice or the exploitation of women who sex work and recognises the customer as someone who is exploiting these vulnerabilities. Although this does not protect the women, it does go some way to ensuring that they are not criminalised for being the victim.

That being said, murders, like those of the Ripper, continue to focus the spotlight of public imagination on stranger murders. Whilst the available data suggests that stranger murder is a relatively rare phenomenon (Chapter 7), instances such as the Ripper murders have been used to almost rationalise violence against women, by shifting the blame onto the victim, the result of which is to thereby control how women move in the public sphere. For example, if a prostitute is killed, we victim blame by suggesting that they have placed themselves in danger. We tell our women and girls not to go out alone because they might be attacked, and this constrains how women have been able to move around in their local communities. Whether this is done in their best interests or not is entirely incidental. Statistically, men are more likely to be killed in public and by a stranger than women, but murders such as the Ripper murder have convinced us that it is women who are the most in danger from such attacks and so we prevent them from moving around as much as boys and place extra restrictions on their movements in the outside world.

Newly powerful in the late Victorian period and growing in readership, the media, in the form of newspapers, was widely influential in the shaping of public attitudes towards social and political issues, not least matters of morality and public safety. This theme has been explored in detail by Judith Walkowitz (1980) in her works on Victorian prostitution and on London during the late Victorian period. Walkowitz dwells on the various responses to the Ripper murders and the detail with which the newspapers reported the event. Many took the stance that prostitutes traded their "womanhood", or the Victorian ideal of what "womanhood" represented, for some coins with which to assuage their miserable existence, and that the risk of violence, murder and mutilation was simply a feature of the lives that they had chosen. At its most simplistic, reports written largely from the dominant patriarchal perspective, and communicating a terror among the public that women were not safe, either in the tawdry streets of the East End, or further into the affluent West certainly served to keep women under control, indoors, "safe" under the dominance of their males. Through ebullient reporting aimed to maximise sales, this, at the very least inadvertently, had the effect of manipulating the social behaviour of the country's women. This phenomenon has been seen since the early days of the printed press, with stories running on Spring-heeled Jack serving as clear warnings to unaccompanied women that they risked their lives if stepping out of doors without male escorts.

However, as Walkowitz also points out in detail, the responses of different sections of society to the Whitechapel murder reports and the Ripper scandals that dominated the press in the summer and autumn of 1888 were varied. While some were moved to cry out against the social conditions in the East End, others took to denouncing prostitution, considering the victims' choice of lifestyle, regardless of their reasons for becoming prostitutes, as creating the motivating factor of the crimes (victim-blaming). While some took to wanting to protect the community through vigilante patrols, others, notably a few feminists, cried out against what appeared to be a panic that was resulting in women being increasingly more vulnerable and limited by their perceived vulnerability. Some, such as Josephine Butler, expressed their concern that the outrage over the murders would lead to a closure of brothels, repression of prostitution and leave more women homeless and destitute. Others of more puritan persuasion saw little humanity in prostitutes and appeared to care little what became of them. But it was the fear that sensationalist press reports engendered among women that is a prevalent feature of the time. A secondary school teacher in the West End, Mary Hughes, puts it succinctly when she recalls in 1888, "how terrified and unbalanced we all were by the murders. It seemed to be round the corner, although it all happened in the East End, and we were in the West; but even so, I was afraid to go out after dark, if only to post a letter" (Walkowitz, 1980).

The public appeared to thirst for details, fascinated with the developing fantasy of the Ripper and his sexual deviancy demonstrated for them by his mutilation of the female sex organs. The Ripper exposed the prostitutes' sexuality and then destroyed their sexual strength. The same newspapers that fuelled a moral panic with their sensational stories of the murders and the publication of dozens of opinion pieces and speculations were soon reporting violent assaults against a number of women, not all of whom were prostitutes but who were accused of being "whores" and threatened with "I'll do a Ripper on you". The media succeeded in feeding society's fears and fantasies to the extent where gossip was filled with the gruesome details of the murder and people crowded to cheap reconstructions and peep-show exhibits. For many men, the Ripper stories created what Walkowitz termed "a common vocabulary and iconography for the forms of male violence that permeated the whole society, obscuring the different material conditions that permeated the whole society, obscuring the different material conditions that provoked sexual antagonism in different classes" (Warwick and Willis, 2007). While boys felt able to taunt and terrify girls, men felt confident in patrolling the streets while their women stayed "safe" indoors. Women were frightened by the Ripper stories while men felt able to terrorise them, going by the various court cases in which men had taunted their victims with words such as "look out for Leather Apron" (Walkowitz, in Warwick and Willis, 2007).

If one considers the prevalent attitudes towards women in the Victorian era and prostitutes in particular, the laws that were passed and amended in a bid to control the sex industry as it was at the time, the labelling and perpetuating of crimes against women and the desperation and poverty many women were left in, then it is perhaps unsurprising that a crime of this sort was committed. Prostitutes were attacked and killed across the country, often by their customers. This was not unusual, but the frequency and horrific nature of the Ripper murders is what sets them apart. It is likely that society's attitudes at the time combined with the perpetrator's own internal factors, to create a perfect storm from the vortex of which these offences emerged. It may well have been the vulnerability and desperation of the women, the lack of policing, protection and vigilance, the desperation leading to increased risk taking and the narrative of dehumanising prostitutes that tipped the balance and made it possible for the Ripper to enact such awful violence on these women.

If there is a legacy left for the twenty-first century by the Ripper murders, it is that the vocabulary and iconography of sexual violence against women, in particular against prostitutes, continues to dominate the media. The public furore and sensationalist reporting of the Yorkshire Ripper, for example, gives a late twentieth-century example of a very similar media and public response to a set of crimes against prostitutes, including the outbursts of victim-blaming as well as feminist demonstrations protesting the crimes. Yet, the dominant legacy of these more recent incidents continued to be the fear felt by women of being outdoors alone, especially at night, unaccompanied by a man. Modern media, online as well as on television screens and on paper, continues to exploit sexual violence. Female mutilations are depicted in cinema and in video games, violence against women is a regular theme in television dramas, news reports across all media exulting in sensational detail to feed the public's fascination and fears. Films such as *Scream*, for example, give a satirical commentary on how women who have sex and are no longer virginal and pure are often the first to be killed in horror films, highlighting the subtext of many modern films and suggesting a continuing attitude that women should be pure or else the worst conceivable violence might befall them. As recently as in March 2019, online gaming platform Valve announced its decision to ban the game *Rape Day*. At the time of writing, the game's developers were confident of finding a platform for their game. Women, despite the evolution of sexual freedoms, women's rights and empowerment, continue to be seen as victims and continue to feel vulnerable, as vulnerable as the Ripper's victims would have felt when walking those dark streets and alleys of Whitechapel in the hours before their murders.

REFERENCES

Acton, W. (1870), *Prostitution, Considered in Its Moral, Social, and Sanitary Aspects in London and Other Large Cities and Garrison Towns, with Proposals for the Control and Prevention of Its Attendant Evils*, John Churchill and Sons, London.

Agnew, R. (2006), "General Strain Theory: Current Status and Directions for Further Research", p101–123 in *Taking Stock: The Status of Criminological Theory – Advances in Criminological Theory*, edited by Cullen, F.T., Wright, J.P. and Blevins, K., Transaction, New Brunswick, NJ.

Becker, H. (1963), *Outsiders; studies in the sociology of deviance*, Free Press of Glencoe, London.

Durkheim, É. (1997), *The division of labor in society*, Free Press, New York, NY (original work published 1893).

Finnegan, F. (1979), *Poverty and Prostitution: A Study of Victorian Prostitutes in York*, Cambridge University Press, Cambridge.

Fisher, T. (1997), *Prostitution and the Victorians*, St Martin's Press.

Goldman, E. (1910), *The Traffic in Women. Emma Goldman's Anarchism and Other Essays*, Second Revised Edition, Mother Earth Publishing Association, New York and London, p183–200, retrieved from https://www.marxists.org/reference/archive/goldman/works/1910/traffic-women.htm

Jack the Ripper's letter to the *Central News Agency*, 18th September 1888, cited in Gilman, S., "'Who Kills Whores?' 'I do,' Says Jack: Race and Gender in Victorian London", in *Jack the Ripper*, ed Warrick. A. and Willis, M. (2007), *Jack the Ripper: Media, Culture, History*, Manchester University Press, Manchester, p215.

Kinnell, H. (2008), *Violence and Sex Work in Britain*, Willan Publishing, Devon.

Mayhew, H. et al. (2005), *The London Underworld in the Victorian Period: v. 1: Authentic First-person Accounts by Beggars, Thieves and Prostitutes*, Dover Publications Inc.

Rubenhold, H. (2019), *The Five: The Untold Stories of the Women Killed by Jack the Ripper*, Penguin Random House UK, London.

Ryan, M. (1839), *Prostitution in London, with a Comparative View of that of Paris and New York, as Illustrative of the Capitals and Large Towns of all Countries; and Proving Moral Depravation to be the most Fertile Source of Crime, and of Personal and Social Misery; with an Account of the Nature and Treatment of the Various Diseases, caused by the Abuses of the Reproductive Function*, H. Bailliere, London.

Ryder, S.P., Anderson, R., Chisholm, A. and Scott, C., "Casebook: Jack the Ripper", copyright Stephen P. Ryder and Johnno, 1996–2020, Thomas Schachner, retrieved from https://www.casebook.org/ripper_letters/

Scoular, J. (2004), "The 'subject' of prostitution: Interpreting the discursive, symbolic and material position of sex/work in feminist theory", *Feminist Theory*. 5; 343, DOI: 10.1177/1464700104046983.

Stead, W.T. (1885), "The Maiden Tribute of Modern Babylon", *Pall Mall Gazette*, 4th–13th July 1885.

Tait, W. (1840), *Magdalenism: An Inquiry into its Extent, Causes and Consequences of Prostitution in Edinburgh*, P. Richard, Edinburgh.

Talbot, J.B. (1844), *The Miseries of Prostitution*, J Madden and Co, London.

Walkowitz, J.R. (1980), *Prostitution and Victorian Society: Women, class and the state*, Cambridge University Press, Cambridge.

Walkowitz, J.R. (1992), *City of Dreadful Delight: Narratives of sexual danger in late Victorian London*, Virago Press, London.

Warwick, A. and Willis, M. (2013), *Jack the Ripper: Media, Culture, History*, Manchester University Press, Manchester.

7

VIOLENCE AGAINST WOMEN THEN AND NOW

*Cruelty, like every other vice, requires no motive outside of itself;
it only requires opportunity.*

George Eliot

To say that there are many reasons for anger and violence would be both an understatement and an unhelpful statement. In this chapter, we try to explain violence, particularly violence towards women using the cognitive psychological approach and we can then examine some of the current statistics of violent crime in the UK. There are numerous approaches which explain violence and anger, but the cognitive approach focuses on the thought processes of the offender which is helpful in trying to understand what drives violence against women. A particularly useful text for us as we tried to understand violence was Aaron T. Beck's (1999) book *Prisoners of Hate*, which uses cognitive theory to make sense of anger, hostility and hate; all of which are features of the social strains in late nineteenth century Britain, such as the hostility towards the Jewish and Irish communities, the attitudes towards women and the features of the Jack the Ripper crimes themselves.

The cognitive approach in psychology posits that humans are information processors where information or stimuli is entered, processed by our thoughts and beliefs that we hold about the world and an output such as a behaviour is the result. The internal thoughts and beliefs that we have are derived from schemas, which are a set of core beliefs and rules about an object, person or situation that we learn about over time. As we learn new things about that object or situation, this new information is assimilated into our schemas with the impact of either consolidating or changing our attitudes and opinions about the object. These schemas can be adaptive and help us function in the world or they can be maladaptive and prevent us from functioning to the best of our ability. For example, an adaptive schema after failing a test might be to organise a resit, revise harder and seek extra tuition. A maladaptive schema in this situation might be to become angry with the assessors, get into arguments with tutors and possibly give up on trying to pass. In these examples the schemas are driven by different core self-beliefs, beliefs about the world. The adaptive schema may say, "it's OK to fail, you are not a failure", "you are capable of doing better". The maladaptive schema may hold negative core beliefs that "you are useless", "you are a failure", "the world thinks that I am a failure". These different beliefs about the world and themselves can lead to people having different emotions and outward behaviours and can have an impact on self-esteem or the need to protect one's self-esteem. In the adaptive case, the person's self-esteem has not been diminished as they are not taking the failure as a fundamental failing in themselves and are trying to rectify the situation. In the maladaptive case, the person believes they are fundamentally a failure, that others are working to harm them and make them fail. These core beliefs, both adaptive and maladaptive, are the result of interactions between personality traits and environmental factors such as good or bad experiences and positive and negative support from caregivers and significant others.

People who can be angry and people who can be violent are more likely to hold rigid beliefs about the world such as "nobody can be trusted", "people should not disrespect me", "people are controlling", "everybody is against me". When these rigid beliefs are combined with poor self-esteem it can lead to extreme behaviour; for example, if someone's self-esteem is violated in some way, it produces a huge violent outburst in order to reinstate self-esteem, feel better and punish the other for violating one of the rigid rules or beliefs held. Because of these core beliefs, people like this often misinterpret the behaviour of others as antagonistic, they are hyper-vigilant to threats to their self-esteem and have an attention bias to threatening or disparaging behaviour, meaning that they focus on behaviour that could be threatening rather than also seeing non-threatening behavioural cues in an interaction.

Underlying violent responses are often the offender's perception or misperceptions of himself and other people. As a result of the interactions between personality traits and environmental factors, an individual may develop a cluster of antisocial concepts and beliefs. This shapes his/her interpretation of other people's words and actions, and their personal sense of vulnerability is reflected by a hypersensitivity to specific kinds of social confrontation or disparagement. For example, the core beliefs of the offender lead them to negatively appraise a situation; this drives a desire to restore self-esteem, but they have also learnt through their experiences that this can be done using violence. Crucial to this process is the activation of hostile beliefs within a schema which are activated when an event strikes at a person's specific vulnerability such as rejection or disparagement.

Stereotypes are developed by our minds in order to guide our perceptions of people and help interpret their behaviour quickly (Lippmann, 1922; Allport, 1954). This helps us make quick judgments which have an evolutionary basis, such as keeping us safe from others and reacting quickly to threats or danger. This can lead to oversimplifying a situation or distortion of a situation and eventually to bias (negative appraisals). Greater competition for resources creates greater competition between groups and therefore increased bias and stereotyping. This can be seen in the poverty and lack of suitable food and housing in the 1880s, leading to the stereotyping and hostility against Jews, the Irish and the upper or lower classes depending on which group you belonged to. This can also be linked to the current climate around the world where there is fierce competition for housing, energy, food and education, exacerbated by agendas of austerity. In London and elsewhere, this competition is engendering hostility towards those people who are seen as a drain on the limited resources such as immigrants, people on benefits or requiring social housing and even religious stereotyping; where in 1880s London this was Judaism, in current London this is now Islam. On the other side, hostility, then as now, is also directed towards the wealthy, as they are seen as contributing to the poor conditions of the lower class or having escaped the burden that the lower classes are bearing. The language used to do this, frames the groups as them and other, us and the enemy. Once an enemy has been created then violence towards them can be justified and moralised; it lifts inhibitions against discrimination and even violence that the individual might usually hold and removes the psychological block to committing crimes, even murder, against the enemy. The groups doing this see themselves as the victims and are protecting their own rights.

It is important to note that paranoid groups and persons with paranoid delusions, both share the common factor that they are vulnerable or feel vulnerable and therefore feel they need to react violently to punish or neutralise the enemy before they come to harm. As we move to looking at violence and hostility at a more individual level, it is helpful to also consider whether Jack the Ripper could have held hostilities towards women because they made him feel "vulnerable". Was he attacking women or prostitutes to punish them? Were these crimes the result of a thought process that was "attack or be attacked"? This attack could be humiliation, not being respected or being made to feel embarrassed by women and therefore a threat to his self-esteem that needs to be resolved with a huge action such as murder in order to feel that his self-esteem has been restored?

Men who harm women are more likely to attribute negative intentions to them such as "she was trying to swindle me", "trying to trick me", "trying to embarrass me", "she is trying to control me" (Eckhardt and Cohen, 1997, in Beck, 1999). Many violence-prone men believe their wives or women are their property and use violence to exact total obedience. However, they may also attribute day-to-day activities and conversations as pressure or criticism or they may be focused on behaviours which confirms their maladaptive belief (selective attention) that the woman can't be trusted, for example seeking signs of infidelity and acting jealously, all of which can be a flash point to violence in order to protect their self-esteem or achieve their goal of gaining total obedience through violent means. For example, in a hypothetical scenario, there is a perceived wrong to a male by a female which is magnified by his maladaptive beliefs. This damages his self-esteem, and he believes that only violence will rectify this or restore his power/self-esteem in the relationship. Because of these maladaptive beliefs there is a hypersensitivity to threats to the balance of power such as in the customer-supplier situation of sex workers. Appearing to be submissive, weak or powerless lowers self-esteem and makes him feel vulnerable to further violation. Violent behaviour serves as a form of self-protection. This also coincides with the person's beliefs about the desirability and acceptability of violence as a response (pro-violent beliefs) as well as over-generalising the actions of others such as "all women are cruel and are untrustworthy", misinterpretation of other motives because they are appraising the situation in a negative way based on their maladaptive core beliefs and holding others responsible for the harm done to them and their subsequent violence.

In exploring violence towards sex workers in modern times, Hilary Kinnell (2008) interviews sex workers about their experiences and explores the given reasons of men convicted of violence towards sex workers. It is interesting to note in her work that perpetrators of violence towards sex workers often described a hatred for sex workers and felt they were justified in their violence towards them. The theory posited for this, is that society's use of labels legitimises violence towards sex workers (Miller and Schwartz, 1995). Our use of language for women including sex workers has often been blamed for encouraging inappropriate and even violent behaviour towards them; words such as slag, slut and whore, all words that are derogatory and dehumanising but that also carry sexual connotations. Women, especially sex workers, have often been referred to as trash, bitches and scum, and it is thought that this legitimises poor behaviour and violence towards them by referring to them as being less than animals and worthless as rubbish. Kinnell points out that equating sex workers with rubbish is often reflected in the way the bodies of murder victims are treated; Kinnell gives an example of a sixty-three-year-old sex worker from Hull, UK, who was beaten, dragged face down along a pavement and dumped in a bin, and in the case of Jack the Ripper, discarding the bodies in the gutter illustrates what he may have thought of these women and their value in society.

The theories about violence against women are supported by the statistical evidence and one way of reviewing the statistics regarding violence against women is by using the British Crime Survey. This is an annual audit of the victims of crimes committed in England and Wales and is a useful source of information regarding current crime rates and the experiences of the victims. Reviewing this data allows us to build a picture of murder in present-day England and Wales which we can compare to data from the time of the Jack the Ripper murders. A review of the recent data (British Crime Survey, 2019) at the time of writing demonstrates some interesting statistics regarding murder in general and then murder with a female victim more specifically.

Originally, there were 671 homicides recorded by the police in 2018/19; this is a decrease from the previous year. The number of male victims fell by 11% and the number of young victims (sixteen to twenty-four years old) fell 24%. Interestingly, the number of female victims of homicide increased by 10%, and this was "the second consecutive annual increase and the highest number since the year ending March 2006". Female victims (aged sixteen years and over) were more likely to be killed by a partner/ex-partner (38%, eighty homicides), while male victims were more likely to be killed by a friend or acquaintance (27%, 105 homicides). The most common method of killing continued to be by a sharp instrument, with 259 homicides by this method with a homicide rate of eleven per million population, the rate for males (fifteen per million population) is around double that for females (eight per million population). This data demonstrates that women are less likely to be killed by a stranger in modern society than men but are far more likely to be killed by a partner or ex-partner or by an acquaintance. In fact, data from the British Crime Survey 2019 states that the number of male victims of murder has increased every year since the 1970s, whereas the number of female victims has remained relatively stable. The report states that as in previous years, children under a year old had the highest rate of being the victim of homicide (forty-five offences per million population) compared with other age groups.

There were differences recorded in the report between males and females in the pattern of relationships between victims and suspects. Almost half (48%) of adult female homicide victims were killed in a domestic homicide. This was an increase of twelve homicides compared with the previous year. In contrast, 8% of male victims were victims of domestic homicide (thirty) in the latest year. This was an increase of six homicides compared with the previous year. In almost four in ten female homicide victims aged sixteen years or over, the suspect was their partner or ex-partner (38%, eighty homicides). This was an increase of seventeen homicides compared with the previous year. Over the last ten years there was an average of eighty-two female victims a year killed by a partner or ex-partner. In contrast, there were only 4% of male victims aged sixteen years and over where the suspect was their partner or ex-partner (sixteen homicides). For adult male victims, the suspect was most likely to be a friend or social acquaintance (27%, 105 men). The suspect was less likely to be a friend or social acquaintance when the victim was female (8%, sixteen women). In 37% of female homicides recorded in the year ending March 2019, no suspect had been identified for the offence at the time of analysis (seventy-six victims). The percentage of male victims with no suspect identified was similar, at 31% (124 victims).

The most common method of killing continued to be by knife or another sharp instrument. There were 259 sharp instrument homicides recorded in the year ending March 2019, of those men were the most common victims (198 victims) and women (sixty-one victims). The second most common method of killing was "kicking or hitting", accounting for 106 homicides (16% of the total). As in previous years, the majority (75%) of victims killed in this way were male. Around one in six (17%) of female victims were killed by "strangulation, asphyxiation" (forty-one victims); this was the second most common method of killing for female victims. In contrast a much smaller proportion (3%) of male victims were killed in this way. Differences in methods of killing by sex of victim are likely to reflect differences in victim/suspect relationships. The use of a knife for killing is still more common today than in previous decades, although it is interesting that asphyxiation or strangulation are more common methods of killing women than men.

In the year ending March 2019, just over half (51%, 341 offences) of all homicide cases resulted from a quarrel, a revenge attack or a loss of temper. This was a similar proportion compared with previous years. This proportion was higher where the principal suspect was known to the victim (64%), compared with when the suspect was unknown to the victim (38%). There was little difference between male and female victims. Murder for theft or gain accounted for 7% of homicides (forty-seven offences), and 5% (thirty-one offences) occurred during irrational acts. This is a small proportion overall that can be attributed to people committing offences of murder who might have a mental disorder or be otherwise unable to act rationally.

Female victims were most likely to be killed in or around a house or dwelling or residential home (71%, 170 offences for year ending March 2019). This compares with 39% of male homicides (168 offences). Just under a third (30%) of male homicides took place in a street, path or alleyway (129 offences) compared with only 6% of female homicides (fourteen offences). Not only do these patterns reflect differing victim-suspect relationships and the circumstances of the homicide, but they also demonstrate the rarity of offences such as a those committed by Jack the Ripper, in that it is men who are mostly victims of murder outside of the home than women.

In summary, today's data demonstrates that men are more likely to be the victim of murder than women, that women are more likely to be killed by someone they know, murder by a stranger is relatively rare and the use of knives is still one of the most common methods of killing than any other. Women are more likely to be killed in the home than men, making the Ripper murders in the street and by a stranger all the more rare. It stands to reason that it is more likely that the women knew their killer or were familiar to him in some way.

Honeycombe (2011) reviewed crimes against and crimes by women for his book *Murders of the Black Museum*. He records that female victims are most likely to be killed by someone they knew, and this statistic is around 50% and this corresponds with current statistics above of 44%. Between 1900 and 1949 29% of persons found suspected of murder committed suicide whereas today this is down to 5%; 21.4% of persons found guilty of murder were also judged to be insane or unfit to plead whereas today, patients with schizophrenia, psychosis or other disorders in the UK committed a total of 870 homicides between 2004 and 2014, approximately 11% of all killings in that time (Flynn, Appleby and Shaw, 2016).

In the 1880s, police recorded crime was different from what it is today and limited in many ways. One has to look at the available court data in order to get some idea of the number and type of offences being committed, but of course this means that there is likely to be a huge number of crimes not reported, recorded or sent to court. We know this as the dark figure of crime, and we can assume that this will be a significant percentage of crime at the time. Data from hearings at Thames Police Court in 1887, the court that would have covered Whitechapel and still does today, states that 84% of violent crime convictions were committed by males and 16% by females. The nature of these violent incidents was, 22% male on male, male on female 45%, with 23% of those being domestic violence, 4% female on male and 28% female on female. In the 1880s the Old Bailey[3] heard 221 cases of violence against women including assault and battery which came under the offence of "Breaking the Peace", fifty-eight cases of female on male and forty-three of female on female. There were 455 cases of killing, which included murder, manslaughter and infanticide. Of these, 308 (67%) were males and 126 (27%) were female; in 105 (23%) of these cases the perpetrator was male and the victim female, 190 (42%) were male on male, thirty-three (7%) were female on male and forty-nine (10%) were female on female. Only 162 of the 455 killings were murder, fifty-one (31%) were male on female, fifty-six (34%) were male on male, thirteen (8%) were female on male and eighteen (11%) were female on female; the rest were undetermined.[4] Compared to the data from the British Crime Survey in 2018/19, one can see that the numbers of murders and the numbers of female victims have not changed drastically over

---

3   Hitchcock, Shoemaker, Emsley, Howard, and McLaughlin. et al., The Old Bailey Proceedings Online, 1674-1913 (www.oldbaileyonline.org, version 7.0, 24 March 2012).
4   https://www.oldbaileyonline.org/forms/formStats.jsp

the last 150 years. It is still the case that women are more likely to be killed by a male then as now, and that more men than women are the victims of murder, so how is it that women are still led to believe that they are at risk of being the victims of violence more frequently than men? One has to question what the role of the media, social stereotypes and the myths of social violence have had on the freedom of women in the public sphere over time.

Current research that is being conducted is demonstrating that violence towards sex workers often occurs at the point of payment, including homicide. This could be due to issues with value: did the customer feel they were getting value for money, did they feel that they should not have to pay for sex and therefore use violence as a way of avoiding payment and retaining some self-esteem of their own? Kinnell's research also gives examples of men posing as customers to get close to sex workers and then commit violence but again the violence is occurring around the point of payment. From the Jack the Ripper literature, there is limited suggestion that there was any sexual contact between the perpetrator and the victim; however, we know from witnesses that they see the victims talking to the possible perpetrator. Could Jack the Ripper have been posing as a customer to get close to his victims? Could violence have come from a want of their money or a disagreement about payment?

We also know from research as well as cases from the 1880s, that sex workers were the targets of criminal gangs, who would attack them and take their earnings. One victim in 1888, Emma Smith, was thought at one point to have been one of the Jack the Ripper victims. Earlier one evening she had been attacked, sexually assaulted and robbed by a criminal gang, of her earnings from prostitution, and later that day died in hospital as a result of her injuries (*Lloyds Weekly Newspaper*, 8th August 1888, secondary source from Gray, 2013). From this we can say that not all violence towards sex workers is motivated by hate but some is motivated by gain. In Kinnell's research, we see that risk of homicide is determined by location and isolation with street work being the most risky and then being alone indoors with a client.

Modern research into criminal profiling supports this. David Canter and Gabriella Salfati have conducted a number of studies to develop criminal profiling using geographical and statistical methods. Their work draws links between the environment where the offence takes place and the relationship between the victim and perpetrator profiling. Canter (1994) explored Peter Sutcliffe's murders and was able to demonstrate that the offences took place close enough to home for him to be familiar with the area but far enough away from his actual home not to raise suspicion. As he gained in confidence, he was able to range further afield, with a variety of potential areas where the perpetrator may have been operating from. This leaves the relationship of the perpetrator to the victims to be explored. Peter Sutcliffe and Steve Wright (Ipswich murders) both chose sex workers as they are vulnerable and are an opportunistic victim. Other serial killers in the USA also chose sex workers due to the easier opportunities but some have been known to be predatory and to hunt and select their victims for very specific reasons. Was Jack the Ripper opportunistic or a predator? This would depend on his likely relationship with the victims.

Using theories of violent behaviour by researchers such as Zillmann (1979), Fesbach (1964) and Salfati and Canter (1999) were able to determine perpetrator characteristics using the statistical association between crime scene behaviours and characteristics of the perpetrators. Zillmann suggested that at extreme levels of emotional arousal, cognitive or thinking processes are greatly impaired and hostile or aggressive behaviours are likely to be used impulsively; however, if these behaviours have been well learnt over the years, what might appear impulsive might actually be an automatic behaviour based on the schemas that we described earlier in the chapter. Fesbach posited that perpetrators can be classified into two types of aggression; hostile or Expressive and Instrumental, and these are distinguished by the goals or rewards offered to the perpetrator. For example, hostile or expressive aggression can be motivated by an anger-inducing scenario such as an insult, disrespect or physical attacks with the aim to make the person suffer or right the perceived wrong. Instrumental aggression comes through the desire for something such as an object, money or status. These theories support Kinnell's work, as it describes both types of aggression against sex workers: gangs attacking sex workers for their takings and vigilantes and customers attacking sex workers due to a perceived slight. Disrespect or re-addressing the power imbalance in the customer-sex worker relationship. Using these theories and statistical methods Salfati and Canter were able to develop typologies of perpetrators of homicide: the Expressive (Impulsive) Offender, the Instrumental (Opportunistic) Offender and the Instrumental (Cognitive) Offender.

The Expressive (Impulsive) Offender often had a past of impulsive offences such as previous violence, public disorder and drug offences. There were aspects of conflict against people which suggest they may have difficulties dealing with people in a socially acceptable manner and may resort to violence when difficulties arise in social interactions or interpersonal relationships. The Instrumental (Opportunistic) Offender is one that is using violence for gain but is opportunistic and takes their chances when they arise. This typology has a history of thefts and burglaries; however, what was interesting was that in most cases, the victim was known to the offender. This means that the offender could be watching people they know and waiting for an opportunity to rob them or attack them for whatever their goal or gain might be. The benefit of this for the offender is that their victims may not suspect that they intend harm towards them and in trusting them may make themselves more vulnerable, such as wandering in dark alleys and the streets of Whitechapel in the early hours of the morning. The Instrumental (Cognitive) Offender was thought to have chosen aggression and violence as a lifestyle and usually have spent time in prison and have antisocial associations. This suggests that violence is a way of life for them, and they would be well known in their community and amongst their social circles for their use of violence and aggression.

Salfati and Taylor (2006) used these methods to explore sexual violence and sexual homicides. They developed a model where sexual violence and sexual homicide make up parts of a continuum. There were three main categories which determined the relationship between the victim and offender during the offence: Exploitation, Control and Violence. The Exploitation category included characteristics such as foreign objects inserted into the victim, stealing items of value from the victim and stealing non-identifiable items from the victim. Control included variables such as binding the victim, blindfolding the victim, ripping the victim's clothing, using a weapon and being forensically aware. Finally, the Violence category included multiple wounds to the victim, non-controlled violence and the offender using something from the scene as a weapon. We don't have information about Jack the Ripper that would help us to categorise which of these violent and sexual violent categories he might come under; however, what these typologies do help us with, is understanding some of the motivations, thoughts and behaviours behind violence towards women and violence towards sex workers in particular.

But what about female perpetrators of violence? Data gathered from the British Crime Survey has shown that in general, the nature, severity, frequency, and victim characteristics of violent offences committed by women are significantly different from those committed by men. Other research has demonstrated that female violence less often results in serious injuries and is less visible and subtler, manifesting more often as relational violence, child abuse or violence towards relatives (Monahan et al., 2001; Nicholls, 2001; Robbins, Monahan and Silver, 2003, in Webster, 2007). The most common victims of violence by adult women are partners or children and the most common victims by girls are siblings and peers (Batchelor, 2005). There are several explanations for this (Bennett, Farrington and Huesmann, 2005), but a commonly cited explanation is the different method of socialisation, whereby boys are encouraged to act assertively while girls are encouraged to bond with others (see for example Brownie, 2007). In adulthood, women are more likely to describe themselves in terms of their relationship with others rather than in terms of their individual characteristics (Cross and Madson, 1997). Furthermore, women seem to have different motives for violent offences; female violence is more often reactive and relational and less often characterised as instrumental than male violence and occurs more commonly within the context of social relationships (Crick and Grotpeter, 1995; Monahan et al., 2001; Nicholls, 2001; Odgers et al., 2005; Robbins et al., 2003, in de Vogel and de Ruiter, 2005). Claimed motives for violence by women are, for example, jealousy, self-defence and feeling disrespected by others (Kruttschnitt and Carbone-Lopez, 2006). Women, in comparison to men, are more likely to use knives or so-called personal weapons, such as hands and teeth, when they commit violence (Koons-Wit and Schram, 2003).

In the past, motives for offences committed by girls were more often seen in the social sphere or within relations (revenge, jealousy and gossip) than in boys. In a recent US study of the explanations for violent offences by girls as seen by probation officers, the three most frequently cited explanations for girls were: 1) emotional outburst; 2) relational violence; and 3) history of abuse (Fusco et al., 2011, in de Vogel and Stam, 2014). For boys, these three explanations were not once mentioned. The three most frequently cited explanations for violent offences for boys were: 1) ego-driven; 2) peer pressure; and 3) survival. However, this research also demonstrated that there is a subgroup of girls/young women who seem to show more "masculine" forms of violence. In this subgroup of females, instrumental aggression, hostility, committing robberies and criminal gang membership is more prevalent (Babcock, Miller and Siard, 2003; Batchelor, 2005; Bottos, 2007; MacKenzie and Johnson, 2003, in de Vogel and Stam, 2014).

Whilst violence towards women has always been disapproved of in society, it has also been the case that "what happens behind closed doors stays behind closed doors". Violence between men and women has been common in communities where there is poverty, stress and close living quarters. What makes the Jack the Ripper murders unique is that it brought violence against women onto the streets of London where it was there for all to see, and it could not be brushed under the carpet of Victorian propriety. It was not that it was violence towards women per se, but the severity and the perceived sexual nature of the violence towards these women. It was the extent of the violence and the extreme mutilations that led to public outrage and horror, not necessarily the fact that a prostitute was killed. This reflects what we already know about the prevalent attitudes in Victorian and present-day society towards sex working and about how violence was allowed to go unpunished. In the case of the Ripper murders, the victim was depersonalised by society to the extent that it was the details of the murders and not the loss of a woman's life that became the focus of the narrative that, with a few exceptions, persists to this day.

REFERENCES

Allport, G.W. (1954), *The Nature of Prejudice*, Addison-Wesley, Cambridge, MA.

Batchelor, S. (2005), "'Prove me the bam!': Victimization and agency in the lives of young women who commit violent offences", *The Journal of Community and Criminal Justice*, 52, 358–375.

Beck, A.T. (1999), *Prisoners of Hate. The Cognitive Basis of Anger, Hostility and Violence*, Perennial, Harper Collins, New York, p125–132 and 150–164.

Bennett, S., Farrington, D.P. and Huesmann, L.R. (2005), "Explaining gender differences in crime and violence: The importance of social cognitive skills", *Aggression and Violent Behavior*, 10(3), 263–288, http://dx.doi.org/10.1016/j.avb.2004.07.001

Canter, D. (1994), *Criminal Shadows: Inside the Mind of the Serial Killer*, Harper Collins, London.

Cross, S.E. and Madson, L. (1997), "Models of the Self: Self-Construals and Gender", *Psychological Bulletin*, 122, 5–37, https://doi.org/10.1037/0033-2909.122.1.5

de Vogel, V. and de Ruiter, C. (2005), "The HCR-20 in personality disordered female offenders: A comparison with a matched sample of males", *Clinical Psychology & Psychotherapy*, 12, 226–240, doi: 10.1002/cpp.452.

de Vogel, V. and Stam, J. (2014), "Exploring the Criminal Behavior of Women with Psychopathy: Results from a Multicenter Study into Psychopathy and Violent Offending in Female Forensic Psychiatric Patients", *International Journal of Forensic Mental Health*, Volume 13, 2014 – Issue 4, retrieved from https://www.tandfonline.com/doi/ref/10.1080/14999013.2014.951105?scroll=top on 12th August 2018.

Fesbach, S. (1964), "The function of aggression and the regulation of aggressive drive", *Psychological Review*, 71, 257–272.

Flynn, S., Gask, L., Appleby, L. and Shaw, J. (2016), "Homicide-Suicide and the role of mental disorder: a national consecutive case series", *Social psychiatry and psychiatric epidemiology*, 51, 6, p877–884.

Gray, D.D. (2013), *London's Shadows*, Bloomsbury Academic.

Honeycombe, G. (2011), *Murders of the black museum: 1875–1975. The dark secrets behind more than a hundred years of the most notorious crimes in England*, Gordon John Blake Publishing.

Kinnell, H. (2008), *Violence and Sex Work in Britain*, Willan Publishing, Devon.

Koons-Witt, B.A. and Schram, P.J. (2003), "The prevalence and nature of violent offending by females", *Journal of Criminal Justice*, 31, 361–371.

Kruttschnitt, C. and Carbone-Lopez, K. (2006), "Moving beyond the stereotypes: Women's subjective accounts of their violent crime", *Criminology*, 44, 321–351.

Lippmann, W. (1922), *Public Opinion*, Harcourt, Brace and Company, New York, retrieved 3rd May 2016, via Internet Archive.

Miller, J. and Schwartz, M.D. (1995), "Rape Myths and Violence Towards Street Prostitutes", *Deviant Behaviour*, 16, 1, 1-23. DOI: 10.1080/01639625.1995.9967984, retrieved from https://www.researchgate.net/publication/248985276_Rape_Myths_and_Violence_Towards_Street_Prostitutes on 8th December 2018.

Office for National Statistics (2020), "Homicide in England and Wales: year ending March 2019", released 13th February 2020, retrieved from https://www.ons.gov.uk/peoplepopulationandcommunity/crimeandjustice/articles/homicideinenglandandwales/yearendingmarch2019

Salfati, G.C. and Canter, D.C. (1999), "Differentiating Stranger Murders: Profiling Offender Characteristics from Behavioral Styles", *Behavioral Sciences and the Law*, 17: 391–406.

Salfati, G.C. and Taylor, P. (2006), "Differentiating sexual violence: A comparison of sexual homicide and rape", *Psychology, Crime & Law*, April 2006, Vol. 12(2): 107–125.

Webster, C.D. and Bloom, H. (2007), *Essential Writings in Violence Risk Assessment and Management*, Centre for Addiction and Mental Health.

Zillmann, D. (1979), *Hostility and aggression*, NJ Lawrence Erlbaum, Hillsdale.

8

WOMEN AND CRIME: THEN AND NOW

'Poverty is the parent of revolution and crime.'

Aristotle

*'There are crimes of passion and crimes of logic.
The boundary between them is not clearly defined.'*

Albert Camus

The Victorian criminal underworld has reached a level of notoriety through the writings of novelists and journalists and filmmakers that has enthralled audiences for decades. Inevitably, among the criminals that lived and "worked" the streets of the East End of London in the late Victorian period, were many women.

The involvement of women in crime in the Victorian era was seen as part of the criminal underworld and compounded the view that women needed men to ensure they remained moral and pure. However, exploring women's crime in more depth as something that stands in its own right rather than as a part or even by-product of a male-dominated underground crime world brings to light some interesting similarities and differences in crimes between genders. It also serves to shed some light on the possibility and likelihood that the Ripper might have been female. To explore this fully, we have drawn upon current research into female crime; largely because there are only limited studies on the motivations and factors related to female offending during the late Victorian period. Statistics across cultures and time have been consistent in reporting that men commit more criminal acts than women. There are numerous theories which offer explanations for this sex difference including evolutionary, psychobiological and social reasons. Discussing these in detail is beyond the scope of this book; however, it is relevant to the premise of this book to explore some of these theories and consider how they might relate to crime in the Victorian era and specifically to some of the theories on the identity of Jack the Ripper, such as the mad doctor or female serial killer theories.

Gottfredson and Hirschi's (1990) "general theory of crime" states that individuals with lower levels of self-control are more likely to be involved in criminal behaviour. This theory was tested in a gender sensitive context by Burton et al. (1998), who found that low levels of self-control are associated with criminal activity; for example, self-control was highly positively correlated to criminal behaviour in both genders but was especially significant for males. For females, the relationship between self-control and criminality became significant when opportunity was introduced; however, opportunity was not a significant indicator of male criminal behaviour, suggesting that women have less opportunity than men to commit crime and female criminality increases when opportunities present themselves. This has social connotations for female criminality. For example, recent research indicates an increase in crime perpetrated by women including violent offences, and it has been suggested that perhaps women's changing societal roles and socialisation may be offering more opportunity for criminality, such as being away from the family home and out in the workplace, pubs and bars, and thereby reducing these differences between male and female offending (Weizmann-Henelius, 2006).

We can relate this to the late Victorian era where women's social role was also changing. The industrial revolution was driving more women into the workplace, more women were taking up professions as well as education and some were driving moves towards greater independence, by living alone or with other women and walking the streets "unchaperoned", women were using alehouses and hostels unaccompanied, and it was likely that greater opportunities for offending presented themselves. The Victorian concept of woman was that a woman had to be pure, either a wife or fully chaste, and an evident increase in female-perpetrated crime is likely to have fuelled an increase in social anxieties regarding the dangers of changes to the accepted female role. The Jack the Ripper narrative, as has been explored in Chapter 1, actively played to those fears, the sensationalisation of the events by the media accelerating a state of moral panic in the nation, heightening fears in city communities that women should not be outdoors unaccompanied. This in turn served to restrict the movement and growing independence of women; the message being played out was, to all intents and purposes, "if you are a woman that steps out of line, you will meet a very bad end". To the Victorian mind, women criminals alongside prostitutes, were an extreme and an abhorrent form of woman and one which overstepped the boundaries set for them by the prevalent patriarchy.

Turning specifically to violent offending, evolutionary theories of aggression focus on the use of aggression as a means of ensuring reproduction, gaining status and resources, and protecting territory. Theories of aggression are often cited when discussing sex differences in criminality. In particular, there are two theories on the role of testosterone in aggression and competition among males that are frequently cited. The first one is the Challenge Hypothesis, which states that testosterone increases during puberty, facilitating reproductive and competitive behaviour which would include aggression, and that this occurs as a result of evolution. Therefore, it is the challenge of competition in relation to testosterone among males that facilitates aggression and violence. Studies conducted have found direct correlations between testosterone and dominance, especially among the most violent criminals in prison, who had the highest testosterone levels (Archer, 2006; Ellis and Hoskin, 2015).

The second theory is known as the evolutionary neuroandrogenic (ENA) theory of male aggression (Ellis and Hoskin, 2015). Testosterone and other androgens have evolved to masculinise a brain in order to be competitive even as far as being a risk to harming others. By doing so, individuals with masculinised brains as a result of pre-natal and adult life testosterone and androgens enhance their resource acquiring abilities in order to survive, attract and copulate with mates as much as possible. In this theory, crime can be seen as an extreme form of adaptation to gain status and acquire more resources.

As the purported evolutionary role of females is to nurture and develop social bonds with others in order to ensure the survival of herself and her young, overt aggression is not thought to be necessary except as a self-defence mechanism (Swan et al., 2008). It is thought that women are more likely to use direct aggression in private, where other people cannot see them, and are more likely to use indirect aggression (such as passive-aggressive behaviour) in public. Female violence is more often reactive and relational and less often characterised as instrumental (Crick and Grotpeter, 1995; Monahan et al., 2001; Nicholls, 2001; Odgers et al., 2005; Robbins et al., 2003). If we return to the earlier referenced research regarding adolescent female violence whose motives included emotional outburst, relational violence, and history of abuse (Fusco et al., 2011), Quinsey (2002) found males, regardless of age, engaged in more physical and verbal aggression, whilst females engaged in more indirect aggression such as rumour spreading or gossiping. The studies also found that males tend to engage in more unprovoked aggression at higher frequency than females.

The theories and research thus far discussed open the door for the potential of a female Ripper. Motivations such as jealousy or an emotional outburst could have led to an extremely violent attack on the victims who would likely have been known to them. As noted in the previous chapter, offender profiling suggests elements of the Ripper murders which were expressive of emotionally driven violence, but other aspects were related to a more calculated attack. Following the evolutionary and biological theory, it is difficult to see how a male Ripper would have needed to harm these women in order to satisfy needs such as competition and territory, although one could understand how such violence could have been ego-driven. However, these theories alone are simplistic, and it is likely that the violence witnessed in the Ripper murders was driven by psychological and social mechanisms.

Women's violence can also be explained by psychosocial models such as social learning theory and feminist theories. Social learning theory was initially articulated by Bandura (1978) and is used to explain a variety of behaviours including violence. This theory suggests that modelling of others' behaviour through observation is central to the development of behaviour including violence. For example, children who are witness to, or experience, violence learn to also use violence to control or gain power over others, as well as to express emotion and punish others. Exposure to violence over time can desensitise people to violence and these can end up viewing violence as part of everyday life. These behaviours have to be rewarded in order to be maintained. The importance of modelling in the development of violent behaviours has been empirically established in the social psychology, arena where experimental designs have routinely shown that girls and boys who observe aggressive behaviour are at risk for behaving violently themselves (Moretti, Obsuth, Odgers and Reebye, 2006). Social learning theory would posit that women learn to become violent by being exposed to it. This exposure could come from their own victimisation and traumatic experiences of violence (Babcock, Miller and Siard, 2003), learning that violence can be used to gain control and power over others, and in gaining control over others they tend then to victimise other women and children or family members. Reinforcement alone is not enough to maintain behaviours; however, cognitions can, such as pro-violent attitudes, maintain this behaviour. For example, Grant and Butler (1998) found that young women who were violent held more antisocial beliefs than their non-violent peers, and others have reported violent women to misinterpret environmental cues in a manner conducive to violence (e.g., hostile attribution bias) (Leschied, Cummings, Van Brunschot, Cunningham and Saunders, 2001). Equally, women can be violent due to disrespect and jealousy as well as self-defence and for economic purposes, and for that reason, other theories such as personality theories can be helpful to understanding violence in women.

Theories examining the over-controlled and under-controlled personality constructs emphasise that factors both internal and external to the individual are instrumental in predicting violence. Megargee (1966) initially identified these personality styles among male juvenile offenders and found the under-controlled personality to be particularly characteristic of aggressive boys and, where characteristics included lower inhibitions against aggressive behaviour, increased likelihood of aggressive responses when frustrated or provoked. Over-controlled aggressors, on the other hand, were far less common but tended to be more characteristic of young men who committed extremely violent crimes such as homicide. These offenders showed lower overall rates of aggression and a more docile demeanour. It was hypothesised that these men inhibited feelings of anger to such a degree that it resulted in anger accumulating over time and through repeated provocations, with the end result ultimately being an explosion of anger and violence, but on a much less frequent basis.

In 1995 this theory was extended to women by Ogle et al. (1995), who theorised that the socialisation processes teach women to inhibit expressions of anger, thereby compelling them to internalise negative affective states such as guilt, hurt and depression, rather than externalise it as anger. As a result of these societal inhibitions, women are prevented from developing culturally appropriate ways of expressing feelings of anger. Furthermore, it is proposed that, as the number of stresses in a woman's life increase, such as motherhood, poverty, unemployment and messages of societal devaluation, inadequate means of dealing with these stressors leads to pent-up negative emotions which may eventually surpass their inhibition threshold and erupt in violence. Research by Verona and Carbonell (2000) provides support for this dispositional style among violent women, with most females who are violent tending to be one-time violent offenders who present with an over-controlled personality.

Feminist theories contend that female violence is a reaction to male dominance and abuse, and the patriarchal values of society that epitomise men and devalue women's roles.

The Feminist Ecological Model (FEM) addresses the complexity of women's violence, taking into account interactions between social, historical, institutional, and individual factors in understanding their behaviour (Das Dasgupta, 2002). The FEM suggests that gender and culture will influence how individuals interact with their family and immediate environment (Ballou et al., 2002), therefore the use of violence is suggested to be influenced by exposure to violence in the family of origin, in the community in which one resides, and cultural depictions of violence (Jonson-Reid, 1998). By referring to these theories, it could be construed that the Ripper murders could have been committed by a female who perhaps withheld her anger against prostitutes for so long that she eventually reacted violently. However, the weight of the research suggests that this is still more likely to be a male rather than female response.

According to the Old Bailey Records, in the year from January 1888 to January 1889, women had been arrested for 101 offences. Of these, theft was the most common (twenty-five) followed by deception (twenty). However, there were eleven cases recorded of killing involving women. There were seven instances of infanticide (also listed as murder, manslaughter and concealing a birth). In all cases, the women were found not guilty by reason of "puerperal mania" or by reason of insanity and either committed to an asylum or the care of their parents. There is no record of women killing men and there are three instances of a woman killing another woman (murder and manslaughter). Again, the verdicts were not guilty by way of insanity or lack of evidence. In one instance, the judge agreed with evidence from the doctor that this woman suffered from epilepsy, and this could lead her to act in an unconscious way during a petit mal and not be aware of her actions.

According to the Office for National Statistics Report (March 2019), Female victims were most likely to be killed in or around a house or dwelling or residential home (71%, 170 offences for year ending March 2019). This compares with 39% of male homicides (168 offences). Just under a third (30%) of male homicides took place in a street, path or alleyway (129 offences) compared with only 6% of female homicides (fourteen offences). As we have seen in the previous chapter, these patterns reflect differing victim-suspect relationships and the circumstances of the homicide. More females are killed in the home by their partner, whereas more males, whilst known to their attacker, might be killed outside of the home. Despite these statistics which are repeated year on year by the Office of National Statistics, it remains the case that society believes that women are in danger outside the home due to the fear generated by crimes such as those of the Ripper, and the augmentation of similar fears that were perpetuated by urban legends such as those of Spring-heeled Jack. However, the reality is that women are at greater risk of harm in their own home than they are in public.

Swan et al.'s (2008) review published in the journal *Violence and Victims* found that more serious and violent abuse was perpetrated by men and women's physical violence was more likely motivated by self-defence or fear while men's was motivated by control. A 2011 systematic review from the *Journal of Trauma Violence Abuse* also found that the common motives for female on male domestic violence were anger, a need for attention or as a response to their partner's own violence. Another 2011 review published in the *Journal of Aggression and Violent Behaviour* also found that, although minor domestic violence was equal, more severe violence was perpetrated by men. It was also found that men were more likely to beat up, choke or strangle their partners, while women were more likely to throw something at their partner, slap, kick, bite, punch or hit with an object. In the context of the Ripper murders and the nature of the violence committed against these women, it is theoretically more likely that the perpetrator was male rather than female.

There continue to be differences observed in the nature and context of violence between males and females. For example, Robbins, Monahan and Silver (2003); Strand and Belfrage (2001); and Teasdale, Silver and Monahan (2006) all conducted studies which demonstrated that men tend to engage in more overt acts of violence, while violence committed by women is more often likely to be covert and to occur within the context of relationships both intimate and non-intimate. Differences also exist with respect to the types of offences for which men and women tend to be arrested. For example, women are less likely than men to be arrested and convicted for a sexual violence. Women also tend to be less likely than men to use weapons (Greenfeld and Snell, 1999). Unlike men, women do not generally commit crimes in pairs or in groups, and they are less likely to use weapons (Greenfeld and Snell, 1999; Kruttschnitt, Gartner and Ferraro, 2002). Some crimes are virtually unique to women, such as neonaticide. Violent offences tend to also happen in the context of the home rather than out on the street, and victims tend to be family members such as children and partners (Batchelor, 2005). The rate of offending for other crimes is drastically differentiated by the sex of the perpetrator, for example, sexual offending (4–5% are women, Cortoni and Hanson, 2005), stalking (15–20% are women, Meloy and Boyd, 2003) and familicide, where 95% of perpetrators are male (Wilson, Daly and Daniele, 1995), are predominantly perpetrated by one gender or the other. In contrast, other forms of violence are more evenly distributed across the sexes, such as child abuse and partner abuse (Archer, 2000; Hamel and Nicholls, 2007).

The research indicates that whilst female violence towards adults, including other females does occur, the context is usually domestic, with the location usually in the home and the victim usually a family member or child, unlike the Ripper murders themselves. Whilst this does not discount that there could have been an exception to the rule as we will explore below, the likelihood is low. There has been limited research in the past on female serial killers; however, Eric Hickey of Fresno State University (Hickey, 2009) interviewed sixty-four female serial killers in the USA, identifying characteristics of women who murdered in a series through poisoning, shooting and stabbing their victims. The profile of these women was that the majority were white middle- and upper-class and typically killed between seven and ten victims. They were more likely to murder family members rather than strangers and the most prevalent motive for murder was money. There has been other research to support this; for example, Farrell, Keppel and Titterington (2011) reviewed newspaper reports of ten American female serial killers and found that they tended to operate for a substantially longer time than their male counterparts, 80% knew their victims and nursing as a profession was over-represented as an occupation in female serial killers.

Harrison (2015) used media coverage of female serial killers to identify characteristics and found that almost all (92%) knew their victims, almost all were white and their most common means to kill was poison, while the primary motive for murder was money. Nearly two thirds were related to their victims, nearly one third killed their significant others and about 44% killed their own biological children. More than half the sample killed children, and about one quarter killed those who were elderly or infirm, those who had little chance of fighting back. In the UK, Honeycombe (2011), in his book *Murders of the Black Museum: 1875-1975*, found that between 1843 and 1955 there were thirty-seven women poisoners out of sixty-eight other women who were hung for murder, most of whom came from towns rather than the countryside. Therefore, although it is not beyond reason that the Ripper could have been female, it seems unlikely. Each of the victims would have needed to be known to the female ripper and there would probably have needed to be an intimate or familial link. Evidence of motives such as jealousy or money would need to have been identified through the crime scene, it is much more likely that poisoning rather than violence would have been used and the murders are more likely to have taken place in the home.

Throughout this chapter there have been allusions to the most common types of people who were victims of female murderers, children. Infanticide was the most common murder committed by women of the time and much of this was due to the social and economic pressures faced by women in the new industrialised society. To bring up a child in these conditions, outside of marriage would have brought with its social shame and even deeper poverty or complete destitution, so it was not uncommon for women to commit infanticide or to pass their children on to baby farmers.

Despite the attitudes at the time regarding women and their mental health, judges tended to be lenient when there was evidence of puerperal psychosis in infanticide cases. Cossins (2015) suggests that women frequently used the insanity defence if accused of murdering their children, but this defence had to be supported by psychiatrists who often considered lack of denial and lack of subterfuge around the crime, as symptoms of insanity. Verdicts involving puerperal insanity seemed to agree that such women represented the very antithesis of womanhood yet also allowed them to be treated with compassion. Cossins posited that madness and infanticide could be seen as part of femininity and maternity and this could be why there was some leniency demonstrated in these verdicts. Physical and mental fragility were widely agreed to be latent in all women and was greatly strained at childbirth, which often resulted in collapse and madness; Victorians believed that it was this combination that typified puerperal insanity, that madness was a part of motherhood and was therefore redeemable. Female perpetrators of infanticide with puerperal insanity were ultimately forgiven by society and redeemed, and yet so many other crimes committed by females, including sex working, were not redeemable. For example, from the Old Bailey Records between 1888 and 1889 there were six cases of infanticide: in one case the judge states:

> *From the evidence of MR. HOLLAND HODGSON WRIGHT, Surgeon, of Ostring Road, Kentish Town, it appeared that at the time the prisoner committed the offence she was suffering from puerperal mania, and was not accountable for her actions, and also that the injuries might not have been inflicted until after the death of the child. NOT GUILTY.*

In another case the judge states:

> *RUTH NEWMAN (21) PLEADED GUILTY to unlawfully endeavouring to conceal the birth of her child. She was stated to have always borne a very respectable character, and Mr. Wheatley, the Secretary to St. Giles's Christian Mission, undertook to place her in the care of her mother. — To enter into her own recognisances to come up for judgment if called upon. She was also charged, upon the Coroner's Inquisition, with the murder of the said child, but the Grand Jury having ignored the bill, no evidence was offered on the Inquisition, and a verdict of NOT GUILTY was returned.*

This demonstrates a leniency on the part of the judges as well as from the jury, the social peers of the women on trial. It demonstrates that society understood and agreed that women who committed these types of crimes were suffering and were not responsible for their actions.

Another form of infanticide came from baby-farming practices. Technically, baby farming was illegal but was permitted to continue as it was recognised as an underground, silently acknowledged public service or as filling a social need. In a time when there was no access to contraception, and there were many women working as prostitutes to make ends meet, unwanted pregnancies were common and access to safe abortions almost completely non-existent. Some women would choose to pay baby farmers to care for their infants instead. This would allow the woman to continue working and not be pushed into even more desperate poverty. Baby farmers at the time would have been known as foster mothers or nannies and would take money to feed, clothe and care for the children. Whilst there were likely to have been some decent foster mothers, there were records of children in desperate poverty, neglected and malnourished. Some children were sold to wealthy couples who were unable to have children of their own, and in many more cases, children died or were killed. One such case was the case of Margaret Waters, who in 1870 was found guilty of murdering sixteen children in her care and was sentenced to death by hanging. This crime outraged society, but it was acknowledged that in the Victorian mind-set, such women were providing a service, and according to Darwinian Theory, the weakest were perishing. Whilst it is not known what differentiates a woman who would commit this crime from those who would commit violence, we can assume that money remains at least one of the motivating factors and it is likely that antisocial attitudes and a lack of empathy mediated this appalling behaviour.

It can be seen that across the ages, different types of crime have been attributed differently to women than to their male counterparts and to an extent this is the same for violent crimes perpetrated by women. These crimes are differently motivated and differently perpetrated leading to the conclusion that although violent crime is not uncommon amongst women and applying violence such as the killing of children is possible, the likelihood that the Ripper murders would have been conducted by a woman is very limited although not entirely impossible. It is more likely that these murders towards women, with the level of violence and the location of the crimes were much more likely to be perpetrated by a man. It is also clear that there is a disconnect between what is true and evidenced by statistics of violence towards both men and women, and society's common understanding of who are victims and when. Society has used the fear of violence, such as that committed by the Ripper and others throughout modern history, to keep women and children "safe" at home, but at home is precisely where the majority of this violence towards women and children occurs. It is therefore inevitable to speculate whether the relating of these stories of violence is a means of controlling the movements and actions of women and children or whether society at large is genuinely not aware of the statistical reality of violent homicide. If they were, the question must be posed: would the narrative be changed, and would males be kept indoors, safe at home, or always escorted, chaperoned and supervised, when outdoors?

REFERENCES

Archer, J. (2006), "Testosterone and human aggression: an evaluation of the challenge hypothesis", *Neuroscience and Biobehavioral Reviews*, 30 (3): 319–45, doi: 10.1016/j.neubiorev.2004.12.007.

Babcock, J.C., Miller, S.A. and Siard, C. (2003), "Toward a typology of abusive women: Differences between partner-only and generally violent women in the use of violence", *Psychology of Women Quarterly*, 27, 153–161.

Ballou, M., Matsumoto, A. and Wagner, M. (2002), "Toward a feminist ecological theory of human nature: Theory building in response to real-world dynamics", in Ballou, M. and Brown, L.S., *Rethinking mental health and disorder: Feminist perspectives* (p99–141), Guilford Press, New York.

Bandura, A. (1978), "Learning and behavioural theory of aggression", in Kutash, L., Kutash, S.B. and Schlesinger, L.B., *Violence perspective on murder and aggression* (p29–57), Jossey-Bass, San Francisco, CA.

Batchelor, S. (2005), "'Prove me the bam!' Victimization and agency in the lives of young women who commit violent offences", *The Journal of Community and Criminal Justice*, 52, 358–375.

Bottos, S. (2007), "Women and violence: Theory, risk and treatment implications", Research report No. R-198, Research Brand Correctional Service Canada, Ottawa, ON, Canada.

Burton, V.S. Jr., Cullen, F.T., Evans, D.T., Alarid, L.F. and Dunaway, G.R. (1998), "Gender, Self-Control and Crime", *Journal of Research in Crime and Delinquency*, 35, 2, 123–147.

Cossins, A. (2015), *Female Criminality: Infanticide, Moral Panics and The Female Body*, Palgrave McMillan, London.

Crick, N.R. and Grotpeter, J.K. (1995), "Relational aggression, gender, and social psychological adjustment", *Child Development*, 66, 710–722.

Das Dasgupta, S. (2002), "A framework for understanding women's use of nonlethal violence in intimate heterosexual relationships", *Violence Against Women*, 8, 1364–1389.

Ellis, L. and Hoskin, A. (2015), "The evolutionary neuroandrogenic theory of criminal behavior expanded", *Aggression and Violent Behaviour*, 24: 61–74, doi: 10.1016/j.avb.2015.05.002.

Farrell, A.L., Keppel, R.D. and Titterington, V.B. (2011), "Lethal ladies: Revisiting what we know about female serial murderers", *Homicide Studies*, 15, 228–252, doi:10.1177/1088767911415938.

Fusco, S.L., Perrault, R.T., Paiva, M.L., Cook, N.E. and Vincent, G. (2011), "Probation officer perceptions of gender differences in youth offending and implications for practice in the field", paper presented at the 4th International Congress on Psychology and Law, Miami, March 2011.

Gottfredson, M.R. and Hirschi, T. (1990), *A General Theory of Crime*, Stanford University Press.

Grant, I. and Butler, S. (1998), "The relation between anger and antisocial beliefs in young offenders", *Personality and Individual Differences*, 24, 759–765.

Greenfeld, L.A. and Snell, T.L. (1999), "Bureau of Justice Statistics special report: Women offenders.", United States Department of Justice, Washington, DC.

Harrison, M.A., Murphy, E.A., Ho, L.Y., Thomas, G. and Flaherty, C.V. (2015), "Female serial killers in the United States: means, motives and makings", *The Journal of Forensic Psychiatry and Psychology*, 26, 3, 383–406.

Hickey, E. (2009), *Serial Murderers and Their Victims*, 5th ed., Wadsworth Publishing Co Inc, Belmont.

Honeycombe, G. (2011), *Murders of the black museum: 1875–1975. The dark secrets behind more than a hundred years of the most notorious crimes in England*, John Blake Publishing.

Jonson-Reid, M. (1998), "Youth violence and exposure to violence in childhood: An ecological review", *Aggression and Violent Behaviour*, 3, 159–179.

Kruttschnitt, C., Gartner, R. and Ferraro, K. (2002), "Women's involvement in serious interpersonal violence", *Aggression and Violent Behaviour*, 7(6), 529–565, https://doi.org/10.1016/S1359-1789(01)00045-3

Kruttschnitt, K. and Carbone-Lopez, K. (2006), "Moving beyond the stereotypes: Women's subjective accounts of their violent crime", *Criminology*, 44, 321–351.

Leschied, A.W., Cummings, A.L., Van Brunschot, M., Cunningham, A. and Saunders, A. (2001), "A review of the literature on aggression with adolescent girls: Implications for policy prevention and treatment", *Canadian Psychology*, 42, 200–215.

MacKenzie, A. and Johnson, S.L. (2003), "A profile of women gang members in Canada", research report No. R-138, Research Brand Correctional Service Canada, Ottawa, ON.

Marland, H. (2004), *Dangerous Motherhood: Insanity and Childbirth in Victorian Britain*, Palgrave Macmillan, Basingstoke, Hampshire.

Megargee, E. (1966), "Undercontrolled and overcontrolled personality types in extreme antisocial aggression", *Psychological Monographs*, 80, 1–19.

Monahan, J., Steadman, H.J., Silver, E., Appelbaum, P.S., Robbins, P.C., Mulvey, E.P., Roth, L.H., Grisso, T. and Banks, S. (2001), *Rethinking risk assessment: The MacArthur study of mental disorder and violence*, Oxford University Press, Oxford.

Moretti, M.M., Obsuth, I., Odgers, C.L. and Reebye, P. (2006), "Exposure to maternal vs. paternal partner violence, PTSD, and aggression in adolescent girls and boys", *Aggressive Behaviour*, 32, 385–395.

Hitchcock. T., Shoemaker. R., Emsley. C., Howard. S., and McLaughlin. J., et al., The Old Bailey Proceedings Online, 1674-1913 (www.oldbaileyonline.org, version 7.0, 24 March 2012).

Nicholls, T.L. (2001), "Violence risk assessment with female NCRMD acquittees: Validity of the HCR-20 and PCL:SV", unpublished master's thesis, Simon Fraser University, Vancouver, British Columbia, Canada.

Odgers, C.L., Moretti, M.M. and Reppucci, N.D. (2005), "Examining the science and practice of violence risk assessment with female adolescents", *Law and Human Behaviour*, 29, 7–27.

Office for National Statistics (2020), "Homicide in England and Wales: year ending March 2019", released 13th February 2020, retrieved from https://www.ons.gov.uk/peoplepopulationandcommunity/crimeandjustice/articles/homicideinenglandandwales/yearendingmarch2019

Ogle, R.S., Maier-Katkin, D. and Bernard, T.J. (1995), "A theory of homicidal behaviour among women", *Criminology*, 33, 173–193.

Quinsey, V.L. (2002), "Evolutionary theory and criminal behaviour", *Legal and Criminological Psychology*, 7 (1): 1–13, doi:10.1348/135532502168324.

Robbins, P.C., Monahan, J. and Silver, E. (2003), "Mental disorder, violence and gender", *Law and Human Behaviour*, 27, 561–571.

Strand, S. (Belfrage, H.) (2001), "Comparison of HCR-20 Scores in violent mentally disordered men and women: Gender differences and similarities", *Psychology Crime and Law*, 7, 1, 71–79. doi:10.1080/10683160108401784.

Swan, S.C., Gambone, L.J., Caldwell, J.E., Sullivan, T.P., Snow, D.L. (2008), "A review of research on women's use of violence with male intimate partners", *Violence and Victims*, 23, 3, 301–314, doi:10.1891/0886-6708.23.3.301, ISSN 0886-6708. PMC 2968709, PMID 18624096.

Teasdale, B., Silver, E., Monahan, J. (2006), "Gender, Threat/Control-Override Delusions and Violence", *Law and Human Behaviour*, DOI 10.1007/s10979-006-9044-x.

Verona, E. and Carbonell, J.L. (2000), "Female violence and personality: Evidence for a pattern of over-controlled hostility among one-time violent female offenders", *Criminal Justice and Behaviour*, 27, 176–195.

Weizmann-Henelius, G. (2006), "Violent Female Perpetrators in Finland: Personality and Life Events", *Nordic Psychology*, 58(4), 280–297, http://dx.doi.org/10.1027/1901-2276.58.4.280

9

WOMEN'S MENTAL HEALTH AND TREATMENT

'How very little can be done under the spirit of fear.'

Florence Nightingale

A casual internet search using the terms "victims", "mental illness" and "Jack the Ripper" will quickly reveal long lists of resources ready to discuss the psychological profile of the murderer and all those potential "Jack the Rippers". The focus of much of the material at the fingertips of the enquiring public is entirely on the perpetrator, the murderer, the figure of mystery that has fascinated people for well over a century. The focus seems to be almost invariably on the man, the male protagonist in the tragedy of at least five, possibly more, women. And yet each of the victims, along with a multitude of women among whom they lived, had endured trauma, ill health and the crushing poverty that must have had powerful negative impacts on their mental health. All the victims were known to enjoy drink. Substance abuse is nowadays recognised as a form of self-medication, a means to numb the stress, anxiety, depression and a prop to get through each difficult day. It is also the cause and the symptom or deeper problems, with alcohol affecting mental health as much as it does physical health.

Jack the Ripper's victims were not merely coincidental victims of a spree by a knife-wielding maniac as some of the popular tales especially in the film and media industry would have us believe. These women were victims of circumstance, of socioeconomic and political conditions, and of the difficulties they encountered in lives that were out of their control.

Rubenhold (2019) meticulously researches what available information there is on the lives of the Ripper's victims and is one of the few works in the Ripper lexicon that focuses primarily on the lives rather than the gruesome deaths of these tragic women. She puts forward the traumas they must have endured in their lives, such as divorce, abandonment, being forced into prostitution, domestic violence, poverty, homelessness, deaths of children, siblings, the suicide of a parent… a plethora of highly stressful situations that today would have seen them in therapy and in Victorian times saw them on the streets. Mary Ann Nichols, for example, had to endure her husband's love affair with a neighbour, as well as financial difficulties and the hardships of multiple pregnancies. That she turned to drink for solace is hardly unexpected. Leaving her husband and children meant her life descending into a chaos from which there would be no return. Annie Chapman experienced the untimely death of four of her younger siblings from a scarlet fever epidemic when she was just an impressionable teenage girl. She also experienced the trauma of her father committing suicide by cutting his own throat just a few years later. Drink proved to be a way for Annie to deal with the trauma and the bleak emotions of the time when there was no other help than perhaps prayer. Drink was her prop and her downfall, destroying the relationships she had with her husband and later with her own family. Elizabeth Stride was infected with syphilis at a young age, possible by her employer or someone in her employer's household when she worked in domestic service, a world where it was common for men to abuse the powerless female employees. She was obliged to work as a prostitute and could never quite disengage from this lifestyle until she was butchered by the Ripper. A victim of abuse and a harsh, discriminatory society that blamed the woman's impurity over the men's unrestrained sexual impulses for the spread of venereal disease, Stride must have been a victim of emotional trauma and suffered mental illness.

Mental illness was not as understood in the 1880s as it is now, and mental health treatment has changed dramatically over the years. In simplistic terms, before 1850, mental illness was seen as being an evil in the soul and as a degradation of moral values. Up until 1830, we hear anecdotal stories of treatments such as exorcisms and trepanning in order to release the demons from the body of the patient, the use of manacles and restraint as well as a whole range of other harsh treatments which by modern standards are considered barbaric. After 1850, mental illnesses were seen as forms of disease and were treated as such by doctors instead of by priests.

1850 is an interesting date as it seems to mark a significant change in medical views of mental illness, and it is important to clarify why this was the case. During the 1840s Charles Darwin was completing much of his work on geological change. By 1844 he had completed his voyage on the *Beagle* and written his first edition of his findings, which was well received and contributed to our current theories of evolution. Whilst the work of Darwin has had a vast impact on our understanding of the evolution of man and our environment, his theories also had an impact on the understanding of social classes, ethnicity and gender differences. Darwin commented that the people he met and studied from the tribes in South America were a less evolved version of white British men. He reasoned that because their technological developments were less than that of Darwin's culture, the people must be less evolved. This had an impact on British society and how they translated this theory into their daily lives.

Darwin's theory was not in isolation and neither did it shape attitudes in a vacuum. Cesare Lombroso was a psychiatrist who employed Darwinian Theory to develop a method of predicting criminality and madness by examining the facial characteristics of people. He hypothesised that, as madness and criminality were hereditary, then physical characteristics would exist to identify these persons and that trained experts could identify these. Some of these characteristics included unsymmetrical conformation of the head, peculiarities of the eyes and head, and irregularities of the features. This did not take into account features of people's social environment such as poverty, malnutrition and illness, which could also affect a person's physical characteristics alongside their inherited features. Further to this, at the time of the Jack the Ripper murders, Forbes Winslow, a psychiatrist of the time, thought he could identify madness and murderers using physiognomy and offered to do this for the murders. However, he was widely discredited, and this claim eventually led to him being made a prime suspect.

As mentioned in Chapter 6, attitudes to women were already largely focused on women being pure and virginal, and Lombroso was already generating theories of crime in Italy based on the physical attributes of offenders. Theories such as those of Darwin and Lombroso served to engender an attitude to offending and mental illness which was characterised by class and gender divisions. Women were seen as weaker and less evolved than men and therefore more susceptible to becoming mentally ill. Explanations of women's mental illness at the time centred around women's sexual activity and sexual maturity. This is in keeping with Victorian social attitudes where women were expected to be pure; mental illness, therefore, must, according to prevalent theorising, be caused by women's sexual capacity.

One theory, developed from earlier theories of the "wandering uterus" or Histeron, suggested that women's mental illness was linked to significant periods in their sexual development: menstruation, pregnancy and menopause. Due to this and to their perceived weaker evolutionary development, women were seen as more susceptible to mental illness than men. This would provide an explanation as to why many of the mental illnesses and crimes linked to women were considered sexual in nature and fits with contemporary attitudes towards women. The majority of women's offences in the Victorian era were vagrancy, drunk and disorderly and soliciting (Gray, 2010). There are, of course, instances of female perpetrators of murder, particularly child murder or baby farming, which we touch on in Chapter 8. The perception of criminal offences was often dictated by the perception of social order (class and gender). For example, women brought to court for violent offences were treated harshly as they were seen to have transgressed law and womanhood (the Victorian ideal of women).

In this chapter, we explore how attitudes to women influenced how they were understood and treated from a mental health perspective. It is through learning about the differences in the treatment of women that it becomes clear how class and social role expectations of women contributed to poor mental wellbeing and eventually disorders such as depression, puerperal insanity and anorexia nervosa. This exploration will also shed some light into the attitudes prevalent at the time of the Jack the Ripper murders, which goes some way into understanding why some sections of the community – notably the working classes of Whitechapel, the friends and neighbours and acquaintances of the victims – poured their outrage into the streets and formed vigilante gangs, while others – more significantly the chattering middle classes and the wealthy, more puritan sections of society and the establishment – sought to pass a degree of the blame onto the victims, exonerating the incompetency, deliberate or otherwise, of the Metropolitan Police.

The Lunatics Act of 1845 sparked a series of asylum building to accommodate and treat the public. By the 1850s it was recorded that not only had the patient population increased but in particular, the majority of the patient population was recorded as being female. However, by the 1870s these asylums were considered overcrowded, underfunded and understaffed. In the 1870s Darwinian Theory was predominant and, rather than using daily activities to enable patients and treat madness as they may have pre-1840s, the attitude changed and madness was considered a biological weakness, something that was innate and inevitable, the result of genetic predisposition. This attitude is thought to have led to a lack of funding of asylums over the decade. The Darwinist movement in psychiatry meant that doctors were looking to hereditary characteristics to explain madness and behaviour. Some Victorians believed that inheriting certain physical characteristics confirmed that people were "degenerate", and that madness could only be inherited through the mother line due to a woman's weaker evolutionary development (Showalter, 1985).

Both the development of women's social roles in universities and other professions and the rise of study in nervous disorders, hysteria, anorexia nervosa and post-traumatic stress disorder (PTSD) in men led to the development of psychoanalysis in the early twentieth century and an alternative to the asylum and treatments of the past. The asylums were typically used for the poor insane; middle- and upper-class patients continued to be treated at home or in separate private asylums for a fee. In some instances, asylums were segregated not only by disorder but by gender and by class (Davidoff, L'Esperance and Newby 1976; Stark, 1807) and although constructed to be therapeutic, it was considered that paupers should not be placed in luxury as it would spoil them, and they might develop ideas beyond their station (Browne, 1864, in Showalter, 1985). Victorian attitudes towards the class and the poor in particular were derogatory to say the least. The lower class, working poor and the criminal underworld were seen as less evolved, as a threat to the safety, security and status quo of society and the higher classes. Segregation kept the lower classes in their place but also kept the upper classes safe from them. Whilst the higher classes could afford education, housing, clothing and food, the lower classes were left in abject poverty, to be dragged along in the current of the industrial revolution, chewed up and spat out again. In keeping with evolutionary theory, it was felt that the lower-class poor should be left to their own devices, to survive or not as the case may be, and eliminate poverty from Victorian society. It is well noted that people in the Victorian era saw poverty as an issue for people who brought it upon themselves through being amoral and born into poverty and did not see poverty as a social or political problem as we do today. The cornerstones of Victorian psychiatric theory and practice were moral insanity; a deviation of social morals rather than mental illness, moral management; treatments based around re-educating people to live within society's moral values and moral architecture; the building of asylums to manage and control those who require treatment. Victorian psychiatrists persisted in exploring biology and moral degeneration as the causes of insanity and to that end they explored physical and moral management as treatments. This included the person's own willpower and moderation in life rather than living to excess.

There is current evidence to demonstrate that one's social situation can have a direct impact on one's mental health; for example, higher rates of psychosis have been found in people who dwell in inner-city areas where there are higher rates of poverty and crime (Kirkbride et al., 2006; Allardyce, 2001; Lewis et al., 1992; Mortensen, 1999). Incidences of mental illnesses such as depression and anxiety have also been recorded in people of lower socioeconomic status (Royal College of Psychiatrists, 2010). The studies suggest that social stressors such as poverty, lack of social movement and opportunity can impact one's mental health. In addition, maladaptive coping strategies such as alcohol and substance misuse are also linked to these social stressors as well as psychological stressors such as previous traumas, bereavement and attachment issues to name but a few. In 1880s Whitechapel, people were living in squalor, families living in one small room, some people not having any permanent accommodation. They worked long hours and were obliged to supplement their income with further work and prostitution or submit to poverty, starvation, sometimes turning to the use of alcohol and other substances to escape the hopelessness of their lives for a few hours. In today's society there has been a drive towards condemnation of the poor, those seeking benefits and immigrants, not unlike those of the Victorians, by a political ideology which has led to cuts in benefits for those in need, including the disabled. Not even Whitechapel has escaped gentrification, with the poor and homeless being forced away from their communities as rents soar, available affordable housing disappears, and benefits are cut to the bone. There is a strong case for holding the view that social strife leads directly to increases in mental health problems for those of lower socioeconomic status. Of course, this is not to say that people from across the social spectrum do not experience mental health problems – mental health problems have no prejudice when it comes to class or gender – this paragraph is simply suggesting that the evidence demonstrates that those from poorer backgrounds face a higher probability of experiencing mental health problems due to social stressors within their lives.

In modern times, diagnosis of a mental illness is guided using either the DSM-V or ICD-11 diagnostic manuals. In psychology, the tenets of what can be considered a mental illness relies on certain premises: is a person's presentation contravening social norms, is their presentation leading to harm to others, is their presentation causing themselves or others distress, are they failing to function adequately, are they deviating from ideal mental health? It is understandable, looking at these premises, that many persons might fit one or two of these criteria at any point in their lives. The important point is that they fit one or more of these premises and that they meet the criteria for diagnosis using the diagnostic manuals. An example might be that someone may be presenting as chaotic and unstable, unable to hold down work or a home but pose no harm to others and are not distressed with their situation. Another person might be able to function in work but may struggle with relational issues, and in some cases, this might lead to distress for themselves and others, and could even lead to increased risks of harm to themselves and others. There are an infinite number of permutations to this but what needs to remain foremost in mind is that these tenets are very much based in society's cultural norms. A person might pose no risk to themselves or others, may not be distressed and able to function but because their behaviour doesn't fit our usual social norms, society might think this person is "abnormal" and may consider that this is an issue of poor mental health.

Understanding how women's mental illness was diagnosed and treated needs to be considered in the social and cultural context of the time. Even today, there are differences in diagnosis depending on a person's gender and ethnicity. Examples of this include more women than men being diagnosed with Emotionally Unstable Personality Disorder, mood disorders and disorders such as anorexia. More men tend to be diagnosed with Antisocial Personality Disorder but in particular men from minority ethnic backgrounds tend to be more frequently diagnosed with schizophrenia. A 2013 survey on minority ethnic groups groups found that 16% of the 740 respondents had been diagnosed with schizophrenia and, of those, the rates were highest amongst Black Caribbean men and Black African men (Rehman and Owen, 2013), which confirms the results of earlier research suggesting that patients from minority ethnic backgrounds were more likely to be diagnosed with schizophrenia spectrum disorders than white patients (DelBello et al., 2001; Strakowski et al., 1996). Otherwise, rates of diagnosis for serious mental disorders such as schizophrenia and Bipolar Affective Disorder are approximately the same for men and women (World Health Organization). Equally, behaviours and emotional responses that one society might consider abnormal and symptomatic of a mental illness may be perfectly normal to another culture; for example, in some cultures hearing voices is a means of communing with gods or spirits and is seen as a special gift, whereas in western culture this is seen as a sign of psychosis and requiring treatment.

Towards the end of the nineteenth century, developments in psychiatry and the popularity of social Darwinsim, led to the criminal being identified as someone suffering from some form of behavioural abnormality, either inherited or nurtured by parents, which begins to influence penal policy and psychiatry. Penal policy of the 1830s and '40s led to reforms within prisons which included silence and isolation for reflection and moral development. Workhouses and Bibles were included in order to teach virtue and the value of work. However, as Charleroy and Marland (2006) have demonstrated in their research, silence and isolation led to deterioration in the mental health of inmates. This is still the case today, where the sensory deprivation theory (Mason and Brady, 2009) demonstrates how inmates left in isolation and sometimes persons left in police custody cells for long periods of time, who already have a mental illness, will experience a deterioration in their mental state and an increase in signs of psychosis.

In the nineteenth century women could be sent to the asylum for a number of reasons, such as post-natal depression, alcoholism or a social/moral transgression such as infidelity, which was a transgression against Victorian perceptions of womanhood. Other reasons for transfer to asylums at the time were epilepsy, puerperal insanity, anxiety, hysteria (wandering uterus), meloncholia (linked to the menopause) and erotomaina (sometimes linked to the stigma of being a single woman). Since women were seen as being more sensitive to mental illness than men and prone to bouts of hysteria, frequent treatments for this included cold showers, Electroconvulsive Therapy (ECT), medication, occupational therapy such as embroidery and sewing, marriage, silence and refraining from mental activities (Showalter,

1985). A woman who rebelled against Victorian domesticity risked being declared insane. Spinsters and lesbians were considered a danger to society as these women chose an alternative lifestyle without the need for sexual contact with men. They were outside of the social norm of the passive housewife. It was believed the lack of male interaction would make women mentally ill. This is an example of deviation from social norms leading to a label of insanity. Women who deviated from Victorian ideals and social norms could be declared insane and taken to an asylum. Husbands and fathers could consign a woman to an asylum and women did not have the right to appeal, although this did change in later years and into the twentieth century. For example, women could be declared insane if they made an outburst against their male patriarchs due to discontentment or repression. Similarly, a disorder known as "nymphomania" was suggested in order to understand and treat other female behaviours and characteristics within society – for example promiscuity, giving birth to illegitimate children, being the victim of assault or rape, being caught masturbating, or being overly flirtatious – and women diagnosed as such could be placed in an asylum (Showalter, 1987).

This era also saw the development of another mental disorder into the form we know it today. The term "anorexia" was given in 1873 by Sir William Gull to describe women who were significantly underweight and refused to eat. Gull noted that this occurred mostly in women of the upper and middle classes, and it came to be understood at the time, that it occurred in women who wished to exemplify their femininity by being truly passive and weightless beside their husbands and filling the role of the sacrificing Victorian heroine. Being extremely underweight became a status symbol for many women as it proved that they did not need food because they did not need to work. Working-class women had to eat in order to have the energy to work while middle- and upper-class women could afford to be thin. Allbutt (1895 and 1898), a psychiatrist at the time, also described working with women who in particular refused meat and showed associated angry and "lustful" behaviours and rebelliousness, easily putting one in mind of the line in the musical film *Oliver Twist:* "meat ma'am meat, you've been overfeeding the boy", when Mr Bumble arrives to remove Oliver from the funeral parlour. Showalter (1987) gives an example in her book, *The Female Malady*, of a psychiatrist who was attracted to a patient when she was weak and emaciated but after recovery no longer found her attractive. In starving herself, and being weak and vulnerable, she had fulfilled the ideal of the Victorian woman, but once she had put on weight and recovered, he no longer found her attractive as she had appeared to decline in class status. It appears that in many instances, women's mental health at the time, revolved around the empowerment of men. Anorexia in those times, was seen as an attempt to fit the male stereotype of beauty and nymphomania a means of restricting women's behaviour in society. However, as women's roles in the world have changed, so too have psychiatric views of women's disorders.[5]

Many women struggled in a society where they often felt their lives held little meaning. This is unsurprising when we consider that Victorian middle- and upper-class women were considered "pure" with a delicate constitution and their social role was as a mother and Angel on the arm of their husband. Therefore, they were expected to engage in activities which used very little physical or intellectual energy. As a result, many women felt increasing despair and lethargy in their lives, sometimes leading to poor mental health. However other women decided to "slum it" with the lower classes in order to find meaningful work. Florence Nightingale is a particular example of this. She experienced periods of depression throughout her life. In her diaries, she linked this to not being permitted to engage in meaningful work and activities and one can only consider the impact this may have had on her self-esteem and self-efficacy, leading to depressed thoughts and moods. Later in life, Florence Nightingale felt her depression was under greater control when she was able to study, work and contribute to society (Showalter, 1987). This does not appear to be an unusual state of affairs as women from the higher classes were prevented from having meaningful work – this was not considered suitable or part of their social role. In modern society, a means of engaging both men and women in treatment is by using occupational therapy and enabling environments to help people to participate in fulfilling activities that give them a sense of purpose and worth in their lives.

Another mental illness that becomes apparent in the literature of the time is that of puerperal psychosis. This is described in modern times as a postpartum psychosis which lasts a few months and has a very good prognosis and treatment today. However, it can lead to the mother having thoughts of wanting to kill herself and her child and includes familiar features of psychosis, such as hearing voices, paranoia and delusions (Marland, 2012).

---

5   https://www.sciencemuseum.org.uk/objects-and-stories/mental-health

In the instances where women with this disorder went on to kill their child, the legal process of these incidents are discussed in Chapter 8.

According to Marland (2003 and 2004), the experience of mental disorder after birth was not a new concept for women in the Victorian era. Marland notes that many women in the Middle Ages had also recorded episodes of melancholia after giving birth. However, what is interesting is that puerperal psychosis records indicate that the most likely victim of any harm is the child; there does not appear to be a link between puerperal psychosis and harm to adults, although in some instances harm to the husband was recorded but not to the extent of murder. The victims are the children and the women themselves. Today it is noted that puerperal psychosis is not frequently discussed, but it appears that it is more likely to occur in women who have had a mental disorder prior to their pregnancy, which could indicate the presence of another mental disorder as a risk for violence and not the puerperal symptoms themselves.

Marland (2004) also notes that in the Victorian era, the majority of women with diagnoses of puerperal psychosis and other major mental disorders admitted to asylums, were living in poverty. This is supported by psychological theory; for example, the stress-diathesis model suggests that having a pre-dispositional vulnerability, combined with poor resilience and few functional coping skills and stressful life experiences, can place someone at risk of experiencing mental health problems (Ingram and Luxton, 2005; Lazarus, 1993). In the case of Victorian women, these may have had a genetic vulnerability or predisposition to mental illness, but their life circumstances, such as poverty, which is an acute stressor for people, could make them more vulnerable to developing mental illnesses. Marland gives an example of women entering asylums being fed first and foremost on being admitted, as it was believed that women gave their food to their children and to their husbands so they could work (Marland, 2004).

Showalter (1985) has delineated differences in the perception of madness for men and women associated with intellectual and economic pressures on men and the female malady associated with sexuality and the "essential nature of women", as it was seen then. Victorian social roles could be just as hard on men's mental health as it was on those of women. This is acutely demonstrated during and in the aftermath of the First World War. Men were regarded as masculine, stoic, rational, brave and heroic, and the opportunity of war was peddled as a means for men to demonstrate their bravery. But in the context of war, men struggled under the pressure of these social perceptions and living with the extreme violence they were experiencing on the battlefield. It is thought that by the end of the war, approximately 80,000 men had been seen for symptoms that we would now know as Post-Traumatic Stress Disorder (PTSD). Many men found themselves afraid, pushed to emotional limits and experiencing emotional "weakness" which indicated the development of disorders such as PTSD. Psychiatrists looked to biological explanations, but when Myers, who was studying shell shock in soldiers, could not find one single biological mechanism, it was felt that poor genetics and poor recruitment practices were to blame. Even then, officers were found to be just as susceptible and eventually the trauma of war was held to blame. Still the class divide is ever present, and it was recorded by eminent psychiatrists at the time, including Myers and W.H. Rivers, that officers were frequently diagnosed with nervous disorders, whereas soldiers were more frequently diagnosed with mania or hysteria. This latter was akin to being effeminate or cowardly as these types of diagnoses and attributes were more commonly associated with women before the First World War.

There were also gender differences in the treatment of mental disorders for women and men. Women were seen as emotional, weak and dictated to by their sexuality and sexual organs, so treatment was different to that of men, who were seen as logical and coherent. Showalter (1985) dedicates an entire chapter in her book to some of the excruciating treatments aimed at women because of the belief that madness was driven by the uterus. This included leeches on the cervix and removal of the clitoris – today we would call this a form of Female Genital Mutilation (FGM). This was due to the theory that the uterus and women's periods were responsible for their mental vulnerability. There was a fear of female sexuality, and the uterus was responsible for women wanting sex – this went against the preconceived social roles and societal presentation of women as angelic, pure beings. This meant treatment focused on managing and even reducing periods, and women who were teenagers or menopausal were treated particularly poorly because these points in a woman's development were considered the time when their uterus affected their minds the most. Other forms of treatment included marriage, silence and reflection, remaining bed bound and not being permitted to read or work so as to allow their minds to rest, participating in what were seen as feminine pastimes as part of their moral management. Rebellion against this regime would lead to solitary confinement, sedation and being plunged into cold baths. In contrast, men received treatments akin to what we know today as enabling environments where they could walk outside, participate in sports, work and learning activities with the belief that men needed to use their minds and needed to work and be useful in order to fulfil the male social role of the Victorian era.

Female perspectives on insanity and treatment are limited; however, diaries from famous women such as Florence Nightingale and Charlotte Bronte include their experiences of depression as well as what treatments were offered to them. Florence Nightingale notes that her depression deteriorated further and further under the standard treatment method of bed rest and no brain stimulation and did not improve until she was able to convince others to let her work and study. This suggests that mental illness was linked as much to their social roles, self-esteem and belief about purpose and usefulness as much as it could be linked to a biological ailment. The written experiences of women such as Florence Nightingale supports modern research, still being conducted today which demonstrates that deteriorations in the mental health of patients and prisoners from the use of separation, isolation and segregation for behavioural management. In terms of current research, we would know this effect as the sensory deprivation theory (Mason and Brady, 2009), whereby removing normal stimuli from the environment can lead to experiences of psychosis.

These examples of treatments as cited above are behaviourist in nature under a facade of being medical treatments. In psychology there are different approaches to understanding the human experience, broadly these are biological, psychodynamic, cognitive, behavioural, and humanistic. The types of treatment preferred in Victorian society are either biological – focusing on controlling physical elements through medication, ECT, lobotomy or removal or the clitoris – or behavioural in nature – using reinforcement or reward and punishment to increase wanted or socially acceptable behaviour and to extinguish unwanted behaviour. For example, unwanted behaviour is extinguished through punishment (removal of the clitoris to extinguish rebellious or over-sexualised behaviour, cold baths and solitary confinement). The success measured by these psychiatrists is seen as outward behaviour change; however, it could be argued that this did not change their thinking or emotions but only changed their outward behaviour such as rebelliousness. It does not necessarily provide evidence of recovery. There appears to be little consideration of cognition or emotion in the treatment of mental illness until later in the century with the advent of the psychodynamic approach and talking therapies. Today, treatment is based on research evidence and patient need, and in extreme cases ECT is still used. Medication is used widely but both men and women have the same right to the same types of treatment, which include medication, talking therapies, enabling environments and psychologically planned environments within hospitals and community treatment services with the focus of the treatment being on its impact on emotional wellbeing, recovery and behaviour change.

When we focus on Jack the Ripper's victims, rather than taking the more popular perspective of speculating on the killer's identity and mental state, we have opted to explore the victims' mental health, addressing what life may have been like for them, what common factors in their lives all the women experienced and from here, to consider the possible psychological issues these women may have had. This may better explain their circumstances and possibly exonerate them from their reputation of being self-appointed victims, as much to blame for their murders as whoever had wielded the knives that killed them.

Mary Ann Nichols was married to a printer from Oxford, and they rented a home in a Peabody Estate in Stamford Street in London. They appear to have had a temporary separation twelve years after their marriage. The reasons for this are unknown, but her alcohol abuse is suspected as the main culprit. Their relationship finally ended in 1880 and it appears Mary's decline started here. She was registered in a workhouse in Lambeth before moving in with her next partner; however, this relationship also failed, and she was back in the workhouse. Her hard work in the workhouse led to her being offered a position as a servant in one of the wealthier houses. However, it is recorded that she ran away after stealing some property and then started working as a prostitute in Whitechapel, probably because there was nothing else she could do to stay alive.

Annie Chapman had been married to a coachman of the nobility and had three children. After the eldest daughter died of meningitis, her marriage collapsed, and it was suspected that her use of alcohol contributed to this. It is thought that Annie's drinking problems started by the end of the 1870s and she may have miscarried up to five children because of her alcohol abuse. One of her sons was also disabled and she went to London originally to seek medical help, returning two years later saying that she had given up alcohol. Unfortunately, she started drinking again soon after returning to the family home. After her daughter's death it is said that her drinking became so bad that she was expelled from her home by her husband's employers and moved to London. She was also said to have been unwell herself and may have been dying of a disease of the lungs and brain. Although her partner continued to support her after their separation, after he died, she had to resort to prostitution as well as selling flowers and matchsticks to survive.

Elizabeth Stride was Swedish and had married an Englishman, although in her early life in Sweden it is thought she had turned to prostitution after having been sexually abused by her then employer and turned out of her work as a domestic servant, and therefore also out of her home. It is thought that her family died in a maritime accident, although she also claims that her husband died in the sinking of the *Mary Alice*. However, this was eventually proven to be untrue. Elizabeth had been running a coffee house, but she and her husband separated in 1884 because of Elizabeth's drinking and she turned to prostitution when he died two years later.

Catherine Eddowes was from Wolverhampton originally and also separated from her husband, and it is suspected this may also have been to do with her drinking. It is believed that she was already an alcoholic by the time they married when she was twenty-six. She had three children who all attended school and was working as a laundress. Eddowes and her husband split, with her husband citing her drinking as the main reason for the ending of the relationship. She then moved to Whitechapel and began working as a prostitute to supplement other low-paying jobs.

Mary Kelly was younger than the other victims and had a son who lived with her. It is reported that she felt very down at the time of her death and had made comments on the night of her death referring to ending her life if she was unable to make any money. Kelly was from Limerick, Ireland, and was one of eight children. The family moved to Carmarthenshire and there she eventually married a local man who died in a mining accident. It is said that she moved to Cardiff and became the lover of a doctor. From here she fell into prostitution and eventually moved to London. She is also meant to have escaped being trafficked to France as a sex worker where she was imprisoned in a brothel.

One interesting feature of all these cases, apart from Mary Kelly, is the abuse of alcohol prior to the separation of their significant relationships. What is a shame is that there is limited information about the victims' lives and their personal development, childhood and teenage years to help us understand why they turned to alcohol; what painful thoughts, feelings and experiences were they trying to mask and escape from by using alcohol? Other common features are bereavements, particularly that of significant others and children. Unresolved bereavement has close links with depression and anxiety as well as the use of alcohol and other substances as a coping mechanism. It ought to be noted that the availability of alcohol might also have been a contributing factor and it must be wondered what the impact would have been had other substances, such as heroin and crack cocaine, been as widely available as alcohol at the time. In addition, we have noted in other chapters, how easy it was for women to fall into prostitution, and one would expect that, despite seemingly making a rational choice about this, the impact of prostitution in these desperate circumstances on self-esteem and self-worth in particular, would also have further contributed to the use of alcohol to escape those painful self-appraisals.

Another feature that is common among Jack the Ripper's victims is these women's inability to manage their relationships, both significant relationships and those that would enable them to have steady, stable employment. This inability to manage relationships can be caused by a number of developmental issues which we can only speculate about here as we have no relevant or associated information about these women. One aspect is parenting style; with the industrial revolution and adults working all hours of the day and night causing significant stress in the household, parenting styles could have been particularly harsh, and children may have been exposed to and been the victims of domestic violence. This would teach these women maladaptive strategies for being in relationships such as confusion over appropriate and inappropriate expression of emotions and behaviour towards others and for coping in relationships which may have led them to drink. They may have witnessed alcohol being used by parents as a means of coping with relationship and work-life stresses. Alternatively, parents had little time to spend with children and this may have led to a neglectful parenting style, the impact of which is that the children's fundamental emotional needs may not have been met, and without learning how to express and address these needs, these women may have grown up unable to express what they need from a relationship and may not have learnt how to act in relationships and manage these stresses, which eventually may have led to alcohol use.

Finally, it is very likely that both men and women in this era suffered from high levels of depression and anxiety due to the social situation and poverty, and it is likely that many men and women used alcohol as a means of escape and coping. Issues of bereavement would have been rife due to the high mortality rate and access to support very low. What separates these women is that we can note difficulties in their relationships and interactions with others. Whilst this is also likely to be a feature of many women and men of the time, could their poor relationship experiences and low self-esteem have contributed to their vulnerability as potential victims for the ripper to prey upon? Mary Kelly herself appeared desperate enough to want to consider suicide if she could not make money on the night of her death and the others needed money for boarding. Out of desperation they headed to the streets of Whitechapel, which they knew to be dangerous, carrying all their thoughts about their experiences of social and relational interactions, their failures, their needs, their self-appraisals and agreed to have sex with either the first man that offered to pay them, or perhaps the one that offered something different – more money, kindness, a meal, a compliment? Whatever the circumstances, perhaps these psychological and social vulnerabilities made them a more suitable target, a more convenient cohort of victims for the killer, than some of the other women working on those streets on those particular nights.

REFERENCES

Allardyce, J., Boydell, J., Van Os, J. et al. (2001), "Comparison of the incidence of schizophrenia in rural Dumfries and Galloway and urban Camberwell", *British Journal of Psychiatry*, 179, 335–339.

Charleroy, M. and Marland, H. (2016), "Prisoners of Solitude: Bringing History to Bear on Prison Health Policy", *Endeavour*, September 2016, 40(3): 141–147, doi:10.1016/j.endeavour.2016.07.001, PMCID: PMC5053369.

Davidoff, L., L'Esperance, J. and Newby, H., "Landscape with Figures: Home and Community in English Society", in Mitchell, J. and Oakley, A. (1977), *The Rights and Wrongs of Women*, Penguin.

DelBello, M.P., Lopez-Larson, M.P., Soutullo, C.A., Strakowski, S.M. (2001), "Effects of race on psychiatric diagnoses of hospitalised adolescents: a retrospective chart review, *Journal of Child and Adolescent Psychopharmacology*, 11(1), 95–103.

Gray, D.D. (2013), *London's Shadows: The Dark Side of the Victorian City*, Bloomsbury Academic, London.

Ingram, R.E. and Luxton, D.D. (2005), "Vulnerability-Stress Models", in Hankin, B.L. and Abela, J.R.Z., *Development of Psychopathology: A vulnerability stress perspective* (p32–46), Sage Publications Inc, Thousand Oaks, CA.

Kirkbride, J.B., Fearon, P., Morgan, C. et al. (2006), "Heterogeneity in incidence rates of schizophrenia and other psychotic syndromes: Findings From the 3-center ÆSOP study", *Archives of General Psychiatry*, 63, 250–258.

Lazarus, R.S. (1993), "From psychological stress to the emotions: A history of changing outlooks", *Annual Review of Psychology*, (1): 1–21, PMID 8434890, doi:10.1146/annurev.ps.44.020193.000245.

Lewis, G., David, A., Andreasson, S. and Allebeck, P. (1992), "Schizophrenia and city life", *Lancet*, 340, 137–140.

Marland, H. (2003), "Maternity and Madness: Puerperal Insanity in the Nineteenth Century", Centre for the History of Medicine, University of Warwick, retrieved on 15th August 2017.

Marland, H. (2004), *Dangerous Motherhood: Insanity and Childbirth in Victorian Britain*, Palgrave Macmillan, Basingstoke, Hampshire.

Marland, H. (2012), "Under the Shadow of Maternity: Birth, Death and Puerperal Insanity in Victorian Britain", *History of Psychiatry*, 23, 78–90.

Mason, O. and Brady, F. (2009), "The psychotomimetic effects of short-term sensory deprivation", *Journal of Nervous and Mental Disease*, 197 (10): 783–785.

Mortensen, P.B., Pedersen, C.B., Westergaard, T. et al. (1999), "Effects of family history and place and season of birth on the risk of schizophrenia", *New England Journal of Medicine*, 340, 603–608.

Rehman, H.. and Owen, D.W. (2014) Mental Health Survey of Ethnic Minorities, report for Time to Change. London: Ethnos Research and Consultancy.

Royal College of Psychiatrists (2010), "No Public Health without Public Mental Health: the case for action", retrieved from http://www.rcpsych.ac.uk/pdf/Position%20Statement%204%20website.pdf on 14th August 2017.

Showalter, E. (1985), *The Female Malady: Women, Madness and English Culture, 1830–1980*, Little Brown Book Group.

Showalter, E. (1987), *The Female Malady: Women, Madness and English Culture, 1830–1980*, Virago.

Strakowski, S.M., Flaum, M., Amador, X., Bracha, H.S., Pandurangi, A.K., Robinson, D., Tohen, M. (1996), "Racial differences in the diagnosis of psychosis", *Schizophr Res*, 21(2):117–124.

World Health Organisation. (2021). *Gender and Women's Mental Health*. Retrieved from

http://www.who.int/mental_health/prevention/genderwomen/en/

Wallace. W. (2012). *Sent to the asylum: The Victorian women locked up because they were suffering from stress, post-natal depression and anxiety*. Retrieved from http://www.dailymail.co.uk/home/you/article-2141741/Sent-asylum-The-Victorian-women-locked-suffering-stress-post-natal-depression-anxiety.html

10

A COMPARISON OF KILLERS

'Prejudices are what fools use for reason.'

Voltaire

In exploring the type of person Jack the Ripper was most likely to have been and considering some of the alternative theories, such as the Ripper being a female, we have decided to compare some of the features of similar serial murders in the UK. We are being purposefully country-specific here. The reason we are not including other similar crimes that were carried out in other nations is that there is a cultural aspect to the Jack the Ripper narrative that we have been addressing in this book and that we will explore further through the examination of some of the features of these crimes.

In addition to this cultural element to the narrative, the killings that we examine are set within a social context that is particular to the UK: there have been laws enacted that are specifically related to women and sex working in the UK that would have been different and occurred at different times in other nations and which may have had a different impact on women in the public sphere, how sex working was perceived and how crimes against these groups would have been treated. We also had to set a realistic boundary to the numbers of murders that could be compared; even limiting these to murders that had taken place in nations similar to the UK in terms of social, political and economic context, there would have been too many to compare effectively without having also examined the cultural development of attitudes towards women of each nation and of that particular offender. This, we felt, would have proven an unnecessary distraction. The Ripper, whoever he or she might have been, perpetrated the murders in London, in a relatively small geographical district, and, it is generally accepted, in a relatively small timeframe, and this helped us to select the most comparable serial murders to see what we might learn about our unknown killer.

We have also chosen to name them "killers of multiple victims" rather than serial killers as this can then include spree killings; at least two of Jack the Ripper's murders took place on the same night which better fits the features of a spree than one of a series of murders. This way of thinking about the killings can help us include similar murders by other offenders. However, our comparison tables do not include offences where multiple people have been killed, as can happen in family unit killings, murder-suicides, gang violence or corporate manslaughter. These offences simply do not fit the Jack the Ripper narrative, nor do they compare with the manner of the murders.

Below are two tables comparing known killers of multiple victims from the time of the Jack the Ripper murders in the late nineteenth century to the present day. There are columns to present data such as type of victim (male/female/child), manner of their deaths and features of the crime. We have avoided presenting anything on motive for the killing as, without having assessed the person or been involved in the case, this would lack the necessary objectivity. Instead, we would be assuming motive from second or third hand with all the emotion and intrigue and media attention that has been attached to these crimes over time. Motives are notoriously complex. There are never simple, or single motives, such as only killing because pleasure is derived from it, or because of a sexually sadistic drive, or even as a response to a single threatening event. The planning and acting out of these particular murders were driven by complex personalities, mediated by a network of environmental, learning, experiential and attitudinal variables as well as beliefs, drives and influential interactions between people. With this in mind we felt it important not to assume that we can know the motive of the perpetrator without having first-hand contact with them regarding the offence and without having appropriately assessed their motives.

What we are able to do by using tables such as this, is place a large amount of information together in a format that can be easily compared. The facts of the cases are entered into the table and we try to make no assumptions about features or motive. The crimes are listed in chronological order. Female perpetrators have been included in a separate table so that we can examine the strength of relevant theories, such as the possibility of the Ripper having been female, and the likelihood that there was more than one assailant. We acknowledge that these tables are not exhaustive, we have included cases where there was a good deal of available public data and acknowledge that there may be other relevant cases with less publicly available records that have not been included here.

A Comparison of Killers

Table 1, Male British Killers of Multiple Victims from 1860 to 2018

Name	Year	Gender/Gender of Victim	No of Victims Killed/No of Victims Survived	No of Victims Female Sex Workers	Features of the Crime	Reported or Possible Psychiatric Diagnosis/Mental Health/Psych History	Previous Offending History	Police Intervention (Capture/Conviction)
Blackout Ripper	1942	Male/female	4/2	2	Used the blackout during the Blitz of the WWII to make his attacks. Used strangulation and then mutilation of the bodies post-mortem.	None known.	Not known, although it is thought that two other murders during air raids in 1941 could have been committed by him.	Spree killer over six days rather than a serial. Due to the sexualised nature of the mutilation of the bodies, links were drawn between him and Jack the Ripper.
Ian Brady	1963–65	Male with female partner/male and female (children)	5/0	0	Sexual nature and torture element to the crimes. Committed with Myra Hindley.	Difficult childhood and interest in authoritarian regimes and sadistic writers.	Burglary and other crimes considered "petty crimes" at the time, spent some time in prison.	Police informed by someone who was close to them, and they had bragged to.
Fred West	1967–87	Male with female partner/females	12/0	0	Sexual element to at least eight of the murders. Murder method was mixed and included stabbing and asphyxiation. Fred and Rosemary West remained undetected until the mid-1990s.	Evidence of change in mood suggested after traumatic brain injury when he was an adolescent.	Theft, child abuse, images of child sexual abuse, domestic violence.	After sexually abusing his daughter, she confided in a friend whose mother informed the police. Their children were taken into care immediately and investigations began. Police continued to investigate the disappearances of his daughters and others, and this eventually led to a warrant to fully investigate the house.

161

Peter Sutcliffe (Yorkshire Ripper)	1975–81	Male/female	13/7	7	Blunt force trauma and stabbing.	Paranoid schizophrenia.	Four violent attacks on lone women using a blunt instrument to incapacitate and a knife to slash and stab.	Caught after a long spell where he had been interviewed four times and police criticised for their handling of the case.
Harold Shipman	1975–98	Male/female	250/unknown	Unknown	Poisoning (overdose of medication). As a GP had access to many elderly patients. Approximately 80% of his victims were elderly females. Stole jewellery and forged wills leaving money to himself.	None identified.	Unknown.	He was caught after the daughter of one of the patients he killed questioned a new will that his mother had apparently made. Police became involved and this led to the identification of the Shipman murders. Subsequently took his own life.
Camden Ripper	2002	Male/female	3/0	1	Stabbing and dismemberment. Sexual positioning of the bodies post-mortem which included taking lewd photographs.	Reported personality disorder by the media.	It has been suggested that he had been violent towards his wife before they broke up and he moved to London. It is thought that at least two other murders of prostitutes could be linked to him and as many as six more murders.	A homeless man found the body parts of women in a bin and forensic evidence led to the perpetrator. He was caught when collecting his insulin from hospital and resisted arrest, causing serious injury to the officers.

A Comparison of Killers

Name	Years	Victim sex	Victims/ Survivors	Children	Method	Childhood	Prior offences	Additional notes
Levi Bellfield	2002–04	Male/female	4/1	0	Use of a blunt instrument such as a hammer and hitting one victim with his car.	Not known/confidential and not available in public records or reporting.	He has also been charged with the attempted murder of another woman and the kidnapping and false imprisonment of a second and rape of yet another woman, but the jury failed to reach verdicts on these charges.	Dramatised recently in the series *Manhunt*. He was caught through investigation work linking his wheel-clamping van to areas where the murders happened. He was eventually linked to the abduction and murder of Millie Dowler.
Suffolk Strangler	2006	Male/female	5/0	5	Victims were all sex workers who struggled with drug and alcohol addiction. It is thoughts they were killed by strangulation or asphyxiation.	None known although known to have built up gambling debts and tried to take his own life twice. His mother left the family when he was six years old, and his father believes this might have affected his views on women.	Had been using prostitutes since the 1980s. He had been convicted of theft in 2001.	Identified through the national DNA database. These attacks forced the government to review their laws to protect sex workers and see them as vulnerable victims instead of criminals. Soliciting is now illegal and the focus on prostitution is to help them to stop sex working; however, the law on drugs remains the same.
Crossbow Cannibal	2009–10	Male/female	3/0	3	Details are not fully known but one of his victims was shot with a crossbow and stabbed. He dismembered the bodies.	Media reported at the time a historic diagnosis of "Schizoid Psychopathy". Psychiatrists had warned that he fantasised about becoming a serial killer and had taken a university course exploring serial murder.	Served three-year prison sentence of stabbing a shop manager and had been previously arrested for violent offences including holding a knife to a female.	He was seen on a CCTV camera that he had set up outside his housing association flat.

Table 2, Female British Killers of Multiple Victims from 1860 to 2018

Name	Year	Gender/ Gender of Victim	No of Victims Killed/ No of Victims Survived	No of Victims female Sex Workers	Features of the Crime	Reported or Possible Psychiatric Diagnosis/Mental Health/ Psych History	Previous Offending History	Police Intervention (Capture/ Conviction)
Mary Ann Cotton	1860–73	Female/male and female children, family members (husbands)	21 (11 children and 2 husbands, her mother)/2	0	Arsenic poisoning.	None known.	None known.	Police suspicion led to an investigation.
Margaret Waters	1866–70	Female/male and female (children)	19/unknown	0	Drugged with opium. Baby farming.	None known.	None known.	Police officer who visited the home found some of the babies.
Amelia Dyer	1869–96	Female/male and female (children)	400/unknown	0	Left to die through neglect. Godfrey's cocktail which was opium and alcohol mix. Baby farming.	None known.	None known.	Identified after the body of a baby was found in the River Thames.
Catherine Flanagan and Margaret Higgins	1880–83	Female/male and female family members	7/unknown	0	Arsenic poisoning to claim funeral society money.	None known.	None known.	Coroner's report identified arsenic poisoning.

A Comparison of Killers

Mary Ann Britley	1886	Female/male and female children, family members (husbands)	3/0	0	Poison	None known.	None known.	Closeness of the deaths led the police to be suspicious and they investigated.
Elizabeth Wilson	1955–57	Female/male (husbands)	4/0	0	Phosphorus poisoning (plant/weed killer).	None known or not publicly available.	None known.	Police became suspicious and exhumed the bodies, which were examined by the coroner.
Myra Hindley	1963–65	Male/male and female (children)	5/0	0	Sexual nature and torture element to the crimes. Committed with Ian Brady.	None known or not publicly available.	None known.	Police informed by someone who was close to them, and they had bragged to.
Rosemary West	1967–87	Female with male partner/female	10 (only charged with 10 out of the 12)/0	0	Sexual element to at least eight of the murders. Worked as a prostitute. Murder method was mixed and included stabbing and asphyxiation. Fred and Rosemary West remained undetected until the mid-1990s.	Admitted to having been sexually abused as a child which could have led to abnormal sexual development, trauma and eventually possible personality disorder, but this is not confirmed.	Child abuse, imagies of child sexual abuse, domestic violence.	Rose was implicated in the abuse of her children and their neglect. Their children were taken into care immediately and investigations began. Police continued to investigate the disappearances of Fred's daughters and others, and this eventually led to a warrant to fully investigate the house.
Joanna Dennehy	2013	Female/male	3 (lover, and two housemates)/2	0	Stabbing.	Media reports suggest psychopathic, anti-social and borderline personality disorders.	Convictions for assault and owning a dangerous dog.	Caught after two days on the run after the bodies of her initial victims were found.

From looking at these tables, we can see that, from the time of Jack the Ripper, there have been at least eight other known male killers of multiple victims, of which three have also drawn the label of "Ripper", presumably due to similarities in the crimes. There have been five instances of known female killers of multiple victims before Jack the Ripper began his attacks and four since, none of which have been given the label "Ripper". This strongly suggests that there may be a difference in how this label is used by society at large as a form of identifying a killer "type" in the popular imagination.

We decided to more closely examine those who were given the label "Ripper" by the media. We started with the Blackout Ripper, who killed four women, two of whom were known sex workers (Rowland, 2014). These murders were perceived to have a sexual nature to them due to post-mortem mutilations to the sexualised areas of the female victims' bodies, thus bearing a strong similarity to our Jack the Ripper killings.

Next, we took up the case of the Yorkshire Ripper. Seven of his thirteen victims were sex workers, and the victims were hit with a blunt object or stabbed (Kinnell, 2008). There appeared to be some instances of mutilations to some of the victims post-mortem; however, this was not the norm for his crimes. It appears the label "Ripper" was attributed by the media because the victims were all women, including some sex workers, and due to a hoaxer, who claimed he was a "Jack the Ripper-type" offender and was dubbed "Wearside Jack". This person was eventually caught and charged with perverting the course of justice (Herbert, 2006), but this event demonstrates the powerful hold that Jack the Ripper still had on cultural consciousness eighty-seven years after the original murders; the killing of women still invoked frightening images of the Ripper preying on women who are out alone at night, from what, by this time, ought to have been considered no more than a folk legend.

One hundred and twelve years after Jack the Ripper murdered women in London, the Camden Ripper killed three women, one of whom was a sex worker. In these killings, the bodies had been posed in sexualised positions; they had been stabbed and dismembered.[6] The other listed male offenders either have a female accomplice, their manner of killing is different from stabbing, or their victims are not females alone but also include children. It appears that to earn the title of "Ripper", offenders must be male, and their victims female where at least some of the victims are sex workers, the mode

---

6   https://courtnewsuk.co.uk/anthony-hardy/

of killing must include using a knife in some way and the victims' bodies need to be sexually mutilated post-mortem.

Of the female killers listed in the table, none have been popularly labelled "Ripper". One, Joanna Dennehy, used stabbing as a method of killing. Rosemary West was suspected to sex work on occasion, and it was noted by officers and the press that there was a sexual element to the murders (Sounes, 1995). However, she, too, has not been labelled a "Ripper" and neither was her partner, Fred West. As is the case with Myra Hindley and Ian Brady, however, their victims were children. In fact, none of the female killers of multiple victims listed above, targeted sex workers. Their victims were either husbands, female family members or children, and, in most cases, poisoning was the method used. This supports the data we saw in an earlier chapter, which stated that random female on female murder is relatively rare, that female offenders tend to offend in the home and their victims are predominantly people they know, such as family members, in particular, their children. Males tend to target females who are alone or perceived as vulnerable, such as sex workers. This is likely to be due to their availability, their vulnerability on the fringes of society and because they are perceived by some as an affront to society and therefore violence towards them has a justification: they are worthless; no-one will care. It therefore seems highly unlikely that Jack the Ripper was female, although it is not entirely impossible that Jack the Ripper had an accomplice that was female.

Referring back to the tables, in the events listed where there were accomplices, in only one event were there two women involved. Two were male and female partnerships, and none were male partnerships. The difficulties in considering cases with accomplices is that their interactions and behaviours become enmeshed, and it can often become difficult to tease apart who was the lead and who was the accomplice or whether the actions were co-lead. What can reliably be said is that, despite there being two people involved, the numbers of victims did not double in comparison to single killers; there were no additional violent elements in comparison to single killers and sex workers were not the main victims.

In the case of Jack the Ripper, it is sometimes thought likely that there had been an accomplice due to the "double event" and the speed at which the two murders were committed despite the physical distance between them. In the cases described in the table, it is clear that single killers are more than capable of achieving this alone, without the help of an accomplice, and that with the murders where there is an accomplice, the victims appear to be younger and more vulnerable, more time taken over the killings and more effort to subvert the criminal justice process to avoid detection.

Included in the table is a column on psychiatric diagnosis/mental health/psychological history. We have included this so that we can consider the possible characteristics of the people listed as well as explore the likelihood that Jack the Ripper might have been a "mad doctor", as some eager Ripper enthusiasts claim.

There is one very clear example in our table of a doctor taking the lives of others, Dr Harold Shipman. However, it is important to observe that, as far as is known, he had no psychiatric diagnosis, and we know little about his psychological history or mental health. What is known is that his method of killing was very calculated and considered, and it is widely believed that he killed in order to gain access to money, property and heirlooms left to him in wills that he forged after his victims' deaths (Whittle and Richie, 2000). This killer was a person with a significant level of training where his learning and experience enabled him to plan and carry out his plan well enough that he got away with killing for many years. In comparison to the Jack the Ripper murders, Dr Shipman used a discrete method of killing that would be quiet and difficult to detect. This is in stark contrast to the method of killing in the Jack the Ripper murders, which left the victims brutalised and in the street for all to see.

In contrast, people listed in the table who are not doctors and who have a possible mental health diagnosis can be seen to be more chaotic; victims escape, or evidence is found quickly, or they struggle to hide and cover their offending and therefore come to the attention of the police more quickly. This suggests that Jack the Ripper would have been less likely to have been a doctor who had been trained to be thoughtful and considered in his approaches. He is perhaps more likely to present with some of the psychiatric diagnoses or psychological traits that are seen in the other people listed in the table.

By thinking about mental disorder using the definition from the Mental Health Act (1983, amended 2007) as "any disorder or disability of mind", we can start to think about what cognitive and emotional problems might be affecting a person's behaviour and how this behaviour might manifest. For example, some mental disorders are associated with significant cognitive and emotional control impairment such as schizophrenia or bipolar affective disorder at the manic phase, and this would make the commission of planned offences and avoidance of capture, very difficult. On the other hand, a disorder such as psychopathy might be associated with lower emotional availability and empathy, and therefore the planning and committing of offences might be easier without guilt or moral considerations to slow them down. Depending on the disorder, a person's offending behaviour might seem chaotic or organised. Mental disorders where there is a lack of capacity and cognitive deficits would lead to more chaotic and disorganised offending. For example, someone experiencing mania, psychosis or a mixture of positive and negative symptoms of schizophrenia might be experiencing thought disorder, where their thoughts are racing or conversely being blocked but their remaining thought processes are guided by delusional beliefs and paranoid ideation, so their corresponding behaviours might be observed to be bizarre, irrational or chaotic in nature.

Someone with a personality disorder also might be observed to have chaotic behaviour, for example, persons with antisocial personality disorder or borderline personality disorder. In DSM-V (2013), personality disorders are defined in this way:

> *An enduring pattern of inner experience and behaviour that deviates markedly from the expectations of an individual's culture, is pervasive and inflexible, has an onset in adolescence or early adulthood, is stable over time and leads to distress or impairment.*

Clinicians often take a bio-psycho-social approach to understanding the development of personality disorders and examine the interaction between genetic and biological factors, psychological factors and a person's environment to the development of personality disorder. Clinicians tend to agree that a history of mental disorder in a person's family can predispose them to the development of a personality disorder; however, it could be argued that familial mental ill health could also provide an environmental risk factor. Other risk factors that have been linked to the development of personality disorder have been adverse childhood experiences such as physical, sexual and emotional abuse, witnessing or being exposed to violence, familial or parental conflict, inconsistent parenting or authoritarian parenting style and poor caregiver attachment, to name a few.

A person with antisocial personality disorder (ASPD) as described in DSM-V (2013) might struggle to manage their emotions, including difficulty managing angry outbursts. They are also characterised by being impulsive, engaging in risk-taking behaviour, being callous or manipulative, lacking in empathy and difficulties in managing interpersonal relationships. Someone with borderline personality disorder (BPD, also known in ICD-10 as Emotionally Unstable Personality Disorder) is characterised by unstable relationships with other people, unstable sense of self and unstable emotions, for example intense or uncontrollable emotional reactions that often seem disproportionate to the event or situation, black and white thinking, impulsivity and self-damaging behaviour (DSM-V, 2013).

Psychopathy is also often associated with violent crime, and the word "psychopath" is often used when describing murderers especially those who have killed multiple victims. The word "psychopath", as used by the media, propagates images of an unfeeling, bloodthirsty monster, who preys on vulnerable victims and takes pleasure in causing them immense pain and distress. Whilst this may be a dramatisation, we should try to separate how the media uses the word and how it is understood in clinical practice.

There is considerable debate over the definition of psychopathy, and it is not yet recognised as a distinct syndrome in its own right in the DSM-V. However, generally speaking, in clinical practice, psychopathy is a personality disorder and shares behavioural symptoms with many of the personality disorders, but mostly emotionally unstable, histrionic, narcissistic and antisocial personality disorder. People who present with high levels of psychopathy are rare and not all commit crime, but those who do are over-represented in the criminal justice system as are people with an antisocial personality disorder.

Developing our definitions and understanding of the characteristics of psychopathy continues to be a difficult path, but two key conceptualisations are useful to address here. Karpman (1941) theorised the primary psychopath versus the secondary psychopath. In this theory, the primary psychopaths were characterised by an affective deficit (lack of emotion), often behaving in a direct yet deliberate manner to increase their gain. This means they are goal-driven and will stop at nothing to achieve that goal even if that means that others are dismissed, stepped on or hurt in the process. It has often been hypothesised but never confirmed, that individuals in large business or even politics may have higher levels of psychopathy than the rest of the population due to certain characteristics useful for their role, such as conning or manipulative traits or lack of empathy that might be required to succeed in those areas.

The secondary psychopath is characterised by symptoms such as poor emotional control, impulsivity and driven by emotional hatred or revenge.

Depending on one's view of the Jack the Ripper crimes, it could be argued that he fits either the primary or the secondary psychopath typology. However, there was no clear advantage in the commission of the murders, no clear goal for advancement or financial gain, therefore it seems that based on this theory the secondary psychopath is a better fit. The crimes demonstrate aspects of poor emotional control and commentators have always agreed that the mutilations to the victims demonstrate a hatred or possible revenge motive. As demonstrated in the earlier chapters, there is evidence of impulsivity; we don't know if he hunted these women over a prolonged period, targeting them after meeting them in a hostel or alehouse in the local area. What we know is they were available and therefore he could make a quick decision based on the conditions of the environment, opportunity and availability. However, in Karpman's conceptualisation, violence for excitement is instrumental or goal-driven, which fits the primary typology, but it contains a reactive, emotional component which fits with the secondary type. If Jack the Ripper was taking pleasure from the violence and mutilations, then he would still fit with the primary psychopath typology.

It is, however, the work of Cleckley (1955) that has gained most momentum and has influenced the ways in which clinicians such as Hare (1991) understand psychopathy. Hare has developed one of the main tools for how we diagnose psychopathy today based on Cleckley's conceptualisation. Cleckley emphasised the importance of maladaptive functioning specifically in the areas of emotion or affect and cognition which would predispose these individuals to engage in antisocial behaviour, and theorised that psychopathy lies on a continuum of severity. He outlined sixteen personality traits to conceptualise psychopathy: superficial charm, absence of delusions or other signs of irrational thinking, absence of nervousness, unreliability, untruthfulness, lack of remorse or shame, inadequately motivated antisocial behaviour, poor judgement and failure to learn by experience, pathological egocentricity and an incapacity for love, poverty in major affective reactions, lack of insight, unresponsiveness in general interpersonal relations, fantastic and uninviting behaviour with or without alcohol, very rarely has someone with psychopathy been found to have taken their own life, impersonal sex life, and failure to follow any life plan. We do not have any evidence from the details of the murders alone to make any suggestion that Jack the Ripper had a psychopathic personality, any mention of this is speculation only, but if in the contemporary witness reports there was anyone mentioned who presents with these characteristics, there is a chance we could be close the mark.

Returning to the tables previously, we can select those killers of multiple victims who were known through them media to have mental disorder diagnoses such as Peter Sutcliffe or may possibly have a mental disorder diagnosis such as Joanna Dennehy. Peter Sutcliffe was diagnosed with paranoid schizophrenia and claimed that he heard the voice of the devil telling him to kill sex workers. Joanna Dennehy, according to some media reports, has been diagnosed with antisocial and borderline personality disorder; she killed three people and seriously hurt another two in a spree over a few days where she killed her lover and housemates and seriously injured two more men in random knife attacks.[7] Whilst there had been an element of planning to these offences, they were disorganised and were acting on impulse, on emotion or, in the case of Sutcliffe, on delusions and hallucinations. Neither was able to hide the bodies of their victims so that they could not be found or hide the evidence well. Both chose available or opportunistic targets. What can be said, is that the violence committed to the victims in carrying out the offence was significant. In contrast, Harold Shipman is a good example of an organised killer. He has no known mental disorder, was well educated and held a professional position. His offending was carefully planned, with the goal of gaining money, possession and property from those he killed with no consideration for the impact on the family. The murders took place over many years, and he was able to evade detection for most of this time. It is Harold Shipman that perhaps better fits the typology of a primary psychopath than any of the other killers.

In forensic psychological practice, typologies can be useful to help start the development of a formulation of the offender; consider how they started out in their criminal behaviour, what factors predisposed them to offending, what precipitated their particular offending behaviour, what factors maintain those behaviours and what factors, if any, moderate or reduce their behaviours. However, as we can see, these typologies are not discrete, and offenders share characteristics between them. Although typologies gather together lots of information on offender characteristics for clinical use, there are elements of the complexity of thinking patterns and the interactions between risk factors and factors that protect someone from committing a crime that are not addressed. The development of individual case formulations is vital to acknowledging that complexity, to aid the understanding of an offender's pathway, their risk to

---

7   https://en.wikipedia.org/wiki/Peterborough_ditch_murders

others and the management of those risk factors. Many psychologists who have worked with the offenders listed in the table, in the modern era, would have had the opportunity to develop formulations. We, sadly, are not able to develop such a formulation for Jack the Ripper as we do not have him or her here to interview or to assess and we know very little about his/her background or behaviours he/she engaged in after the murders. We cannot even be absolutely certain that we know who he/she is. Therefore, typologies become useful in giving us a generic feel for the possible person behind the crime.

Returning to the earlier theories and typologies of violent behaviour from the Violence Against Women chapter, Zillmann suggested that at extreme levels of emotional arousal, cognitive or thinking processes are greatly impaired and hostile or aggressive behaviours are likely to be used impulsively. However, if these behaviours have been well learnt over the years, what might appear impulsive might actually be an automatic behaviour. In these cases, where a perpetrator has lost emotional control and becomes very angry, they fail to be able to use their cognitive management resources and act impulsively, which can lead to violent behaviour towards others.

Fesbach's typologies of aggression – Hostile or Expressive and Instrumental – can also be distinguished in these cases as one can see that Shipman might be more instrumental in his use of violence. Joanna Dennehy may fit the hostile or expressive aggression – perhaps she was insulted by her lover or her housemates, perhaps she felt rejected by them in some way – and this led to an extreme feeling of anger, which inhibited her ability to use any emotional control skills that she might have had which then led to the attacks.

Turning to Salfati and Canter's typologies of homicide – the Expressive (Impulsive) Offender, the Instrumental (Opportunistic) Offender and the Instrumental (Cognitive) Offender – we can see that Joanna Dennehy might fit the Expressive (Impulsive Offender), whereas Peter Sutcliffe overlaps both the Expressive and Opportunistic (Instrumental) offender, and Harold Shipman has aspects of both the Opportunistic (Instrumental) and the Cognitive (Instrumental) without the characteristics of being in prison for previous violence.

When we apply these theories to Jack the Ripper, we can see that what we know from the murders is that there are elements of Fesbach's hostile or expressive typology, there are also elements of all three of Salfati and Canter's typologies as there are elements of Expressive (Impulsive), Instrumental (Opportunistic) and Instrumental (Cognitive). In the Jack the Ripper murders there is evidence of expressive anger in the violence committed to the victims' bodies during the offence and post-mortem; there is evidence of selecting his victim based on opportunity and their vulnerability; he gained something from these killings – he took parts of the body away with him, and he also gained status and accolade as he would have been aware of the media hype around what he had done. Finally, as instrumental cognitive, he may well have had a history of violence and been known in his community but just not as "Jack the Ripper".

However, due to the sexualised nature of the Jack the Ripper murders, we must take into account Salfati and Taylor's categories of the relationship between the victim and offender: Exploitation, Control and Violence. In the Jack the Ripper murders there are elements of exploitation where items belonging to the victims were removed, including organs, and foreign objects being used in a sexually assaultive way post-mortem. There is evidence of control in how the victims' clothes are ripped, the use of a weapon and in being forensically aware. And finally, in the violence category, there were multiple wounds to the victim which in some instances appear chaotic and uncontrolled; however, in the removal of organs, there appears to have been some degree of control exerted. This fits with studies about violent murders in people who have high levels of psychopathy; in a study of 125 murderers, Woodworth and Porter (2002) found that psychopaths were more likely to have sexually assaulted their victims either before, during or after they were murdered. The weapon of choice for psychopathic offenders was a knife and when coding the crime scene for evidence of gratuitous violence (violence that exceeded that which is the level to have killed the individual), psychopaths were found to engage in more gratuitous violence. In a follow-up study (Porter, Woodworth, Earle, Drugge and Boer, 2003), levels of sadistic violence were significantly higher than in murders by non-psychopaths.

Whilst we can speculate that Jack the Ripper may have been a psychopath, had a personality disorder or been an expressive instrumental typology, that is all we can do: speculate. However, we can use what we learn from the Jack the Ripper murders and from the other killers of multiple victims to understand that these cases arise largely due to failures in social structures that allow people to be ostracised, abused, neglected and desperate. These failures provide the right environment for the development of these maladaptive beliefs and thinking styles that lead to extreme cases of violence against the vulnerable and causes people to become the vulnerable. The media's sensationalistic approach to these murderers like Jack the Ripper results in their demonisation and hijacks our understanding of mental health issues preventing us as a society from taking the proper steps to prevent or treat these before someone is harmed and more victims are created.

A TURN OF THE TABLES

Having said earlier that we would not be using killers of multiple victims from other nations in this chapter, we find ourselves having to make one exception.

The exception is Aileen Wuornos (Wuornos and Berry-Dee, 2006), the American female sex worker who killed her clients. Aileen was a sex worker in the USA and was charged with murdering seven of her clients by shooting them at point-blank range. She claims that they tried to rape her during their business interaction, and she was defending herself.

Aileen appears to have had a difficult upbringing, with poor attachment to caregivers, a history of being the victim of physical and sexual abuse, and a history of early drug use and early sexualised behaviour. During the trial she was diagnosed with antisocial personality disorder and borderline personality disorder, reportedly the same as Joanna Dennehy in the UK. Aileen was convicted of murdering six out of seven of the men. She was charged with murder and sentenced to death.

This example demonstrates that there are cultural differences in the method of killing due to the differing gun laws in the USA as opposed to the UK. Both Dennehy and Wuornos have possible diagnoses of personality disorders, and both would have experienced significantly traumatic upbringings to develop these. Both of their victims were males, but with Aileen it could be said that these were stranger murders as these were clients, not flatmates or other people she knew. However, even after the commission of these two sets of crimes and the media storm that surrounded them, there has been no cultural shift to naming them "Jane the Ripper" or for adult males to make sure that they are not out unaccompanied at night or experience the risks to their lives of being in contact with sex workers. Even after these crimes, the culture prevalent today remains that men retain the freedom to move in the public sphere as they wish, despite the statistical evidence that they are more at risk from violent crime than females.

We also feel that it would be remiss of us not to mention the women listed in the table as killers of multiple victims, women who were baby farmers. They have been listed as serial killers in the media; however, we know from earlier chapters that baby farming was a horrendous method of birth and population control. It is unlikely, that as with other killers of multiple victims, these women set out to hunt down tiny vulnerable victims to satisfy an urge to kill, but they were callous enough to end the lives of hundreds of babies through neglect and poisoning in the belief that they were offering a public service or as a means of earning more money in a time when extreme poverty was rife and the disparity between rich and poor enormous. If any of our killers fits the conceptualisation of psychopath, then perhaps it is these women. If any crimes were caused directly by the result of a multiplicity of social malfunctions – extreme poverty, the disempowerment of women through childbirth, the lack of control women were permitted over their bodies and the reproductive capabilities – then perhaps it is the crimes of the baby farmers.

REFERENCES

American Psychiatric Association (2013) *Diagnostic and statistical manual of mental disorders* (5th ed), Washington, DC.

Canter, D. (1994), *Criminal Shadows: Inside the Mind of the Serial Killer*, Harper Collins, London.

Cleckley, H. (1955), *The mask of sanity: An attempt to clarify some issues about the so-called psychopathic personality* (3rd ed), Mosby, St Louis, doi:10.1037/11395-000.

Fesbach, S. (1964), "The function of aggression and the regulation of aggressive drive", *Psychological Review*, 71, 257–272.

Hare, R.D. (1991), *The Hare Psychopathy Checklist-Revised*, Multi-Health Systems, North Tonawanda, New York.

Herbert, I. (2006), "Wearside Jack: I deserve to go to jail for 'evil' Ripper hoax", *The Independent*, 21st March 2006, retrieved 1st June 2020.
Karpman, B. (1941), "On the need of separating psychopathy into two distinct types: The symptomatic and the idiopathic", *Journal of Criminal Psychopathology*, 3, 112–137.

Kinnell, H. (2008), *Violence and Sex Work in Britain*, Willan Publishing, Devon.

Mental Health Act (1983), amended 2007, retrieved from https://www.legislation.gov.uk/ukpga/2007/12/contents on 27th November 2018.

Porter, S., Woodworth, M., Earle, J., Drugge, J. and Boer, D. (2003), "Characteristics of Sexual Homicides Committed by Psychopathic and Non-psychopathic Offenders", *Law and human behavior*, 27, 459–70, 10.1023/A:1025461421791.

Rowland, D. (2014), "The Blackout Killer or the Blackout Ripper", retrieved from https://www.oldpolicecellsmuseum.org.uk/content/new-contributions/the_blackout_killer_or_the_blackout_ripper on the 1st June 2020.

Salfati, G.C. and Canter, D.C. (1999), "Differentiating Stranger Murders: Profiling Offender Characteristics from Behavioral Styles", *Behavioral Sciences and the Law Behavioural*, 17: 391–406.

Salfati. G.C. and Taylor, P. (2006), "Differentiating sexual violence: A comparison of sexual homicide and rape", *Psychology, Crime & Law*, Vol. 12(2): 107–125.

Sounes, H (1995), *Fred and Rose: The Full Story of Fred and Rose West and the Gloucester House of Horrors*, Warner Books, London.

Whittle, B. and Richie, J. (2000), *Prescription for Murder: The True Story of Dr. Harold Frederick Shipman*, Little Brown, p348–9.

Woodworth, M. and Porter, S. (2002), "In cold blood: Characteristics of criminal homicides as a function of psychopathy", *Journal of Abnormal Psychology*, 111(3), 436–445, https://doi.org/10.1037/0021-843X.111.3.436

Wuornos, A. and Berry-Dee, C. (2006), *Monster*, John Blake Publishing Limited, London.

Zillmann, D. (1979), *Hostility and aggression*, Hillsdale, NJ Lawrence Erlbaum.

11

JACK THE RIPPER: SUSPECTS AND THEORIES

'I was not codding dear old Boss when I gave you the tip, you'll hear about Saucy Jacky's work tomorrow double event this time number one squealed a bit couldn't finish straight off. Had not time to get ears off for police thanks for keeping last letter back till I got to work again. Jack the Ripper'

The "Saucy Jack" letter received by Scotland Yard on 1st October 1888

Probably a hoax – in 1888 the police received hundreds of letters from so-called "Jack the Rippers", none of which surrendered the identity of the murderer – this letter from an apparent Jack the Ripper who called himself "Saucy Jack" was one of the few that gave rise to in-depth investigation, and there are still Jack the Ripper experts who believe the letter to be genuine. Whilst this book is not another homicide investigation into the identity of the killer, exploring the theories on the murderer's identity forms an essential contribution to understanding why Jack the Ripper became the notorious semi-mythical monster of the media and the subsequent impact on society, the reverberations of which continue to be felt today. This chapter gathers together the main theories, including some of the many conspiracy theories that have been formulated around the perpetrator in order to demonstrate how the folk demon and urban legend developed. The theories are not given in chronological order but instead are ordered to demonstrate the difficulties that beset each theory over time and the many counterarguments, which has meant that a definitive theory has never been fully formulated and accepted, and therefore no definitive suspect has ever been identified. Nevertheless, as the chapter shows, the crimes instilled deep fear, not just in the community local to Whitechapel, but across the country and beyond, into Europe, the United States and beyond. That fear grew with every murder and was perpetuated with every theory, with each conversation – in print or otherwise – as to the monster that stalked the East End butchering women.

THE THEORIES

John E. Douglas from the Federal Bureau of Investigation (FBI) was given the case to analyse in 1988 using his expertise as an agent. He notes that due to the limited forensic information such as samples, photographs and autopsy details, the original evidence lacks validity. This means that to come to any kind of theory on the identity of the killer or a reasonably accurate profile of the killer, he has had to make some "probable assumptions" about the case. For example, the prostitutes at the time were likely to be victims of crime because of the nature of their lifestyle, they were accessible and also likely to have initiated contact with their attacker and not vice versa. Understanding how the victims lived, what they were like as people and their likely movements and actions leading up to their deaths is part of attempting to drill into the thoughts and personality of the killer. This aspect, Douglas says, is important to understanding a potential perpetrator (Douglas, 1988).

Douglas noticed some distinctive primary areas in the analysis; there was no evidence of sexual assault, victims were killed swiftly, the perpetrator-maintained control of the victim due to a "blitz-style" attack, removed internal organs, there was no evidence of physical torture, there was evidence of post-mortem mutilation, there was a suggestion of possible manual strangulation and the victims' blood was concentrated in small areas. Taken together this suggests a controlled and organised attack rather than a frenzied kill. Douglas notes that the time of death was in the early morning hours on either a Friday, Saturday or Sunday, therefore the perpetrator would most likely have been a local employee working Monday to Friday.

The "first" victim in chronological order of the "canonical" five was attacked near Whitechapel Station. Douglas then indicates that subsequent attacks occurred within a mile of this point in a triangle. This triangle is an indication of a "Secondary Comfort Zone" which occurs when the "Primary Comfort Zone" has been compromised, for example police directing their attention to the Whitechapel Station area. Whitechapel station would have been the primary comfort zone and would be the most likely location for the perpetrator to live or work. There would likely have been unreported attacks in the vicinity of the station or offences that were not attributed to the Jack the Ripper crimes by the authorities who had not made a link. This lack of linking other violent attacks in the area is not necessarily indicative of poor policing or detecting; it is made perfectly possible because the modus operandi of an offender is subject to change depending on the circumstances and over time. A serial killer's preferred method of operation develops gradually as the killer experiments, learns and discovers their particular preferences, and this process takes place over a period of time. It could be the case that other women victims were attacked by different means in the local area during Jack the Ripper's grim apprenticeship as he learned the way he preferred to kill and refined those particular methods that caused him the least trouble and enabled him to enact the most important element of the crime: the ritual of mutilating the victims post-mortem.

Douglas continues his analysis by suggesting that notoriety was not the primary motivation for Jack the Ripper, therefore the letters sent to the police and others (including newspapers journalists) are unlikely to be from the killer because it is more likely that the motivation for committing the crimes is the pleasure derived from the ritual mutilation after the initial killing. This is probably the main reason for the horrific mutilations of Mary Kelly's body. The murder took place indoors for the first time known in the series of murders linked to the same killer and therefore there is a very strong likelihood that Jack the Ripper had the space and time to enact his violent fantasies without interruption. Interestingly, Douglas suggests that the perpetrator would have dressed in better clothing to give the pretence that he had money, and this would have enticed the women to approach him. He could therefore have been a local man with detailed knowledge of the streets and alleys of the Whitechapel area, but dressed as an upper-class visitor. Douglas also suggests that he was likely to be employed somewhere he could vicariously experience his fantasies, for example, as butcher, in an abattoir or a mortuary, as a hospital attendant or a medical examiner's assistant, and he was likely to have used the services of prostitutes often. Douglas continues by suggesting that a hatred and disgust for women could have been fuelled by venereal disease contracted from a prostitute.

Some aspects of Douglas's theory are supported by Trevor Marriott, a former CID detective who added his expertise in practical, modern policing to the growing literature in this area in 2007. Marriott notes that in the case of Mary Ann Nichols, the killer showed signs of organisation in that he lifted the clothing to remove the entrails rather than cut open the clothing. Marriott believes this shows a degree of forethought and planning; with this apparent simple act, the killer demonstrates prior consideration of the best methods to achieve his goal, planning and pre-meditation. The author explains how he feels that the evidence points to a calculated approach to the murders.

Marriott (2007) also considered other motives for the murders based on the prevalent social climate at the time of the murder. He makes the point that at the time of the murders, robbery was dismissed as the reason behind the murders because the acts were too violent and the dismemberment too anatomical in detail. Killings in the course of a robbery were much more likely to be swift if brutal, as with the main motive being to steal, the killing was secondary. The degree of precision in the mutilation of Mary Nichols' body suggested to Marriott that it was the mutilation itself that was the primary motivator (a theory also supported by Douglas).

Marriott also considered the harvesting of body parts. In Victorian times, there were enquiries from medical research establishments and possibly pharmaceutical companies about body parts for testing and research, and Baxter in the Coroner's Court suggests that Annie Chapman's womb was removed for the organ market (Robinson, 2015). Body snatching and this sort of nefarious activity had been known for centuries, so it is possible the murders were motivated by the need to harvest organs, for example the uterus, which was expertly removed in Annie Chapman's case. But Marriott scorns the idea that the murder took place specifically for the harvesting of body parts as there would not have been sufficient time nor light for these very intricate and precise actions to take place at the scene. Instead, he suggests that the removal of body parts took place at the mortuary prior to the post-mortem and with the assistance of the mortuary technicians. This then opens up the possibility of another theory. With the Royal London hospital directly opposite Whitechapel station (within the murderer's primary comfort zone as suggested by Douglas), could the perpetrator(s) have been a person or people working in the hospital who wanted to access organs for research or who wanted to earn money through the delivery of certain organs? It should be noted, however, that some of the murders did not involve the removal of body parts despite increasingly horrific mutilations. The likelihood, therefore, remains that the harvesting of organs was not a motive for these murders.

But what if Annie Chapman's murder was not by the Ripper but was a gangland killing? Marriott explains that in today's crime world people around the globe are ruthlessly murdered to supply the international traffic of organs and body parts and, with large money changing hands, this traffic in human organs is controlled by dangerous gangs. This is one of the facets of organised crime, just like the drugs trade. If Chapman's murder had been a gang crime, the witnesses would never have dreamt of admitting to seeing or hearing anything. Interestingly, the statements made at the inquest and police investigations demonstrated that little was heard by any of the witnesses, and this seems unlikely given that the killer was occupied in cutting out a uterus, a task that required time, light and skill. Could this provide a clue as to the identity and motive of the murderer?

While there are sufficient similarities for the crimes to have been attributed to a single killer that we dub Jack the Ripper, each crime also bears differences, enough to give consideration to whether, if Chapman's killing was a gang murder, the other murders might have been carried out by the same gang but by different members, or by different gangs operating in the same area. Could the dehumanisation of prostitutes as a result of the prevalent social attitudes have led to an acceptance and suggestion that this sort of crime could be carried out with a greater degree of impunity? Did the wombs of prostitutes' matter? While it is known that gangs operated at the time, there is little evidence to suggest that these women were indeed the victims of gang crime. Marriott does not support this particular suggestion and instead offers the possibility that there was just one murderer, and that Jack the Ripper was in fact a seaman. There were ships at dock at the time, the docks were within easy walking distance of the crime scenes, and it would have been easy for a seaman to be familiar with Whitechapel and its prostitutes and to move around without being noticed. Marriott goes further in his attempt to prove his theory by researching into the ships that were in dock and noting that the gaps between the murders also coincided with the times that a certain ship and her crew were out of port. Although this theory does have some merit, it flounders somewhat on the issue of the need for the killer to have been extremely familiar with the complex labyrinth of alleys and streets of Whitechapel and the surrounding area in order to select the right locations for these complex killings and then escape unnoticed, leaving no real physical clues.

In 1976, Stephen Knight and Joseph Sickert co-researched and published a book that used evidence from Sickert's father to identify a conspiracy that points the finger at the Duke of Clarence and a freemasonry-contrived plot which led to the murders. Stephen Knight suggests that three men were responsible for the murders in order to cover up an illegitimate marriage between the Duke of Clarence and a commoner that he had fallen in love with, by killing the women who knew her and who knew about the marriage. Joseph Sickert had diary entries from his grandfather Walter Sickert (the artist) which confirmed this. It was later discovered that Joseph Sickert had lied; however, the notion that there could be a freemasonry conspiracy did not fade and went on to inform subsequent Ripperology theories.

Bruce Robinson (2015) is one of those authors and researchers who has followed the line of there being a link to freemasonry; indeed, he is certain that Jack the Ripper was Michael Maybrick. Michael Maybrick was a leading freemason and public figure at the time with influence at high levels of the establishment, and Robinson has named him as responsible for the framing of his own sister-in-law, Florence Maybrick, for the murder of her husband and his brother, James Maybrick. Robinson suggests that Michael Maybrick hated Florence for having affairs with his other brothers and owing him money. This loathing, combined with a controlling personality, sense of personal invincibility and detailed knowledge of ancient freemasonry rituals, compelled Maybrick to kill women in Whitechapel, prostitutes to whom he would have had easy access, especially via Toynbee Hall where he and others would enjoy shows at the weekend.

Robinson also includes in the series of Jack the Ripper killings the murder of Alice McKenzie, the "Whitehall trunk", the "Battersea trunk" and the corpse of a boy murdered in Bradford, claiming that all of these murders contained clear symbolism associated with freemasonry. There exists a large amount of contemporary evidence to support views suggesting that people at the time were suspicious of what might have been government conspiracies rooted in the class system. The freemasons running the government were gradually convinced that James Maybrick was Jack the Ripper, led to this belief by the clever and scheming Michael Maybrick. He convinced them Florence Maybrick knew about her husband and thus, so Robinson concludes, these influential freemasons found themselves having to silence both; one was murdered, and one spent the rest of her life in prison accused of her husband's poisoning. However, the author believes that officials started to work out the truth and from that point Michael Maybrick disappears from most all freemasonry records and from public life and is not mentioned anywhere else – usefully erased from history.

Robinson did make comment on Stephen Knight's theory of the Duke of Clarence as Jack the Ripper, and he clearly is not the theory's biggest fan. For example, he quotes Joseph Sickert's letter to the *Sunday Times* in 1978: 'It was a hoax, I made it all up, it was a whopping fib and pure invention.' Robinson feels Knight was set up by the police, suggesting that police sources leaked this information into the public domain in order to throw people off the real story. The links between the police and freemasonry are strong and at the time there was a wave of increased interest in the Jack the Ripper story, usefully fuelled by the press' linking of the Yorkshire Ripper with the Victorian murders. Robinson suggests that it was felt that letting out some story of freemasonry involvement in the Jack the Ripper tale would throw the public off the scent of the real killer, rather than encourage continued investigation. It is well recorded that freemasons at the time ruled the law courts and ruled the land, and there has long been a suspicion of corruption and cover-ups of all sorts. For example, Robinson, Rumbleow and Knight mention the Cleveland Street Scandal, where young boys were used in a brothel frequented by MPs, where all the boys were eventually sent to prison, but the punters, MPs and judges included walked free. If Jack the Ripper had been a leading freemason, as Robinson believes, then it would have been critical for the leaders of the country, also freemasons whose oath to the secretive organisation was far more powerful a motivator than their loyalty to the country or even to the rule of law, or the concepts of justice and right and wrong, to act swiftly and in a coordinated fashion, to throw the world off the scent of the real killer. Subterfuge, smoke screens, red herrings, apparent police ineptitudes and a flow of conflicting speculative theories in the press, have served well in the past hundred and more years to create a legend that deflects from any possibility of full, unquestionable identification of the real Ripper.

It did not take long once details of the murders were released in the press, for links to be drawn between the murders and the masonic symbolism in the positioning of the victims' bodies (Robinson, 2015). For example, exploring the account of the death of Hiram Abif; the three ruffians are executed by having their throats cut, their organs thrown over their left shoulder

(Annie Chapman and Catherine Eddowes), their bodies cut in two (the Scotland Yard Trunk – not specifically linked to Jack the Ripper but could be considered a possible victim) and their bowels burnt (Mary Jane Kelly). There are also similarities between the Ezekiel sections of the Bible, important to freemasonry, and details of the harm caused to Mary Kelly, further homage to the masonic elements of the Jack the Ripper story.

However, three other researchers have pointed the finger at Walter Sickert himself as being the elusive Jack the Ripper. The artist was an eccentric who painted images related to the Jack the Ripper murders at the time. Patricia Cornwell (2017) is the most recent author to explore the evidence and has stated that she has DNA evidence that Walter Sickert wrote one of the many Jack the Ripper letters to the police. Sadly, there is no such comparable evidence for the crime scenes, and it would not be beyond the realms of possibility that someone who went so far as to pay to sleep in the room that Jack the Ripper allegedly slept in (according to the landlady who suspected her previous tenant), might also want to put himself further into the shoes of the murderer and write a letter pretending to be him, or perhaps her, as two other theories suggest.

William Stewart, writing in 1939, suggests that Jack the Ripper could have been Jill the Ripper and there was a likelihood that the murders were in fact abortions gone wrong and committed by either an incompetent abortionist hiding her mistakes or a bloodthirsty abortionist taking her opportunities. His evidence for this is that Mary Kelly was three months pregnant when she was killed; however, this is opposed by Dr Thomas Bond's autopsy report, which did not find that Mary Kelly was pregnant. Other considerations were given to perhaps a scorned lesbian lover or wife who found out that her husband had been with a prostitute. A murder committed by Mary Pearcy in 1890 was believed at the time to bear some of the hallmarks of the Jack the Ripper murders where Mary had killed her lover's wife and child by slitting their throats in private and then dumping their bodies in the street. However, the actual case information states that Mary killed the wife by hitting her over the head with a fireplace poker and then cut her head off and the child was smothered. These are not the same hallmarks as those of the considered Jack the Ripper murders and as we have already seen, this fits with what we know about females who commit murder. This theory was supported by Arthur Butler, an ex-detective chief superintendent who wrote a series of articles about this for *The Sun* newspaper in 1972.

Robert Anderson, who was working with Charles Warren at Scotland Yard, is often considered to have tried to turn the populace's thoughts to blaming the Irish or Polish Jews. This created anger in both communities. One of the first suspects, "Leather Apron", was arrested for the death of Annie Chapman. He was known as John Pizer, was a butcher and a Jew, and he went on to successfully sue at least one newspaper for defamation (Robinson, 2015). As has been discussed in a previous chapter there was a strong impulse in the media, which itself reflected Victorian social attitudes, to seek to blame those who were outsiders, "others" – since the murders were so horrific that the highly prejudiced British were prone to consider that only a foreigner could possibly have committed them. A report in the *East London Observer* of 15th December 1888 said:

> On Saturday in several quarters of East London the crowds who assembled in the streets began to assume a very threatening attitude towards the Hebrew population of the District. It was repeatedly asserted that no Englishman could have perpetrated such a horrible crime as that of Hanbury Street, and that it must have been done by a Jew – and forthwith the crowds began to threaten and abuse such of the unfortunate Hebrews as they found in the streets. Happily, the presence of a large number of police... prevented a riot taking place.
>
> Warwick and Willis, 2013

In his essay "Crime and Punishment" in Warwick and Willis, Fishman states that under Sir Robert Anderson, anti-Semitism was rife in the Metropolitan Police. These comments and accusations exemplified what were deeply held prejudices, some of which, given current-day media and political rhetoric, has resurfaced and taken shape in the form of the "hostile environment" leading to scandals such as the forced deportation of the Windrush immigrants, the treatment of European seasonal workers and the refusal to accept child asylum seekers.

THE SUSPECTS

Just a quick look at online search engines and sources reveals a multitude of websites and theories about potential suspects and conspiracies. The Jack the

Ripper Wikipedia page claims there have been one hundred suspects over the years. It is difficult to know who could possibly be right and who could possibly be wrong. In any case, while exploring the merits of each suspect is not within the scope of this book, describing the theories and suspects will continue to give context to the culture and climate of the time, and illuminate aspects of the Jack the Ripper story that go some way to explain the continuing fascination that society has with this series of grisly killings.

According to the police at the time of the killings, there were seven potential suspects: Montague John Druitt, Seweryn Kłosowski, Aaron Kosminski, Michael Ostrog, John Pizer, James Thomas Sadler and Francis Tumblety. Druitt was dismissed as a suspect by Inspector Abberline as the only evidence against him was that he committed suicide shortly after the last murder – or the last of the murders ascribed to Jack the Ripper – and then the killings abruptly appeared to stop. Abberline instead favoured Seweryn Kłosowski who, in 1903, was hung for poisoning three of his wives. However, as we have seen from Douglas in his profiling for the FBI, the purpose behind the murders was the ritual of mutilating the victims. It would be very difficult for someone with such a need, to completely alter their preferred and proven method of attaining the ritual they desire.

Aaron Kosminski was admitted to an asylum in 1891 and it is not thought that his particular manifestation of a psychotic illness would have led him to harm others without giving himself away. This we have also seen in people like the Yorkshire Ripper and others; poor mental health can lead to violent thoughts and actions, but other symptoms can make it very difficult for them to plan to cover their tracks effectively or for very long.

Michael Ostrog was a Russian con man who was identified as a suspect by Macnaghten in 1889; however, there is evidence that places him in France at the time of the murders.

John Pizer, also known as Leather Apron, was a Polish Jew who worked as a boot maker in Whitechapel. He was originally suspected by the other locals and arrested by Sergeant William Thicke but released as he had a sound alibi for the murders.

Again, James Thomas Sadler was at sea at the time of the first four murders even though he was arrested for the murder of Frances Cole, a female friend and thought to be the last Ripper victim although not of the canonical five.

Finally, Francis Tumblety was suspected by later officers investigating the murders, but no evidence was found that he had participated in any.

From looking at this list, it is easy to see how the media and communities at the time would have been infuriated at the lack of success in apprehending the perpetrator.

According to the media of the time, there were a further six suspects: William Henry Bury, Thomas Neill Cream, Thomas Hayne Cutbush, Frederick Bailey Deeming, Carl Feigenbaum and Robert Donston Stephenson.

Bury was executed for killing his wife in 1889 in Scotland, although he had been living in East London prior to that. He admitted to his wife's murder but denied any involvement in the Ripper murders.

Thomas Neill Cream was supposed to have been on the verge of confessing whilst awaiting execution for murder at Newgate Gaol in 1891 when he was interrupted. However, it is well documented that he was in prison in the USA for murder at the time of the Ripper murders and was released early in 1891 after his brother plead for leniency and reportedly bribed the authorities.

Cutbush was a medical student who, according to *The Sun* newspaper at the time, suffered a psychotic episode brought on by syphilis. This has been disproved by Richard Jones,[8] a researcher who transcribed the patient notes from Cutbush's time at Broadmoor. Cutbush was admitted to Broadmoor Hospital in 1891 after stabbing a woman in the backside and attempting to stab a second. Whilst it was considered that he posed danger to others rather than himself, the patient's notes indicate symptoms similar to that of schizophrenia and this would likely have made it difficult for him to meticulously plan attacks. As we see here, he was convicted of stabbing two women in the backside rather than the throat and was quickly apprehended. The true Jack the Ripper evades detection even today. Cutbush is a favoured suspect of A.P. Wolf, author of *Jack, the Myth: A New Look at the Ripper*, written in 1993, Wolfe believed that police at the time dismissed Cutbush in order to protect his uncle, who was a police officer. We cannot help but wonder, perhaps with a tinge of twenty-first-century cynicism, whether the prize and accolade of becoming the officer to catch the Ripper would have outweighed any camaraderie or loyalty that might have existed between police officers.

Frederick Deeming was another murderer suspected by the media. He went on to kill two of his wives and his children and was executed in Australia, but it is thought he was in prison or out of the country at the time of the Ripper murders.

---

8   https://www.jack-the-ripper.org/thomas-cutbush-files.htm

Feigenbaum was a German merchant seaman who has been considered by modern investigators, such as Trevor Marriott, to be the Ripper. He killed a woman in the USA by cutting her throat and it was his lawyer who claimed he was the Ripper. Again, doubt has been cast onto his location at the time of all of the murders.

Finally, Stephenson was suspected by none other than the famous contemporary investigative journalist, W.T. Stead. Stephenson was admitted to the London Hospital in Whitechapel shortly before the murders started and left just after they ended. He showed an interest in the occult and an interest in the murders even, claiming his physician, Dr Morgan Davies, as a suspect. It has, however, been argued that according to shift patterns and rosters, neither man would have been able to leave the hospital at the time of the killings. For those readers who are familiar with the London Hospital in Whitechapel and its proximity to the first murder site, it is not entirely outside of the realms of possibility in the 1880s that someone could leave unnoticed, even a patient.

One final suspect to mention here is Dr Forbes Winslow. As previously mentioned, Winslow had an interest in identifying criminals using physiognomy; however, he also showed an interest in the Ripper murders beyond that of wanting to support this police and inserted himself into the story of Jack the Ripper not just by contacting the police but also by spending night and day in the slums of Whitechapel, speaking to locals and building his own theories and evidence which were then printed in the local newspaper.

There is a lack of clarity in the police reports and evidence collected and a good deal of conflation with the media agenda of the time. It is clear to see, then, why modern authors have tried for themselves to come up with the answers as to why these crimes were committed. Robinson, for example, considers it an error of Ripperologists to confuse "evil" with "insane". He uses Shakespeare's Machiavellian character as an example and that we should be looking to evil rather than insanity. He states that, 'You don't have to be insane to cut people up, you just have to hate enough.' This would certainly fit with our exploration of clinical psychopathy, rather than a person who is experiencing an acute psychotic disorder. Robinson indicates that a lawyer writing at the time stated that people jumped to the conclusion of insanity as the crimes were so barbaric but then he pointed out that many people commit violent acts of barbarity without being "insane".

Robinson states that he believes that Jack the Ripper saw women as either "angels or whores" but describes the violence towards these women as "absolute dominion over, rejection of, hatred of womankind". From the literature, this dichotomy would be typical of attitudes towards women at the time and perhaps suggests that we should look towards the idea of hate, in particular despising the prostitute for bringing the ideal of a woman to the lowest depths as it would have been seen at the time, and this is in line with Hilary Kinnell's book on violence against sex workers (2008). It is interesting to note that the heads of police in some instances blamed the women themselves. Government officials after the resignation of Warren suggested that the women had been "accessory to their own deaths". This links to current views on violence towards women, particularly sexual violence and the literature on rape myths. Again, it was Robert Anderson who suggested their investigation into the Ripper had been defensible and that it was the sex worker's own fault that they had been killed. This attitude was further perpetuated by the class system where concern about the murders expressed by wealthier areas of society was motivated by worry that if prostitutes could not afford to live in the slums and they were unsafe there, then it was only a mere matter of time for these prostitutes to move into more affluent areas. Hilary Kinnell demonstrates that this feeling is not unique to the Victorian era and these same concerns and motivations exist in our society when it comes to sex workers; often communities will react with violence and anger towards prostitutes, forgetting the struggle that has placed the woman in the position in the first place.

The choice and number of theories and suspects associated with Jack the Ripper is wide-ranging, and believers of one theory will express and support this with voluble passion. One cannot help but wonder that, with all the media conflation and the passage of time, it is unlikely the true suspect will ever be uncovered. What is clear, however, is the residual impact Jack the Ripper's murders and the ensuing investigation and incessant theorising has had on society. The continuing search for Jack the Ripper draws his legend into contemporary consciousness so that almost everyone is familiar with the terrifying figure presented, the monstrous perpetrator with an uncanny ability to move unseen in the city and attack women at will then fade into the smog of London as if he had never been there at all. The perpetrator has been romanticised and the competition to be the first to find him has become the modern equivalent of seeking the cities of gold in the Amazon or discovering the location of Atlantis.

What remains are the tragic victims and the sub-story of the victims being blamed for their own deaths, and the deaths of sex workers ever since.

The legacy that Jack the Ripper left was that women alone in public could never be safe, and those who sex worked brought violence upon themselves. In response, women have been accompanied, monitored, chaperoned or not even permitted to move openly and independently in society in order to avoid this perceived horror when, in reality, Jack the Ripper – whoever he was – took advantage of the attitudes towards women, and sex workers in particular, to get away with his crimes with complete impunity. This is the essence of the legend that we, in our own modern society fraught with anxieties and fears, need to heed: that the circumstances and attitudes in our inner cities, are not so far removed from those in Victorian Whitechapel.

REFERENCES

Cornwell, P. (2017), *Ripper: The Secret Life of Walter Sickert*, Thomas & Mercer, Amazon Publishing Inc.

Douglas, J.E. (1988), "Jack the Ripper", Freedom of Information/Privacy Acts Section, Federal Bureau of Investigation.

Fishman, W.J. (1988, 2005), "Crime and Punishment" in Warwick, A. and Willis, M. (2013), *Jack the Ripper: Media, Culture, History*, Manchester University Press, Manchester.

Kinnell, H. (2008), *Violence and Sex Work in Britain*, Willan Publishing, Devon.

Knight, S. (1986), *Jack the Ripper: The Final Solution* (2nd ed), Academy Chicago Publishers, Chicago.

Marriott, T. (2007), *Jack the Ripper: The 21st Century Solution*, John Blake Publishing Ltd.

Robinson, B. (2015), *They all love Jack: Busting the Ripper*, Harper Collins Publishers, London.

Stewart, W. (1939), *Jack the Ripper: A New Theory*, Quality Press, London.

Warwick, A. and Willis, M. (2013), *Jack the Ripper: Media, Culture, History*, Manchester University Press, Manchester.

AFTERWORD

'The deceased has been identified by persons who have known her since she has lived in London, but her relatives, if she possesses any, have not yet communicated with the police.'

The Hull Daily News, 10th September 1888 (speaking of Annie Chapman)

O ur walk through Wanstead Flats past the City of London Cemetery and into a Leytonstone coffee shop on a bitter October afternoon set us on the course to explore the Jack the Ripper story. At the time, we were fuelled not just by coffee, cake and a fascination with the macabre underworld of East London, and, like most other "Ripper" enthusiasts, with a taste for the gothic and the gruesome, but we were also filled with the righteous indignation at the opening of the Museum of Jack the Ripper a few months earlier in August 2015. There had, in fact, been open and public demonstrations against the opening of the museum, with protestors declaring that the museum traded on glorification of violence against women, and in particular, sexual violence against women. The voyeurism, the salacious pouring over images and memorabilia of the butchering of women, had not abated in over 130 years. As women who have in different capacities worked with women who have encountered many difficulties in life, including mental illness, substance abuse, sex working, homelessness and violence, we wanted to somehow add some weight to the counter-perspective of the Jack the Ripper story; the perspective that the victims should be lifted from the incredible ignominy to which they had generally been consigned all these years since their deaths. By exploring the many threads of this complicated story, we wanted to contribute to ensuring their lives were somehow valued.

We set out, then, to discover what we could learn about the women, the people and the East End London of the 1880s. To do this, we needed not just to carry out relevant research and read up various texts and investigate records of the time, we also needed to pull apart the threads of the complex narrative that is the Jack the Ripper story. What is it that this narrative is trying to communicate, was a question we were to ask ourselves over and again. We came to the conclusion that the narrative tells a range of stories: the stories of the individual women; snippets of story of a killer whose identity is not known; the poverty, hardship, racism, class divides and the sense of community of the late Victorian East End; the story of how the media was instrumental in shaping attitudes and behaviour; the story of how prevalent attitudes, morality and social norms affected lives, and in particular, constrained the choices of women. We were surprised that we found many parallels to modern life – if the Victorian East End produced the Ripper once, then the twenty-first-century version could do so again. We discovered that the Jack the Ripper story is part truth, part myth, the killer a combination of man and monster, villain and anti-hero. It is not his identity that matters to us, as much as his actions, the context in which his actions took place, the lives they affected and why those women might have ended up at the sharp end of his monstrous blades.

Writing this book has given us an even greater sense of respect for the victims; these were women, sisters, mothers, daughters, wives and lovers who were taken from their friends and families suddenly and brutally. Theirs were lives already tinged with tragedy and filled with daily hardships, human stories worthy of being remembered.

After we had written much of this book, we encountered Hallie Rubenhold's *The Five: The Untold Lives of the Women Killed by Jack the Ripper*, a meticulously researched book written in clear, accessible language, Rubenhold colours in the sketches that had been left of the victims. She tells each of their stories – or what the evidence would point is most likely to have been experienced in their lives by those victims – with a great deal of respect. We were overjoyed that our own sense that respect for the victims was missing from the Jack the Ripper story was echoed by such an eminent historian and writer as Rubenhold. Similarly, Judith Walkowitz, writing in more academic language, reinforced our initial instincts that the Jack the Ripper story has a misogynistic angle, not just in that the women were victims of extreme violence, probably sexual in its nature, but that the way in which that story has been recorded, remembered and recounted, has also been from a male-dominated perspective, and, to some degree, the voices of the victims have been, until more recently, omitted from their own stories.

Finally, we have become convinced that the murderer, the mysterious "Jack the Ripper" cannot ever be fully and conclusively identified, and, of course, he can never be punished. What we can do, as a society, is to avoid giving rise to those conditions of life that made it far too easy for him to kill, to "rip", these poor, destitute, tragic women. If we, as a society, can achieve that, then the lives of the women, or their deaths, would not have been in vain.

BIBLIOGRAPHY

Acton, W. (1870), *Prostitution, Considered in Its Moral, Social, and Sanitary Aspects in London and Other Large Cities and Garrison Towns, with Proposals for the Control and Prevention of Its Attendant Evils*, John Churchill and Sons, London.

Allardyce, J., Boydell, J., Van Os, J. et al. (2001), "Comparison of the incidence of schizophrenia in rural Dumfries and Galloway and urban Camberwell", *British Journal of Psychiatry*, 179, 335–339.

Allport, G.W. (1954), *The Nature of Prejudice*, Addison-Wesley, Cambridge, MA.

Anonymous, "Mental Illness in the Victorian Era", retrieved from http://waywardvictorian.tumblr.com/post/815439932/mental-illness-during-the-victorian-era on 8th March 2016.

American Psychiatric Association (2013), *Diagnostic and statistical manual of mental disorders* (5th ed), Washington, DC.

Appleby, L., Kapur, N., Shaw, J., Hunt, I.M., Flynn, S., Ibrahim, S., Turnbull, P., Gianatsi, M. and Tham, S. (2016), "National Confidential Inquiry into Suicide and Homicide by people with Mental Illness: Annual Report and 20-year review", Manchester University, a full list of Inquiry reports and publications can be found on the Inquiry website: www.bbmh.manchester.ac.uk/cmhs/research/centreforsuicideprevention/nci-Publications

Archer, J. (2006), "Testosterone and human aggression: an evaluation of the challenge hypothesis", *Neuroscience and Biobehavioral Reviews*, 30 (3): 319–45, doi:10.1016/j.neubiorev.2004.12.007.

Babcock, J.C., Miller, S.A. and Siard, C. (2003), "Toward a typology of abusive women: Differences between partner-only and generally violent women in the use of violence", *Psychology of Women Quarterly*, 27, 153–161.

Ballou, M., Matsumoto, A. and Wagner, M. (2002), "Toward a feminist ecological theory of human nature: Theory building in response to real-world dynamics", in Ballou, M. and Brown, L.S., *Rethinking mental health and disorder: Feminist perspectives* (p99–141), Guilford Press, New York.

Bandura, A. (1978), "Learning and behavioural theory of aggression", in Kutash, L., Kutash, S.B. and Schlesinger, L.B., *Violence perspective on murder and aggression* (p29–57), Jossey-Bass, San Francisco, CA.

Barrett, A. and Harrison, C., *Crime and Punishment in England: A Sourcebook*, Routledge, London.

Batchelor, S. (2005), "'Prove me the bam!' Victimization and agency in the lives of young women who commit violent offences", *The Journal of Community and Criminal Justice*, 52, 358–375.

Beck, A.T. (1999), *Prisoners of Hate. The Cognitive Basis of Anger, Hostility and Violence. Perennial*, Harper Collins, New York, p125–132 and 150–164.

Bennett, S., Farrington, D.P. and Huesmann, L.R. (2005), "Explaining gender differences in crime and violence: The importance of social cognitive skills", *Aggression and Violent Behavior*, 10(3), 263–288, http://dx.doi.org/10.1016/j.avb.2004.07.001

Bloom, C. (2007), "The Ripper Writing: the cream of a writer's dream", in Warwick, A. and Willis, M. (2013), *Jack the Ripper: Media, Culture, History*, Manchester University Press, Manchester.

Bondeson, J. (2000), *The London Monster: A Sanguinary Tale*, University of

Pennsylvania Press, Philadelphia, in Gray, D.D. (2013), *London's Shadows: The Dark Side of the Victorian City*, Bloomsbury Academic, London.

Bottos, S. (2007), "Women and violence: Theory, risk and treatment implications", research report No. R-198, Research Brand Correctional Service Canada, Ottawa, ON, Canada.

Brunvand, J.H. (1981), *The Vanishing Hitchhiker: American Urban Legends and Their Meanings*, W.W. Norton & Company, New York.

Burton, V.S. Jr., Cullen. F.T., Evans, D.T., Alarid, L.F. and Dunaway, G.R. (1998), "Gender, Self-Control and Crime", *Journal of Research in Crime and Delinquency*, 35, 2, 123–147.

Canter, D. (1994), *Criminal Shadows: Inside the Mind of the Serial Killer*, London, Harper Collins.

Charleroy, M. and Marland, H. (2016), "Prisoners of Solitude: Bringing History to Bear on Prison Health Policy", *Endeavour*, 40(3): 141–147, doi:10.1016/j.endeavour.2016.07.001, PMCID: PMC5053369.

Cherry, K. (2019), "The 4 Major Jungian Archetypes", retrieved from https://www.verywellmind.com/what-are-jungs-4-major-archetypes-2795439

Cleckley, H. (1955), *The mask of sanity: An attempt to clarify some issues about the so-called psychopathic personality* (3rd ed), Mosby, St Louis, doi:10.1037/11395-000.

Cohen, S. (1972), *Folk Devils and Moral Panics. The Creation of Mods and Rockers*, MacGibbon, London, in Gray, D.D. (2013), *London's Shadows: The Dark Side of the Victorian City*, Bloomsbury Academic, London.

Cornwell, P. (2017), *Ripper: The Secret Life of Walter Sickert*, Thomas & Mercer, Amazon Publishing Inc.

Cossins, A. (2015), *Female Criminality: Infanticide, Moral Panics and the Female Body*, Palgrave McMillan, London.

Crick, N.R. and Grotpeter, J.K. (1995), "Relational aggression, gender, and social psychological adjustment", *Child Development*, 66, 710–722.

Cross, S.E. and Madson, L. (1997), "Models of the Self: Self-Construals and Gender", *Psychological Bulletin*, 122, 5–37, https://doi.org/10.1037/0033-2909.122.1.5

Curtis, L.P. (2001), "The Pursuit of Angles", taken from *Jack the Ripper and the London Press*, Yale University Press, in Warwick, A. and Willis, M. (2013), *Jack the Ripper: Media, Culture, History*, Manchester University Press, Manchester.

Das Dasgupta, S. (2002), "A framework for understanding women's use of nonlethal violence in intimate heterosexual relationships", *Violence Against Women*, 8, 1364–1389.

Davidoff, L., L'Esperance, J. and Newby, H. (1977), "Landscape with Figures: Home and Community in English Society", in Mitchell, J. and Oakley, A., *The Rights and Wrongs of Women*, Penguin.

DelBello, M.P., Lopez-Larson. M.P., Soutullo. C.A. and Strakowski. S.M. (2001), "Effects of race on psychiatric diagnoses of hospitalised adolescents. A retrospective chart review", *Journal of Child and Adolescent Psychopharmacology*, 11(1), 95–103.

de Vogel, V. and de Ruiter, C. (2005), "The HCR-20 in personality disordered female offenders: A comparison with a matched sample of males", *Clinical Psychology & Psychotherapy*, 12, 226–240, doi: 10.1002/cpp.452.

de Vogel, V. and Stam, J. (2014), "Exploring the Criminal Behavior of Women with Psychopathy: Results from a Multicenter Study into Psychopathy and Violent Offending in Female Forensic Psychiatric Patients", *International Journal of Forensic Mental Health*, Volume 13, 2014 – Issue 4, retrieved from https://www.tandfonline.com/doi/ref/10.1080/14999013.2014.951105?scroll=top on 12th August 2018.

Douglas, J.E. (1988), "Jack The Ripper", Freedom of Information/Privacy Acts Section, Federal Bureau of Investigation.

Ellis, L. and Hoskin, A. (2015), "The evolutionary neuroandrogenic theory of criminal behavior expanded", *Aggression and Violent Behaviour*, 24: 61–74, doi:10.1016/j.avb.2015.05.002.

Emsley, C. (2011), "Crime and the Victorians", BBC History website, retrieved from http://www.bbc.co.uk/history/british/victorians/crime_01.shtml

Farrell, A.L., Keppel, R.D. and Titterington, V.B. (2011), "Lethal ladies: Revisiting what we know about female serial murderers", *Homicide Studies*, 15, 228–252, doi:10.1177/1088767911415938.

Fesbach, S. (1964), "The function of aggression and the regulation of aggressive drive", *Psychological Review*, 71, 257–272.

Fishman, W.J. (1988, 2005), "Crime and Punishment" in Warwick, A. and Willis, M. (2013), *Jack the Ripper: Media, Culture, History*, Manchester University Press, Manchester.

Flynn, S., Gask, L., Appleby, L. and Shaw, J. (2016), "Homicide-Suicide and the role of mental disorder: a national consecutive case series", *Social psychiatry and psychiatric epidemiology*, 51, 6, p877–884.

Fusco, S.L., Perrault, R.T., Paiva, M.L., Cook, N.E. and Vincent, G. (2011), "Probation officer perceptions of gender differences in youth offending and implications for practice in the field", paper presented at the 4th International Congress on Psychology and Law, Miami, March 2011.

Gail de Vos (2012), *What Happens Next? Contemporary Urban Legends and Popular Culture*, ABC-CLIO, Alberta.

Gottfredson, M.R and Hirschi, T. (1990), *A General Theory of Crime*, Stanford University Press.

Goldman, E. (1910), "The Traffic in Women. Emma Goldman's Anarchism and Other Essays", Second Revised Edition, Mother Earth Publishing Association, New York & London, p183–200, retrieved from https://www.marxists.org/reference/archive/goldman/works/1910/traffic-women.htm

Goldsmid, H.J. (1886), *Dottings of a Dosser: Being the Revelations of the Inner Life of Low London Dossing Houses*, T. Fisher Unwin, London, in London, J. (2007), *People of the Abyss*, The Echo Library, Middlesex.

Grant, I. and Butler, S. (1998), "The relation between anger and antisocial beliefs in young offenders", *Personality and Individual Differences*, 24, 759-765.

Gray, D.D. (2013), *London's Shadows: The Dark Side of the Victorian City*, Bloomsbury Academic, London.

Greenfeld, L.A. and Snell, T.L. (1999), "Bureau of Justice Statistics special report: Women offenders", United States Department of Justice, Washington, DC.

Gregg, J.J. (2013), "Murder, Media and Mythology: The Impact the Media's Reporting of the Whitechapel Murders had on National Identity, Social Reform and the Myth of Jack the Ripper", University of Warwick, Undergraduate Research Paper, retrieved from https://warwick.ac.uk/fac/cross_fac/iatl/reinvention/archive/bcur2013specialissue/jones#notes

Hare, R.D. (1991), *The Hare Psychopathy Checklist – Revised*, Multi-Health Systems, North Tonawanda, New York.

Harrison, M.A., Murphy, E.A., Ho, L.Y., Thomas, G. and Flaherty, C.V. (2015), "Female serial killers in the United States: means, motives and makings", *The Journal of Forensic Psychiatry and Psychology*, 26, 3, 383-406.

Henrick, H. (1872), *A Survey of the Irish in England*, edited by Alan O'Day, The Hambledon Press, London.

Herbert, I. (2006), "Wearside Jack: I deserve to go to jail for 'evil' Ripper hoax", *The Independent*, 21st March 2006, retrieved 1st June 2020.

Hickey, E. (2009), *Serial Murderers and Their Victims*, 5th ed, Wadsworth Publishing Co Inc, Belmont.

Honeycombe, G. (2011), *Murders of the black museum: 1875-1975. The dark secrets behind more than a hundred years of the most notorious crimes in England*, John Blake Publishing.

Ingram, R.E. and Luxton, D.D. (2005), "Vulnerability-Stress Models", in Hankin, B.L. and Abela, J.R.Z., *Development of Psychopathology: A vulnerability stress perspective* (p32–46), Sage Publications Inc, Thousand Oaks, CA.

Jack the Ripper's letter to the *Central News Agency*, 18th September 1888, cited in Gilman, S., "'Who Kills Whores?' 'I do,' Says Jack: Race and Gender in Victorian London", in *Jack the Ripper*, Warrick, A. and Willis, M. (2007), *Jack the Ripper: Media, Culture, History*, Manchester University Press, Manchester, p215.

Jonson-Reid, M. (1998), "Youth violence and exposure to violence in childhood: An ecological review", *Aggression and Violent Behaviour*, 3, 159–179.

Joyce, F. (2008), "Prostitution and the Nineteenth Century: In Search of the 'Great Social Evil'", *Re-Invention: A Journal of Undergraduate Research*, Volume 1 Issue 1, http://www2.warwick.ac.uk/go/reinventionjournal/volume1issue1/joyce

Karpman, B. (1941), "On the need of separating psychopathy into two distinct types: The symptomatic and the idiopathic", *Journal of Criminal Psychopathology*, 3, 112–137.

Kinnell, H. (2008), *Violence and Sex Work in Britain*, Willan Publishing, Devon.

Kirkbride, J.B., Fearon, P., Morgan, C. et al. (2006), "Heterogeneity in incidence rates of schizophrenia and other psychotic syndromes: Findings from the 3-center ÆSOP study", *Archives of General Psychiatry*, 63, 250–258.

Knight, S. (1986), *Jack the Ripper: The Final Solution*, 2nd ed, Academy Chicago Publishers, Chicago.

Koons-Witt, B.A. and Schram, P.J. (2003), The prevalence and nature of violent offending by females, *Journal of Criminal Justice*, 31, 361–371.

Kruttschnitt, C., Gartner, R. and Ferraro, K. (2002), "Women's involvement in serious interpersonal violence", *Aggression and Violent Behaviour*, 7(6), 529–565, https://doi.org/10.1016/S1359-1789(01)00045-3

Kruttschnitt, K. and Carbone-Lopez, K. (2006), "Moving beyond the stereotypes: Women's subjective accounts of their violent crime", *Criminology*, 44, 321–351.

Lazarus, R.S. (1993), "From psychological stress to the emotions: A history of changing outlooks", *Annual Review of Psychology*, 44 (1): 1–21, PMID 8434890, doi:10.1146/annurev.ps.44.020193.000245.

Leschied, A.W., Cummings, A.L., Van Brunschot, M., Cunningham, A. and Saunders, A. (2001), "A review of the literature on aggression with adolescent girls: Implications for policy prevention and treatment", *Canadian Psychology*, 42, 200–215.

Lewis, G., David, A., Andreasson, S. and Allebeck, P. (1992), "Schizophrenia and city life", *Lancet*, 340, 137–140.

Lippmann, W. (1922), *Public Opinion*, Harcourt, Brace and Company, New York, retrieved 3rd May 2016 via Internet Archive.

London, J. (2007), *People of the Abyss*, The Echo Library, Middlesex.

MacKenzie, A. and Johnson, S.L. (2003), "A profile of women gang members in Canada", research report No. R-138, Research Brand Correctional Service Canada, Ottawa, ON.

Marland, H. (2003), "Maternity and Madness: Puerperal Insanity in the Nineteenth Century", Centre for the History of Medicine, University of Warwick, retrieved on 15th August 2017.

Marland, H. (2004), *Dangerous Motherhood: Insanity and Childbirth in Victorian Britain*, Palgrave Macmillan, Basingstoke, Hampshire.

Marland, H. (2012), "Under the Shadow of Maternity: Birth, Death and Puerperal Insanity in Victorian Britain", *History of Psychiatry*, 23, 78–90.

Marriott, T. (2007), *Jack the Ripper: The 21st Century Investigation*, John Blake.

Mason, O. and Brady, F. (2009), "The psychotomimetic effects of short-term sensory deprivation", *Journal of Nervous and Mental Disease*, 197 (10): 783–785.

Mayhew, H. (1862), *The Criminal Prisons of London and scenes of prison life. With numerous illustrations from photographs*, London, British Library General Reference Collection 6057.i.7.

Mayhew, H. (1865), *London labour and the London poor: the condition and earnings of those that will work, cannot work, and will not work* (Vol. 1–4), retrieved from https://www.gutenberg.org/ebooks/author/48614

Mayhew, H. and others (2005), *The London Underworld in the Victorian Period: v. 1: Authentic First-person Accounts by Beggars, Thieves and Prostitutes*, Dover Publications Inc.

Mearns, A. and Preston, W.C. (1883), *The Bitter Cry of Outcast London: An Inquiry into the Condition of the Abject Poor*, James Clarke & Co, London, retrieved from http://www.gutenberg.org/ebooks/55316

Megargee, E. (1966), "Undercontrolled and overcontrolled personality types in extreme antisocial aggression", *Psychological Monographs*, 80, 1–19.

Mental Health Act (1983) amended 2007, retrieved from https://www.legislation.gov.uk/ukpga/2007/12/contents on 27th November 2018.

Miller, J. and Schwartz, M.D. (1995), "Rape Myths and Violence Towards Street Prostitutes", *Deviant Behaviour*, 16, 1, 1–23, DOI: 10.1080/01639625.1995.9967984, retrieved from https://www.researchgate.net/publication/248985276_Rape_Myths_and_Violence_Towards_Street_Prostitutes on 8th December 2018.

Monahan, J., Steadman, H.J., Silver, E., Appelbaum, P.S., Robbins, P.C., Mulvey, E.P., Roth, L.H., Grisso, T. and Banks, S. (2001), *Rethinking risk assessment: The MacArthur study of mental disorder and violence*, Oxford University Press, Oxford.

Moretti, M.M., Obsuth, I., Odgers, C.L. and Reebye, P. (2006), "Exposure to maternal vs. paternal partner violence, PTSD, and aggression in adolescent girls and boys", *Aggressive Behaviour*, 32, 385–395.

Mortensen, P.B., Pedersen, C.B., Westergaard, T. et al. (1999), "Effects of family history and place and season of birth on the risk of schizophrenia", *New England Journal of Medicine*, 340, 603–608.

Mulpetre, O. (2018), "Attacking the Devil – W T Stead Resource Site", retrieved from https://www.attackingthedevil.co.uk/pmg/tribute/

Hitchcock. T., Shoemaker. R., Emsley. C., Howard. S., and McLaughlin. J., et al., The Old Bailey Proceedings Online, 1674-1913 (www.oldbaileyonline.org, version 7.0, 24 March 2012).

Nicholls, T.L. (2001), "Violence risk assessment with female NCRMD acquittees: Validity of the HCR-20 and PCL:SV", unpublished master's thesis, Simon Fraser University, Vancouver, British Columbia, Canada.

Odgers, C.L., Moretti, M.M. and Reppucci, N.D. (2005), "Examining the science and practice of violence risk assessment with female adolescents", *Law and Human Behaviour*, 29, 7–27.

Office for National Statistics (2020), "Homicide in England and Wales: year ending March 2019", released 13th February 2020, retrieved from https://www.ons.gov.uk/peoplepopulationandcommunity/crimeandjustice/articles/homicideinenglandandwales/yearendingmarch2019

Ogle, R.S., Maier-Katkin, D. and Bernard, T.J. (1995), "A theory of homicidal behaviour among women", *Criminology*, 33, 173–193.

Porter, S., Woodworth, M., Earle, J., Drugge, J. and Boer, D. (2003),

"Characteristics of Sexual Homicides Committed by Psychopathic and Non-psychopathic Offenders", *Law and human behavior*, 27, 459–70, 10.1023/A:1025461421791.

Psychologist World, "Carl Jung: Archetypes and Analytical Psychology", retrieved from https://www.psychologistworld.com/cognitive/carl-jung-analytical-psychology

Quinsey, V.L. (2002), "Evolutionary theory and criminal behaviour", *Legal and Criminological Psychology*, 7 (1): 1–13, doi:10.1348/135532502168324.

Rehman, H. and Owen, D. (2013). *Mental Health Survey of Ethnic Minorities Research Report. Ethnos Research and Consultancy.*

Robbins, P.C., Monahan, J. and Silver, E. (2003), "Mental disorder, violence and gender", *Law and Human Behaviour*, 27, 561–571.

Robinson, B. (2015), *They all love Jack: Busting the Ripper*, Harper Collins Publishers, London.

Robson, D. (2015), "What Makes an Urban Legend", retrieved from https://www.bbc.com/future/article/20150126-how-to-create-an-urban-legend

Royal College of Psychiatrists (2010), "No Public Health without Public Mental Health: the case for action", retrieved from https://www.rcpsych.ac.uk/docs/default-source/improving-care/better-mh-policy/position-statements/ps04_2010.pdf?sfvrsn=b7316b7_4 on 14th August 2017.

Rowland, D. (2014), "The Blackout Killer or the Blackout Ripper", retrieved from https://www.oldpolicecellsmuseum.org.uk/content/new-contributions/the_blackout_killer_or_the_blackout_ripper on 1st June 2020.

Ryder, S.P., Anderson, R., Chisholm, A. and Scott, C., "Casebook: Jack the Ripper", copyright Stephen P. Ryder & Johnno, 1996–2021, Thomas Schachner, retrieved from https://www.casebook.org/ripper_letters/

Salfati, G.C. and Canter, D.C. (1999), "Differentiating Stranger Murders:

Profiling Offender Characteristics from Behavioral Styles", *Behavioral Sciences and the Law Behavioural*, 17: 391–406.

Salfati, G.C. and Taylor, P. (2006), "Differentiating sexual violence: A comparison of sexual homicide and rape", *Psychology, Crime & Law*, Vol. 12(2): 107–125.

Scoular, J. (2004), "The 'subject' of prostitution: Interpreting the discursive, symbolic and material position of sex/work in feminist theory", *Feminist Theory*, 5; 343, DOI:10.1177/1464700104046983.

Sherman, E. (2016), "The Forgotten Lives Of Jack The Ripper's Victims", updated 11th September 2019, retrieved from https://allthatsinteresting.com/jack-the-rippers-victims

Showalter, E. (1985), *The Female Malady: Women, Madness and English Culture, 1830–1980*, Penguin Books, London.

Showalter, E. (1987), *The Female Malady: Women, Madness and English Culture, 1830–1980*, Virago.

Sounes, H (1995), *Fred and Rose: The Full Story of Fred and Rose West and the Gloucester House of Horrors*, Warner Books, London.

Strakowski, S.M., Flaum, M., Amador, X., Bracha, H.S., Pandurangi, A.K., Robinson, D. and Tohen, M. (1996), "Racial differences in the diagnosis of psychosis", *Schizophr Res*, 21(2):117–124.

Strand, S. (Belfrage, H.) (2001), "Comparison of HCR-20 Scores in violent mentally disordered men and women: Gender differences and similarities", *Psychology Crime and Law*, 7, 1, 71–79, DOI:10.1080/10683160108401784.

Stewart, W. (1939), *Jack the Ripper: A New Theory*, Quality Press, London.

Stead, W.T. (1885), "The Maiden Tribute of Modern Babylon", *Pall Mall Gazette*, 4th July–13th 1885, retrieved from W.T. Stead Resource Site https://attackingthedevil.co.uk/pmg/tribute/

Stearns, P.N. (1978), "A Torrent of Abuse: Crimes of Violence between working class men and women in London 1840–1875", *Journal of Social History*, Vol. 11, No. 3, p328–345.

Swan, S.C., Gambone, L.J., Caldwell, J.E., Sullivan, T.P. and Snow, D.L. (2008), "A review of research on women's use of violence with male intimate partners", *Violence and Victims*, 23, 3, 301–314, doi:10.1891/0886-6708.23.3.301, ISSN 0886-6708, PMC 2968709, PMID 18624096.

Tait, W. (1840), *Magdalenism: an inquiry into the extent, causes, and consequences, of prostitution in Edinburgh*.

Tan, S. (2012), "Transcript of Asylums and Treatments of Mental Illness in the Victorian Era", retrieved from https://prezi.com/r2bguokfl0u2/asylums-and-treatments-of-mental-illness-in-the-victorian-era/ on 8th March 2016.

Tauber, J. (2013), "How cultural perceptions impact the application of laws in the crime of killing in Victorian London: Analysis of Gender in conviction rates 1850–1901", https://www.academia.edu/4852618/Murder_in_Old_Bailey_Records_-_Victorian_England retrieved on 6th June 2020.

Teasdale, B., Silver, E., Monahan, J. (2006), "Gender, Threat/Control-Override Delusions and Violence", *Law and Human Behaviour*, DOI 10.1007/s10979-006-9044-x.

The Daily Telegraph, 20th November 1888, page 3, retrieved from https://www.casebook.org/press_reports/daily_telegraph/dt881120.html on 3rd June 2020 and https://www.britishnewspaperarchive.co.uk/ on 3rd June 2020.

The Guardian, "Slender Man case: girl who attacked classmate gets 25-year hospital sentence", updated 1st February 2018, retrieved from https://www.theguardian.com/us-news/2017/dec/21/slender-man-case-anissa-weier-sentenced

The Star, 8th September 1888, retrieved from https://www.casebook.org/press_reports/star/s880908.html

Verona, E. and Carbonell, J.L. (2000), "Female violence and personality: Evidence for a pattern of over-controlled hostility among one-time violent female offenders", *Criminal Justice and Behaviour*, 27, 176–195.

Walkowitz, J. R. (1980), *Prostitution and Victorian Society. Women, class and the state*, Cambridge University Press, Cambridge.

Walkowitz, J. R. (1982), "Jack the Ripper and the Myth of Male Violence", *Feminist Studies*, 8, 3, 542–574, retrieved from https://www.jstor.org/stable/3177712?read-now=1&refreqid=excelsior%3Afa26ae946c3bc27ae516454dea68f9fb&seq=1

Walkowitz, J.R. (1992), *City of Dreadful Delight: Narratives of Sexual Danger*, University of Chicago Press, Chicago.

Wallace, W. (2012), "Sent to the asylum: The Victorian women locked up because they were suffering from stress, postnatal depression and anxiety", retrieved from http://www.dailymail.co.uk/home/you/article-2141741/Sent-asylum-The-Victorian-women-locked-suffering-stress-post-natal-depression-anxiety.html on 8th March 2016.

Warwick, A. and Willis, M. (2013), *Jack the Ripper: Media, Culture, History*, Manchester University Press, Manchester.

Webster, C.D. and Bloom, H. (2007), *Essential Writings in Violence Risk Assessment and Management*, Centre for Addiction and Mental Health.

Weizmann-Henelius, G. (2006), "Violent Female Perpetrators in Finland: Personality and Life Events", *Nordic Psychology*, 58(4), 280–297 http://dx.doi.org/10.1027/1901-2276.58.4.280

Wescott, T. (2014), "The Bank Holiday Murders: The True Story of the First Whitechapel Murders", Crime Confidential Press, retrieved from: https://www.casebook.org/press_reports/lloyds_weekly_news/18880909.html

Whittle, B. and Richie, J. (2000), *Prescription for Murder: The True Story of Dr. Harold Frederick Shipman*, Little Brown, p348–9.

Bibliography

Wikipedia, "Urban Legend", edited 5th March 2020, retrieved from https://en.wikipedia.org/wiki/Urban_legend

Woodworth, M. and Porter, S. (2002), "In cold blood: Characteristics of criminal homicides as a function of psychopathy", *Journal of Abnormal Psychology*, 111(3), 436–445, https://doi.org/10.1037/0021-843X.111.3.436

Wuornos, A. and Berry-Dee, C. (2006), *Monster*, John Blake Publishing Limited, London.

Zillmann, D. (1979), *Hostility and aggression*, Hillsdale, NJ Lawrence Erlbaum.

World Health Organisation. (2021). *Gender and Women's Mental Health*. Retrieved from

http://www.who.int/mental_health/prevention/genderwomen/en/

Wallace. W. (2012). *Sent to the asylum: The Victorian women locked up because they were suffering from stress, post-natal depression and anxiety*. Retrieved from http://www.dailymail.co.uk/home/you/article-2141741/Sent-asylum-The-Victorian-women-locked-suffering-stress-post-natal-depression-anxiety.html